W9-BCU-911

DISCARD

HOW THE INTERNET WORKS

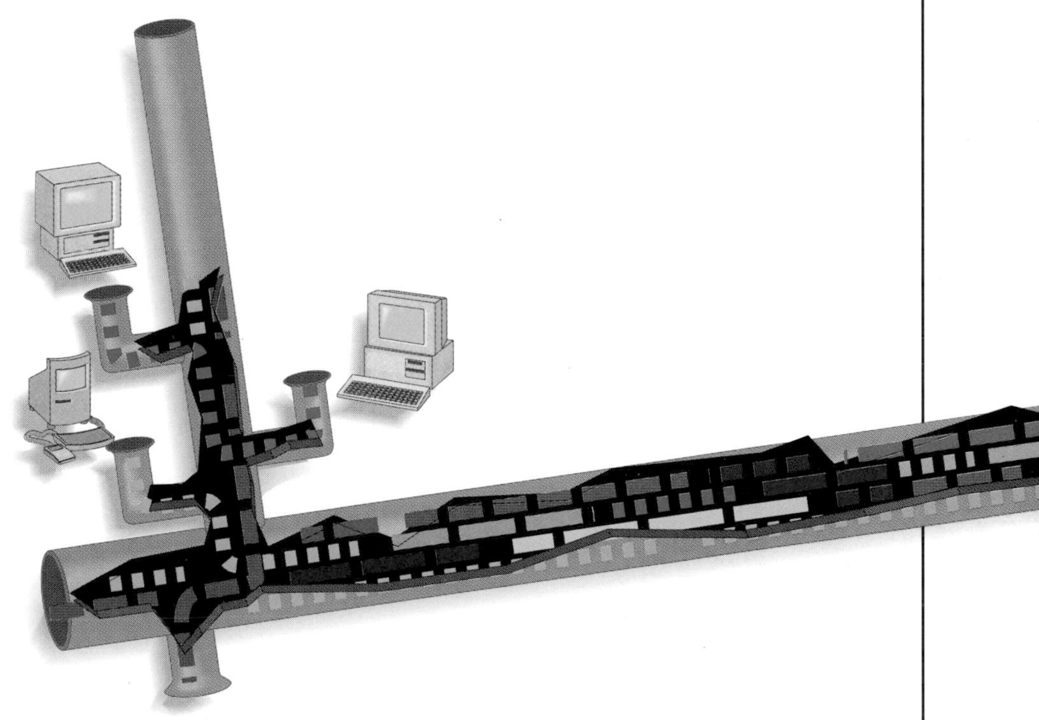

VR
VIDEO
ENTERTAINMENT
INDUSTRY
MAINTENANCE
OSI
RELAY

HOW THE INTERNET WORKS

JOSHUA EDDINGS

Illustrated by

PAMELA DRURY WATTENMAKER

ZIFF-DAVIS
ZD
PRESS

Ziff-Davis Press
Emeryville, California

Development Editor	Valerie Haynes Perry
Copy Editor	Kelly Green
Technical Reviewer	Mark Butler
Project Coordinators	Kim Haglund and Cort Day
Proofreader	Carol Burbo
Cover Illustrator	Pamela Drury Wattenmaker
Cover Designer	Carrie English
Book Designer	Carrie English
Technical Illustrator	Pamela Drury Wattenmaker
Word Processor	Howard Blechman
Layout Artists	M.D. Barrera and Bruce Lundquist
Indexer	Anne Leach

Ziff-Davis Press books are produced on a Macintosh computer system with the following applications: FrameMaker®, Microsoft® Word, QuarkXPress®, Adobe Illustrator®, Adobe Photoshop®, Adobe Streamline™, MacLink®Plus, Aldus® FreeHand™, Collage Plus™.

If you have comments or questions or would like to receive a free catalog, call or write:
Ziff-Davis Press
5903 Christie Avenue
Emeryville, CA 94608
1-800-688-0448

How the Internet Works
PART OF A CONTINUING SERIES

ISBN 1-56276-192-7

Manufactured in the United States of America
10 9 8 7 6 5 4 3 2 1

HOME PLATE

For Kateri and Tony—the next generation of net surfers

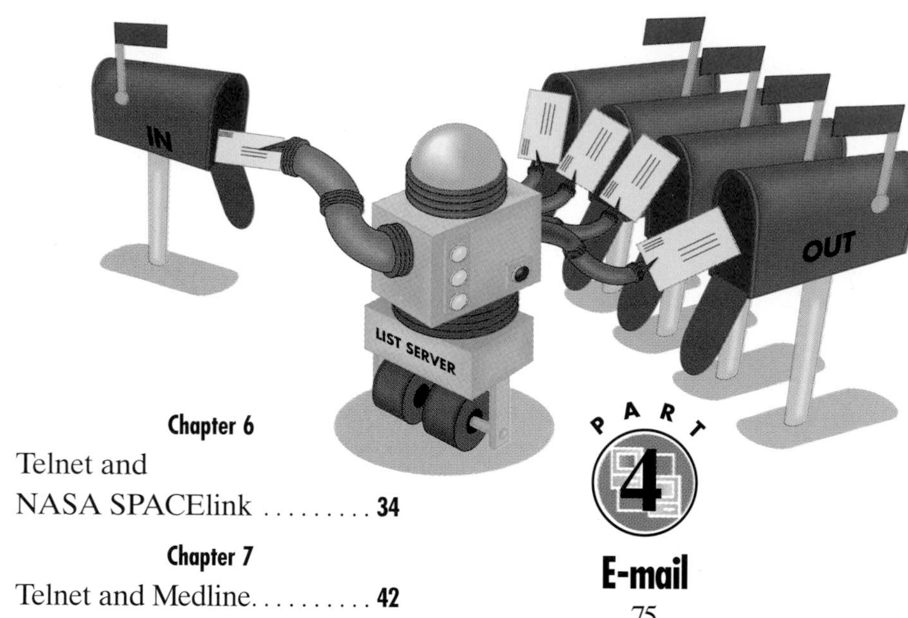
IN
LIST SERVER
OUT

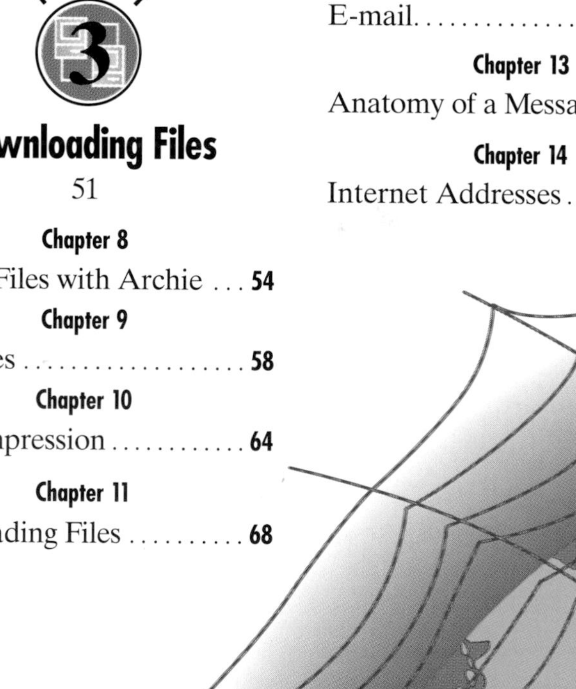
ARCHIE

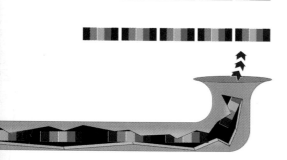

Thanks to Valerie Haynes Perry, development editor at Ziff-Davis Press, for shepherding me through this project. And to Pamela Drury Wattenmaker, illustrator—it was fun to turn in montages of clip art and crayon drawings and to get back illustrations that captured what I was trying to say! And special thanks to the editorial and production team for this project: Kelly Green, copy editor; Kim Haglund and Cort Day, project coordinators; and M. D. Barrera and Bruce Lundquist, layout artists. As a former retail bookseller it was fun for me to watch the choreographed dance involved in getting a book out so quickly.

Thanks to Mike Sabeskis for his support over the years, for turning me on to the *How It Works* series, and for all those times we've bounced ideas back and forth.

Special thanks also to Kathy Henley for her support, for "beta testing" and reviewing my ideas for this book, and for training me in how to think of and explain computer-related topics clearly.

And thanks to the Internet community. I recently heard the statement "There is no encyclopedia on the Internet!" I've found the Internet itself to be an encyclopedic source of knowledge. It is a source of real, live experts, only an e-mail message or phone call away, who are always willing to help you out.

anarchy: 1a: absence of government 1b: a state of lawlessness or political disorder due to the absence of governmental authority 1c: a utopian society of individuals who enjoy complete freedom without government.

—Webster's Ninth New Collegiate Dictionary

The Internet's environment often seems chaotic to the computer tyro who stumbles onto the net for the first time. In fact, the Internet resembles an anarchy in the philosophical sense of the word.

The Internet is a cooperative society that forms a virtual community stretching from one end of the globe to the other. As such, the Internet is a gateway to cyberspace. *Cyberspace* is the electronic infrastructure of the late twentieth century. Cyberspace encompasses a virtual universe of ideas and information we enter whenever we read a book or use a computer, for example. The Internet allows you to travel through cyberspace from your computer using your Mac, Amiga, PC, or SPARCstation, as well as other types of computers. One moment a task on your computer may absorb your attention, the next you may decide to switch between library catalogs spread across several continents. You may then quickly change gears to have an electronic conversation with a friend on the other side of the world whom you'll never meet in person; this could lead to your participation in an electronic forum, along with thousands of others.

Acronyms and terms such as PPP, SLIP, TCP/IP, WAIS, WWW, FTP; and Telnet, e-mail, and gopher often seem to conspire against a simple understanding of the Internet. These acronyms and terms all compete for your attention at the same time. This book is a visual guide to understanding the Internet, its jargon, and how it all works. It will help you get a conceptual handle on the Internet, and will make you comfortable as you explore cyberspace and join the global electronic village.

If you are new to the Internet or to computers, you may elect to read this book linearly, from beginning to end. You can also browse the illustrations, only pausing to dip into the text when a particular topic piques your curiosity. If you are already familiar with the Internet, feel free to read this book in any manner that pleases you. I only hope that whether you are a computer novice or a seasoned net surfer, this book will enhance your understanding of the Internet.

PART 1

WELCOME TO THE INTERNET

CONTENTS

OVERVIEW

FROM YOUR FRONT room, your back office, or your child's grade school, you can turn on your computer, dial a local phone number, and connect with the biggest computer system in the world. It's completely legal. It may even be free. It's the Internet.

The Internet is a network of networks. You can use electronic mail to contact other Internet subscribers. From your computer, you can log in to another computer, called a *remote computer*. The remote computer may be thousands of miles away, and you can run programs on it as if it were in the same room. You can search libraries of software around the world, and transfer that software back to your own computer.

When you connect to the Internet, your computer becomes an extension of what seems like a single giant computer—a computer with branches all over the world. What's really happening is that your computer is talking with one of more than a million other computers. However, these computers don't all talk to each other at the same time. Tens of thousands of networks all over the planet connect them, sending information between computers as needed. Millions of people use this system every day.

PART ONE

This book will give you a taste of what's available on the Internet. The resources that the Internet interconnects and makes available to you, the end user, are tremendous. They also change daily, as new services and computers come on-line, and old computers and resources are taken off-line.

A good way to explore the Internet is to start at home. Whether we know it or not, most of us live near an "electronic town." Local governments and colleges set up and fund these towns, which offer a collection of computer resources to the locals. Chapter 1 will take a closer look at one such town.

Electronic towns pepper the world, and the Internet connects these towns. Many offer similar services, but with a local twist. Other electronic towns offer unique services through various local institutions. Once you've explored what's available locally, in Chapter 2 you can venture out onto the global Internet to explore electronic towns all over the world.

CHAPTER
1

The Electronic Town

SO WHAT CAN you do with the Internet? Let's start by looking at a Free-Net.

A Free-Net brings together the resources of a community or campus. Everyone and everything from regular citizens to public and private schools, government offices, elected representatives, and local businesses; farmer and agricultural experts; community organizations, museums, and other institutions can all be found on the net. This convergence of electronic resources has all the elements of a town—an electronic town. There's a post office, where members have electronic mailboxes from which they can send electronic mail throughout the world. There's a public square, with coffeehouses for one-on-one conversations and podiums and auditoriums for large gatherings. There's a teleport, which enables users to jump to other networks around the world via the Internet. There are weather stations, hospitals, newsrooms, recreation centers, libraries, and much more. In fact, Free-Nets are the libraries of the future.

The Cleveland Free-Net is the original Free-Net, started in the mid-1980s and run by Case Western Reserve University. Technically, it is a metropolitan area network, or "net," reached via the Internet or by a local phone call if you live in Cleveland, Ohio. Case Western Reserve University and the Cleveland Free-Net provide the infrastructure of the electronic town—the administration building, the post office, and the teleport. Other organizations on the net are organizations that exist in the real community. Often these organizations already have local area nets or other computer systems in place. By joining the Free-Net electronic town, these organizations offer their information to many more people, as well as access information from other organizations. The local library system provides the computer with an on-line catalog and library system. The local medical school and hospital do the same with medical information. Computer user groups find electronic homes on the Free-Net. The local, state, and Federal government provide access to more information.

All this is accessible by a simple phone call from your modem, or even from a direct connection to the Internet that your local area network or on-line service may already provide! As you start looking around your community you will probably find your own local electronic town. The Internet has expanded into almost all colleges and universities; even high schools and grade schools are joining. Free-Nets bring the Internet into our own backyards.

An Electronic Town

A Free-Net brings together the resources of a community or campus on your computer. This convergence of electronic resources has all the elements of a town—an electronic town.

Business and Industrial Park As more businesses move into the electronic town you will find more databases and services here.

Home Here's where you start, with your own computer, in your own home.

Schoolhouse This is the home of Academy One, a very low-cost educational resource for students, teachers, and administrators. Many Ohio K-12 schools, as well as schools throughout the country, participate in Academy One. It's open to all schools.

Library You'll find almost all the services of the local library here. Browse the card catalog. See how many overdue books you have. Reserve a book at your local branch—it will be waiting there for you next time you stop by the real library.

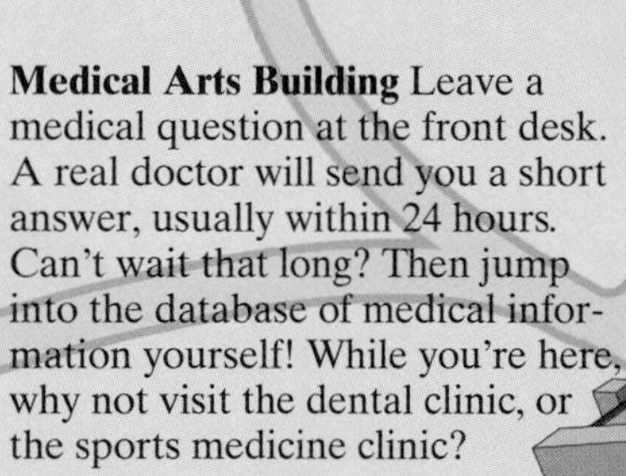

Medical Arts Building Leave a medical question at the front desk. A real doctor will send you a short answer, usually within 24 hours. Can't wait that long? Then jump into the database of medical information yourself! While you're here, why not visit the dental clinic, or the sports medicine clinic?

Community Center and Recreation Area Join in with your neighbors to relax a bit and shoot the breeze. Meet with stamp collectors. Discuss TV trivia. Maybe play an electronic game. Discuss yesterday's basketball game, or that upcoming football game.

COMMUNITY CENTER

ARTS BUILDING

Arts Building Stop in and meet the local artists. You'll find authors, painters, poets, musicians, and much more.

Science and Technology Center Local colleges and computer user groups help run this center. You'll find help for all kinds of computers, plus lots of software.

Government Center Need legal information? Here's the courthouse, with a database of legal questions and answers. Research Supreme Court opinions. Examine the text of historical documents at Freedom Shrine. You can also contact your Representatives from here, or look up 800 numbers for government agencies.

Administration Building Here's where you talk to the people who run the town. Stop in here for general information about helping build the town.

College Campus Register for college on line. Preview next term's class offerings. Leave a message for your favorite teacher. At some campuses you can turn in homework on line, and some classes even meet on-line!

Cafe Stop by the cafe to join in on a conversation. You never know who you might bump into here.

Public Square Gather with the crowd to hear the politicians speak. Give a speech yourself. The podium's open!

POST OFFICE
CAFE

Post Office Check your electronic mailbox for messages, send e-mail to your friend down the street, or to a pen pal in New Zealand. In some towns you have to "buy" stamps to send mail outside of the town.

The Cleveland Free-Net The Cleveland Free-Net, the first Free-Net, was used as the basis for this electronic town. By the time you finish reading this book, some of the features above may have changed, and many more will have been added.

WELCOME TO CLEVELAND FREE-NET cleveland.freenet.edu

The Teleport When you're ready to leave town, you can "beam" yourself anywhere in the global Internet. Turn this page to begin your journey.

CHAPTER
2

The Global Internet

YOU'VE JUST SEEN an electronic town. Many towns offer unique resources: maybe a library specializing in the Civil War, a database of medical journal articles, the world's most accurate clock, television plot summaries, or even a high-end, state-of-the-art supercomputer. Now imagine the planet covered with electronic towns, all linked by the Internet. With your computer you can travel to any of these towns, via the global Internet, without leaving home!

The Internet evolved in part from the connection of supercomputer sites across the United States. The National Science Foundation (NSF), a U.S. government agency that promotes science, wanted to get the most out of their supercomputers. Connecting the sites to each other made the supercomputers more efficient. Scientists, researchers, and engineers could then access the supercomputers from their own labs and offices.

The high-speed networks that connect the NSF supercomputers now form the backbone of the Internet. The *backbone* consists of high-capacity telephone links, microwaves, lasers, fiber optics, and satellites, connecting networks, computer sites, and people all over the world.

NASA SPACElink is an electronic town on the Internet. NASA educational specialists provide teachers with information on space science and the space program. Teachers or anyone interested can find lesson plans, information on the latest shuttle launch, computer images from Mars or the shuttle landing, and much more on SPACElink. If that's not enough, you can also try the European Space Information System, or the Hubble Space Telescope archived exposure catalog, both also available on the Internet!

Libraries are the most visible and numerous resources on the Internet. You can visit college libraries, public and private libraries, national libraries, corporate libraries, scientific libraries, and even virtual libraries with electronic books, all over the world. The U.S. Library of Congress has even developed a virtual library catalog, the L.C. Marvel that you can browse through like any other electronic card catalog. In fact, most libraries will let you browse through their card catalogs, and maybe even check their database of newspaper clippings or other special services. Some let you copy electronic books that are now in the public domain, which have been scanned into a computer. Other libraries, like the Multnomah County Library Association in Portland, Oregon, even let you check out hard-copy books electronically—they send the book to you by U.S. Mail. Of course, they charge the postage for this service to your library card.

There are many other resources available through the Internet. You can visit CURIA, the Irish literature archive, keep track of the Vatican Exhibit, study architecture at the Instituto Universitario de Architettura in Venice, Italy, or buy books from an on-line bookstore. You can participate in politics, communicate directly with people in war-torn areas of the world, or share hobbies with others.

Today, the NSF supercomputer centers are further expanding the power and usefulness of the Internet. They have formed a *metacomputer*, a sort of one-stop shopping center for scientists and engineers. A metacomputer ties supercomputers and other, smaller computers from San Diego to New York together to form a seamless "virtual computer." A carefully arranged team of computers handles problems in areas such as climate change and the scientific visualization of massive amounts of information better than a single computer would. Software at the supercomputer centers determines the best combination of computers to handle such tasks, freeing up valuable computer time for other tasks.

The resources available on the Internet are almost unimaginable. If you were to systematically explore everything that is out there, you'd never finish.

The Internet in the United States

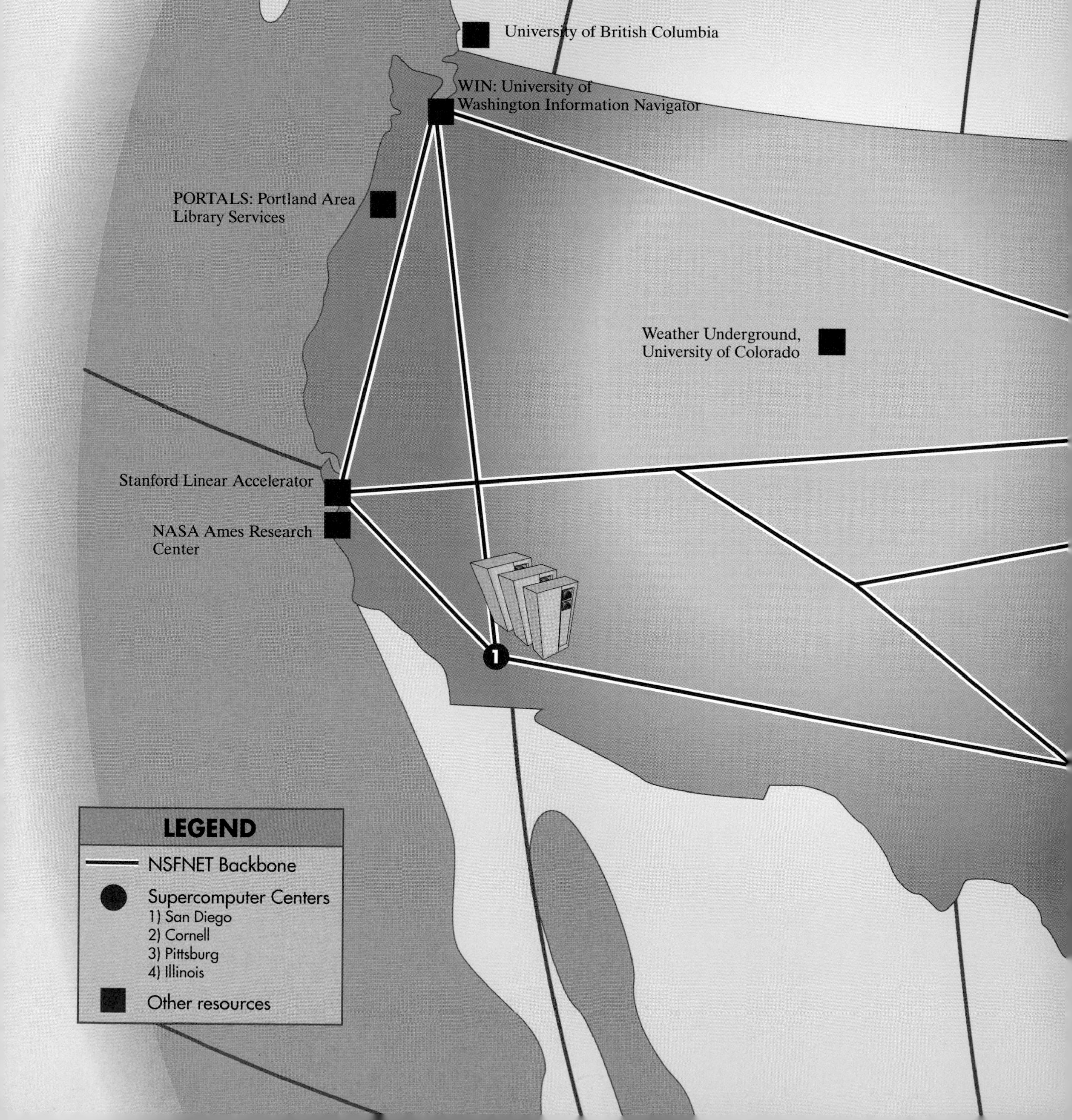

University of British Columbia

WIN: University of Washington Information Navigator

PORTALS: Portland Area Library Services

Weather Underground, University of Colorado

Stanford Linear Accelerator

NASA Ames Research Center

1

LEGEND

NSFNET Backbone

Supercomputer Centers
1) San Diego
2) Cornell
3) Pittsburg
4) Illinois

Other resources

The Internet is a network of networks; each individual network is administrated, maintained, and paid for separately by individual educational institutions and other organizations. The National Science Foundation maintains the NSFNET backbone. The backbone links supercomputers across the country and provides long-haul communications links between different research and educational institutions in the United States and around the world.

Commercial companies called service providers maintain many of the actual communications lines the Internet uses. Universities, research labs, and commerical companies rent connections from these providers, just as you rent a telephone line from the phone company.

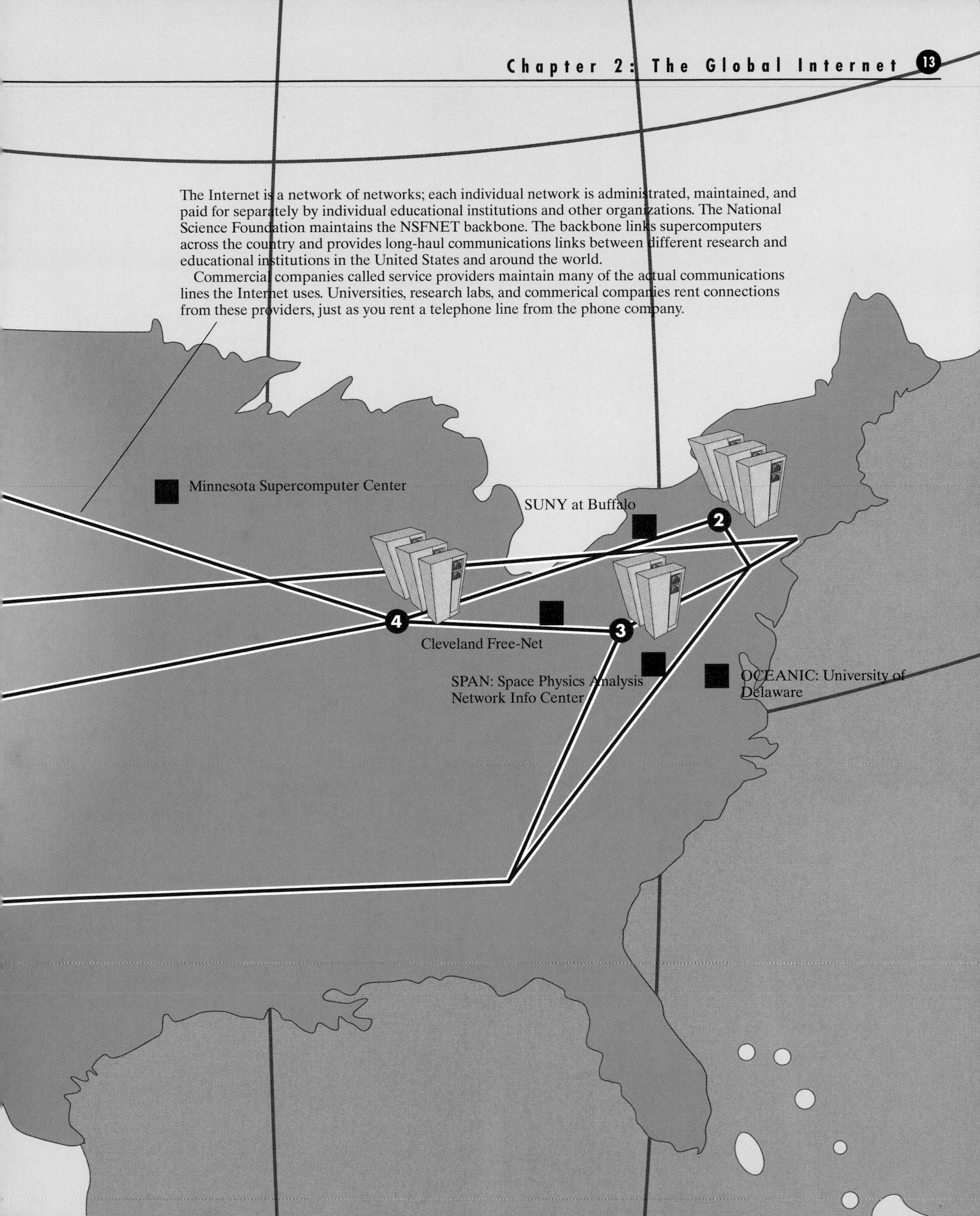
Minnesota Supercomputer Center
SUNY at Buffalo
2
4
3
Cleveland Free-Net
SPAN: Space Physics Analysis Network Info Center
OCEANIC: University of Delaware

The Global Internet

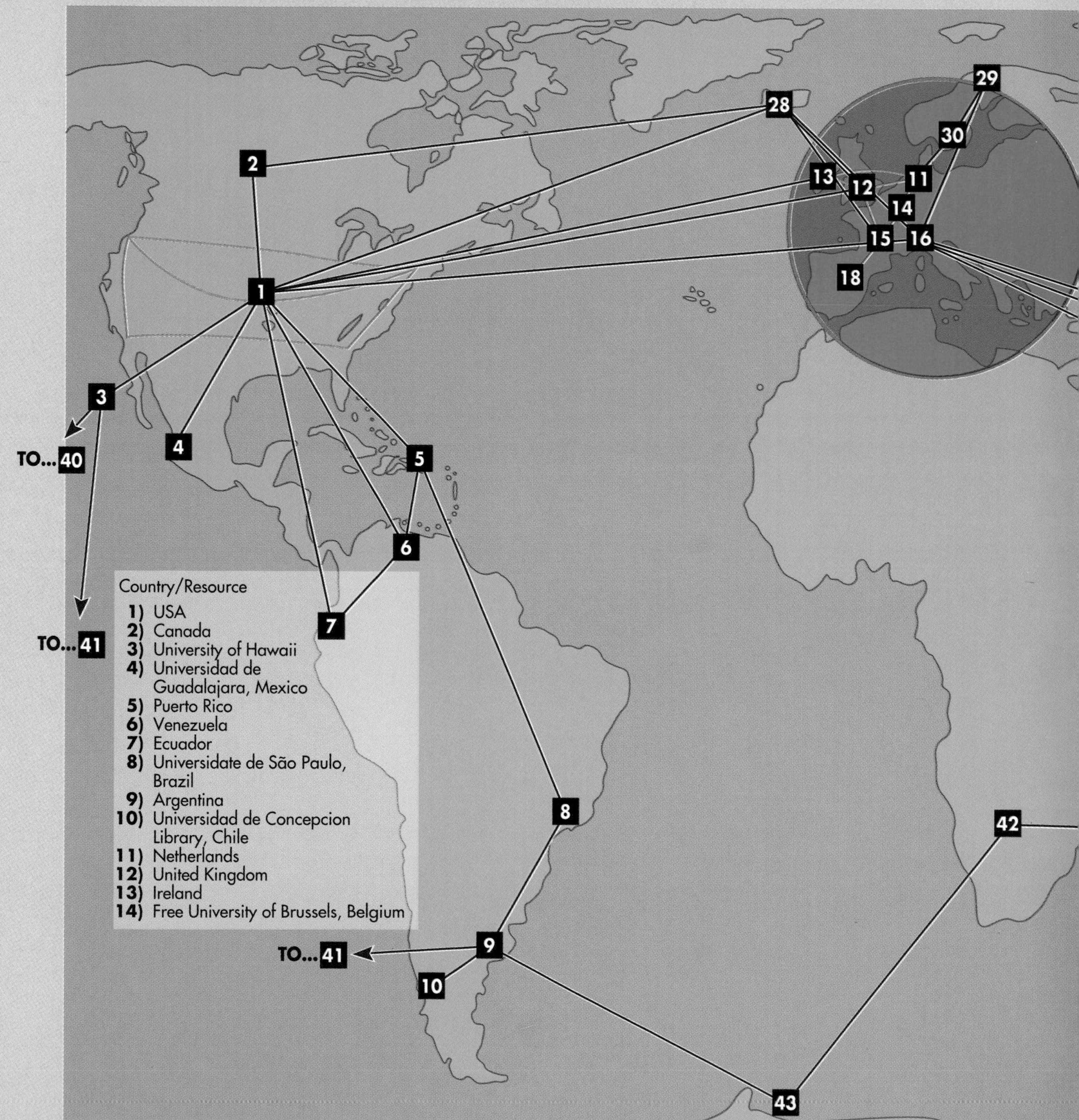

1
2
3
4
5
6
7
8
9
10
11
12
13
14
15
16
18
28
29
30
42
43
TO... 40
TO... 41
TO... 41
Country/Resource
1) USA
2) Canada
3) University of Hawaii
4) Universidad de Guadalajara, Mexico
5) Puerto Rico
6) Venezuela
7) Ecuador
8) Universidate de São Paulo, Brazil
9) Argentina
10) Universidad de Concepcion Library, Chile
11) Netherlands
12) United Kingdom
13) Ireland
14) Free University of Brussels, Belgium

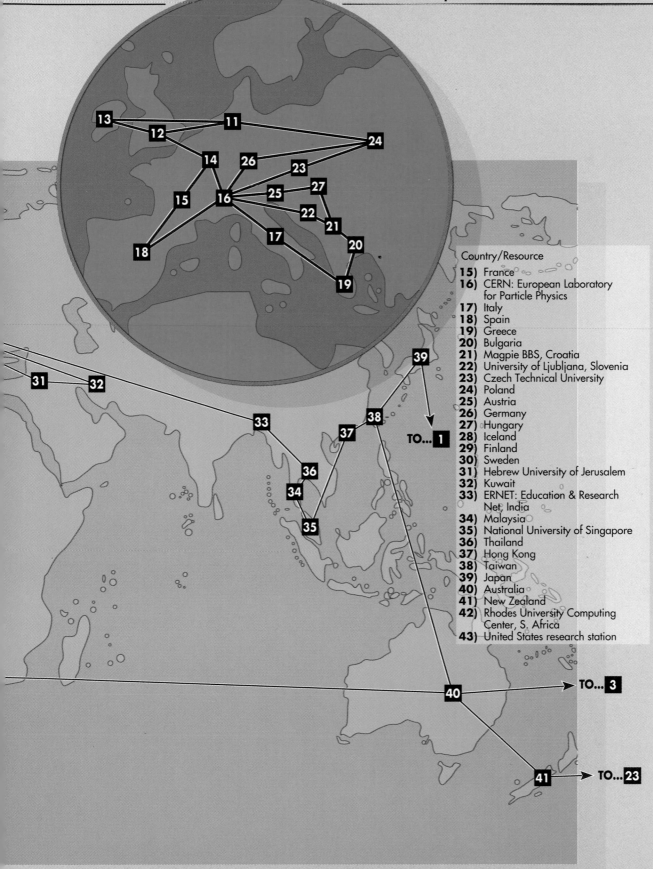

Country/Resource

15) France
16) CERN: European Laboratory for Particle Physics
17) Italy
18) Spain
19) Greece
20) Bulgaria
21) Magpie BBS, Croatia
22) University of Ljubljana, Slovenia
23) Czech Technical University
24) Poland
25) Austria
26) Germany
27) Hungary
28) Iceland
29) Finland
30) Sweden
31) Hebrew University of Jerusalem
32) Kuwait
33) ERNET: Education & Research Net, India
34) Malaysia
35) National University of Singapore
36) Thailand
37) Hong Kong
38) Taiwan
39) Japan
40) Australia
41) New Zealand
42) Rhodes University Computing Center, S. Africa
43) United States research station

TELNET

CONTENTS

OVERVIEW

THE INTERNET AND the telephone system are similar in that you connect your computer to the Internet just as you connect a phone to the phone system. On the Internet, you then dial another computer using Telnet, special software that runs on your computer. *Telnet* connects your computer to a remote host computer which may be located across town or on the other side of the world.

Where the phone system creates a voice connection, the Internet carefully packages into packets the data from your computer. The packets are stamped with the host's address and dropped into an Internet mailbox. Once in the mailbox, streams of packets are sent over any number of paths through the millions of computers and networks between you and the host computer you access using Telnet. This process is called *packet switching*.

This packet-switched network is governed by a host of *protocols*, or rules, that describe what software and hardware should do and how they should work together. The "Internet Layering Model" illustration (Chapter 5) shows how Internet protocols work this magic, which includes the following operations: running the Telnet software on your computer, and interpreting the protocols that transmit packets across a variety of networks to be reassembled into data by the host computer.

PART TWO

You can use Telnet to "log on" to a remote host computer as if you were at a terminal in the next room, although you may also need an account and a password on the host computer. You'll learn how to log on to NASA SPACElink (Chapter 6) and take a look at some of the information NASA makes available to teachers. This information ranges from press releases about the next shuttle launch to computer images from space missions. You'll also learn how to do a literature search after logging on to Medline (Chapter 7), the National Medical Library's database of journal articles and abstracts.

Keep in mind that Telnet is only one of three traditional ways to use the Internet. File Transfer Protocol, or FTP (Part 3), and electronic mail (Part 4) are the other two top-level software applications that let computers on the net talk to each other.

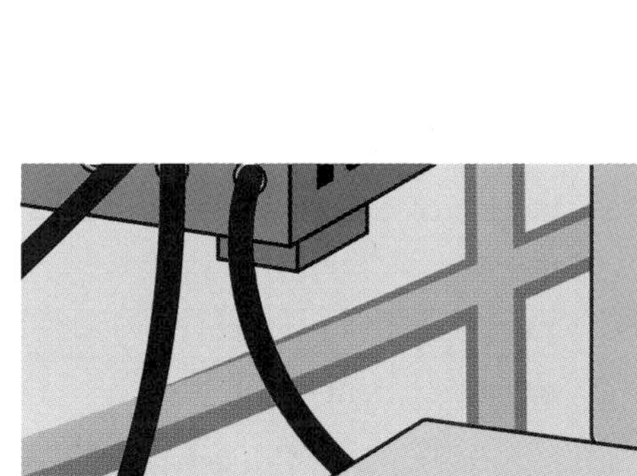

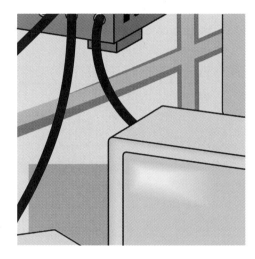

CHAPTER
3

Connecting Networks

PACKETS OF INFORMATION travel across the networks that comprise the Internet. These packets carry information between your computer and a host computer, following a path that leads through many different levels of networks on various types of communications lines. A variety of devices process the packets to help them on their way.

The packets start their journey with a single local computer that may be hooked up by a modem and phone line, or by a direct connection to a campus network. This local computer may also be a *host*, a resource available to other local computers.

Repeaters, hubs, bridges, and gateways are used extensively to transmit data between networks. *Repeaters* simply amplify, or refresh the passing stream of data, extending the distance the data can travel. *Hubs* tie groups of computers together, allowing these computers to take turns talking to each other. *Bridges* link local area networks (LANs), allowing data meant for another LAN to pass through, while blocking in local data. *Gateways* work like bridges, but also translate data between one network type and another.

If the host of the data being sent is a nearby computer, the packets easily reach their destination. If the host is not nearby, routers guide packets on their journey through mid-level networks. *Routers* are intelligent bridges that read the address contained in the first few lines of each packet, then figure out how to best send the packet to its destination, taking into account how busy the network is. Mid-level networks, such as BARRnet (Bay Area Regional Research network), connect LANs via high-speed telephone lines, Ethernet, and microwave links. When a mid-level network is focused in a geographic area, it's known as a regional network. A multisite organization is another form of mid-level network, linking offices of a national or international corporation or agency. A WAN (wide-area network) uses satellite links or other "long haul" connections.

If a packet's destination is another local computer within the mid-level network, the packet is sent on its way. Otherwise, the router then sends the packet to a NAP (Network Access Point) where the packet is quickly shot across the country, or the world, on a backbone. High-speed backbones, such as NSFNET, use special telephone lines, FDDIs (Fiber Distributed Data Interfaces), or other high-speed and high-bandwidth links. Again, routers guide packets on their way to their final destination, where they're passed down to another mid-level network, and finally to the host.

Linking Computers

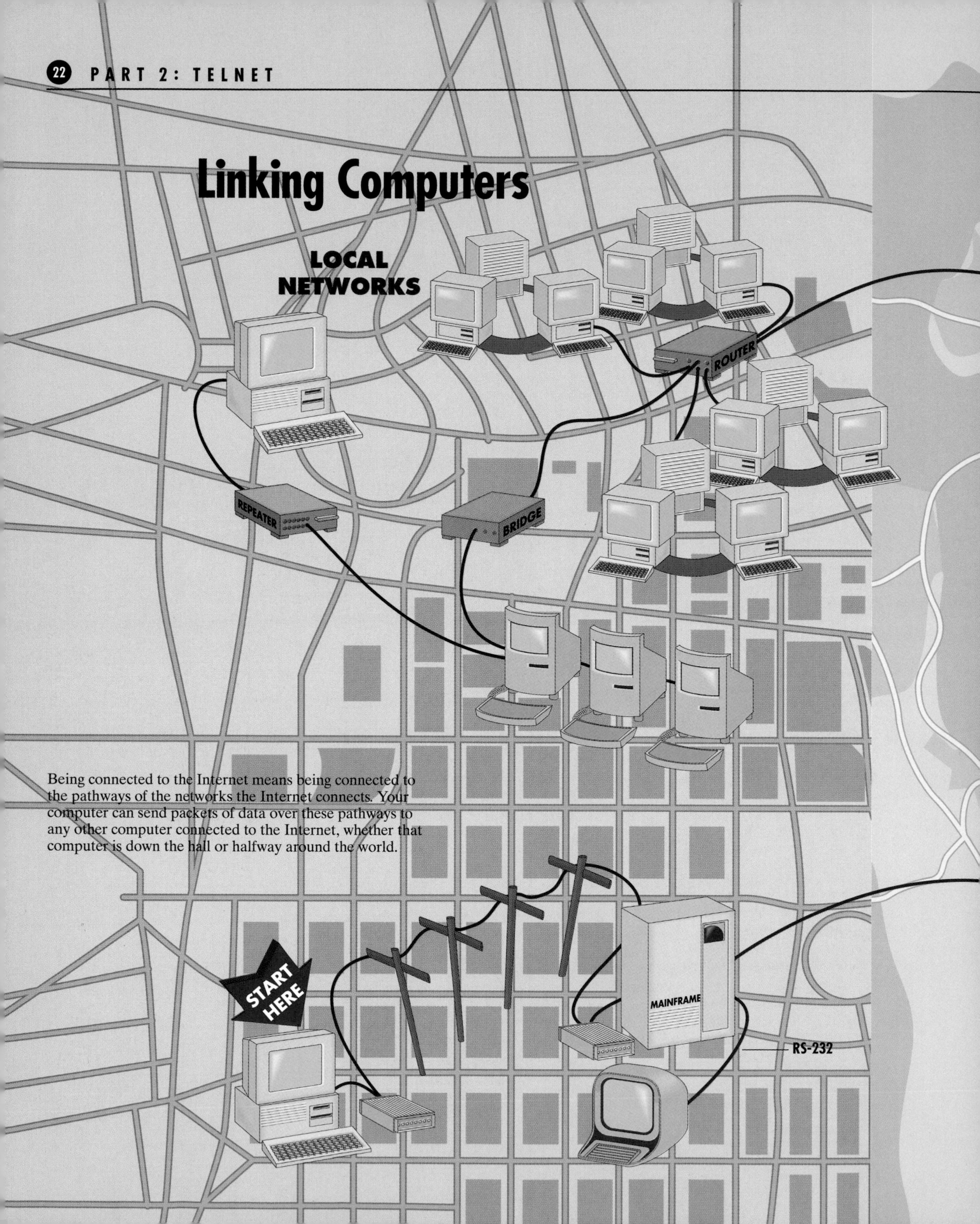
LOCAL
NETWORKS
ROUTER
REPEATER
BRIDGE
START HERE
MAINFRAME
RS-232

Being connected to the Internet means being connected to the pathways of the networks the Internet connects. Your computer can send packets of data over these pathways to any other computer connected to the Internet, whether that computer is down the hall or halfway around the world.

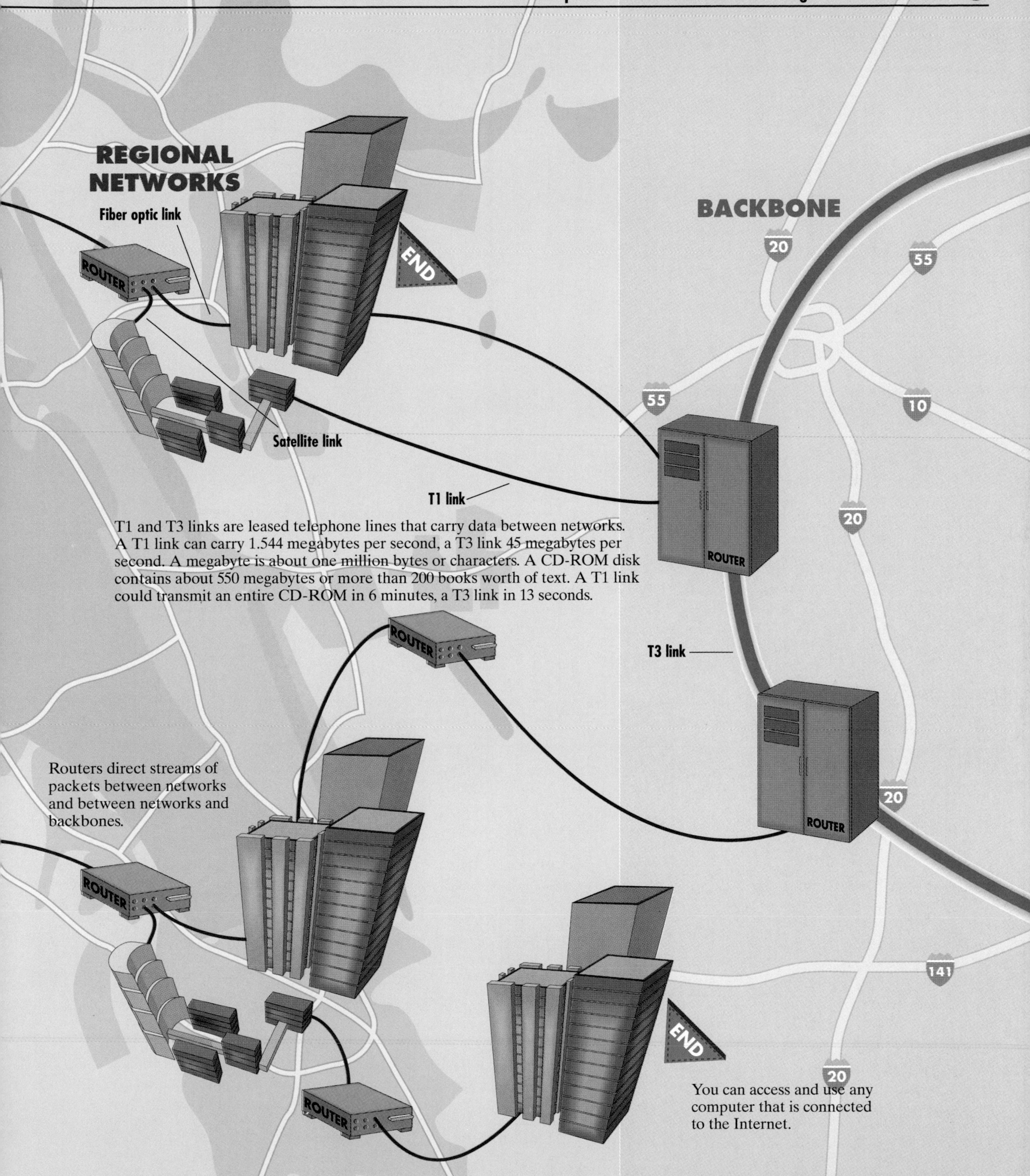
REGIONAL NETWORKS
Fiber optic link
ROUTER
END
BACKBONE
20
55
Satellite link
55
10
T1 link
20
ROUTER
T3 link
ROUTER
ROUTER
20
ROUTER
141
ROUTER
END
20

T1 and T3 links are leased telephone lines that carry data between networks. A T1 link can carry 1.544 megabytes per second, a T3 link 45 megabytes per second. A megabyte is about one million bytes or characters. A CD-ROM disk contains about 550 megabytes or more than 200 books worth of text. A T1 link could transmit an entire CD-ROM in 6 minutes, a T3 link in 13 seconds.

Routers direct streams of packets between networks and between networks and backbones.

You can access and use any computer that is connected to the Internet.

The Internet's Protocols

COMPUTERS ON THE Internet communicate with each other by sending packets of information back and forth. These packets contain chunks of data and special control and addressing information necessary to get the packets to their destination and reassembled into useful computer data. This is all accomplished by Transmission Control Protocol and Internet Protocol, also known as TCP/IP, the common language of the Internet.

A *protocol* is a rule or agreement for network communication procedures. A protocol can also refer to how packets are reassembled into data at a host computer, how signals are transmitted on a phone line, and much more. TCP/IP is the core of the Internet, but only refers to two among many of the protocols you'll find on the Internet.

Protocols are often described in terms of RFCs, or *requests for comments*. RFCs are the working documents the Internet community uses to develop and record technical information. Many Internet computer sites store these documents electronically.

The *Internet layers model* developed by computer scientists diagrams how different layers of protocols are used to connect your computer to the Internet, change data from your computer into packets, and direct these packets to the destination host computer. Once at the host, the data is extracted from the packets and reassembled into data that the host computer can use. The next illustration shows this diagram, and details the way packets are broken down or reassembled at each stage of the game.

There are elaborate systems built into some of the protocol layers to ensure that the data can be reassembled error-free at the packet's destination. For example, the checksum system creates a special code and sends the code along with the data. The original code must be validated by creating another code on the receiving end, which is then compared to the first code. If the two codes don't match, the protocol at that layer on the destination side asks the originating computer to resend the data. At each stage of this process, a direct connection appears to be in place. However, the actual data is carried by streams of packets that may be taking many paths along many different types of networks and devices between your computer and the host you are connected with.

The Internet's Protocols

Your computer sends data to and receives data from a host computer over the Internet. A program such as Telnet breaks up the data into packets. Protocols, which are standards that the computing community has agreed upon, specify how packets should be layered, or packaged, into even smaller packets. Different layers of packets address a variety of software and hardware needs in order to send information over different networks and communications links.

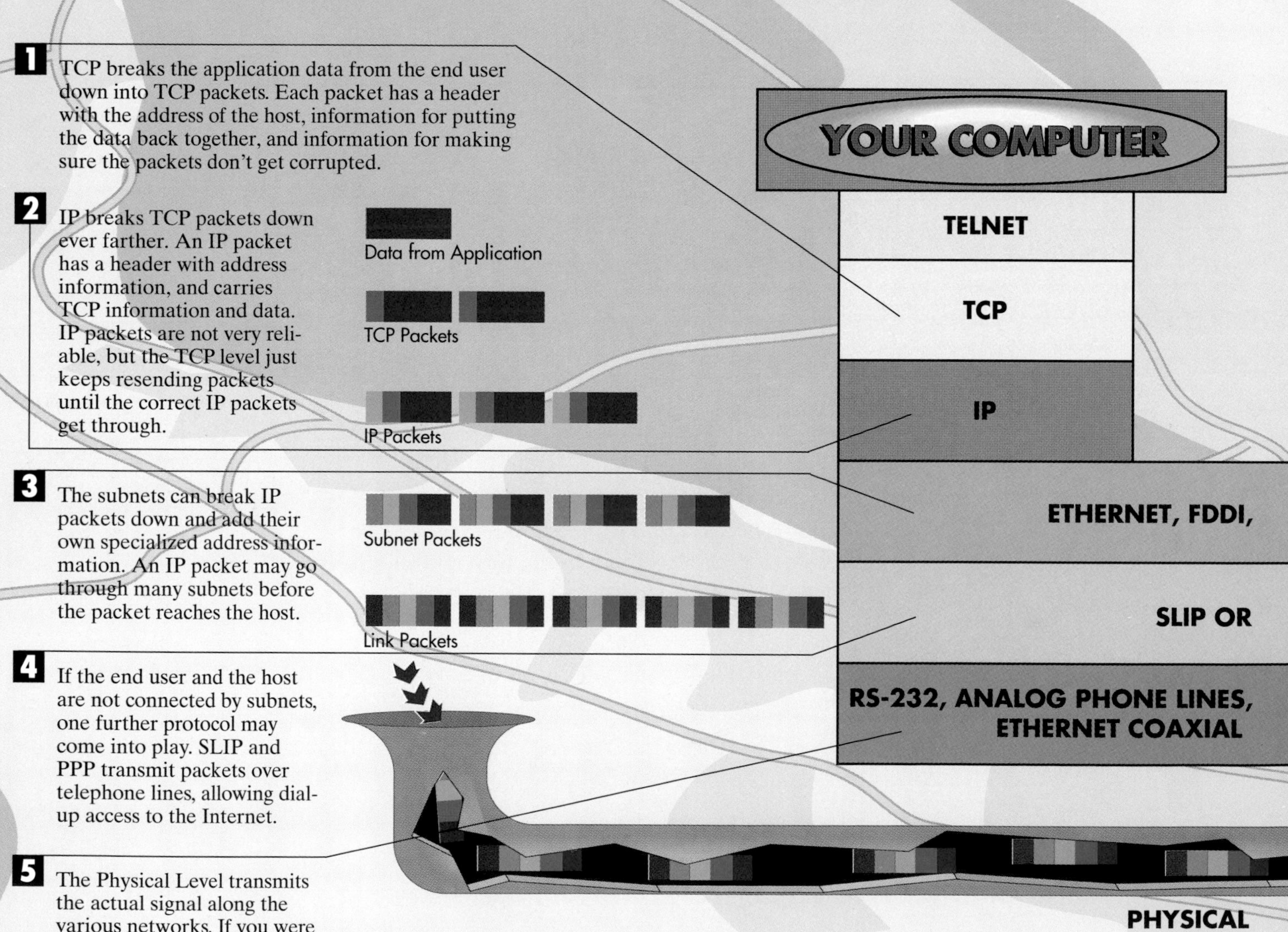
YOUR COMPUTER
TELNET
TCP
IP
ETHERNET, FDDI,
SLIP OR
RS-232, ANALOG PHONE LINES, ETHERNET COAXIAL
PHYSICAL
Data from Application
TCP Packets
IP Packets
Subnet Packets
Link Packets

1 TCP breaks the application data from the end user down into TCP packets. Each packet has a header with the address of the host, information for putting the data back together, and information for making sure the packets don't get corrupted.

2 IP breaks TCP packets down ever farther. An IP packet has a header with address information, and carries TCP information and data. IP packets are not very reliable, but the TCP level just keeps resending packets until the correct IP packets get through.

3 The subnets can break IP packets down and add their own specialized address information. An IP packet may go through many subnets before the packet reaches the host.

4 If the end user and the host are not connected by subnets, one further protocol may come into play. SLIP and PPP transmit packets over telephone lines, allowing dial-up access to the Internet.

5 The Physical Level transmits the actual signal along the various networks. If you were able to look at the signal, all you'd see would be a series of pulses.

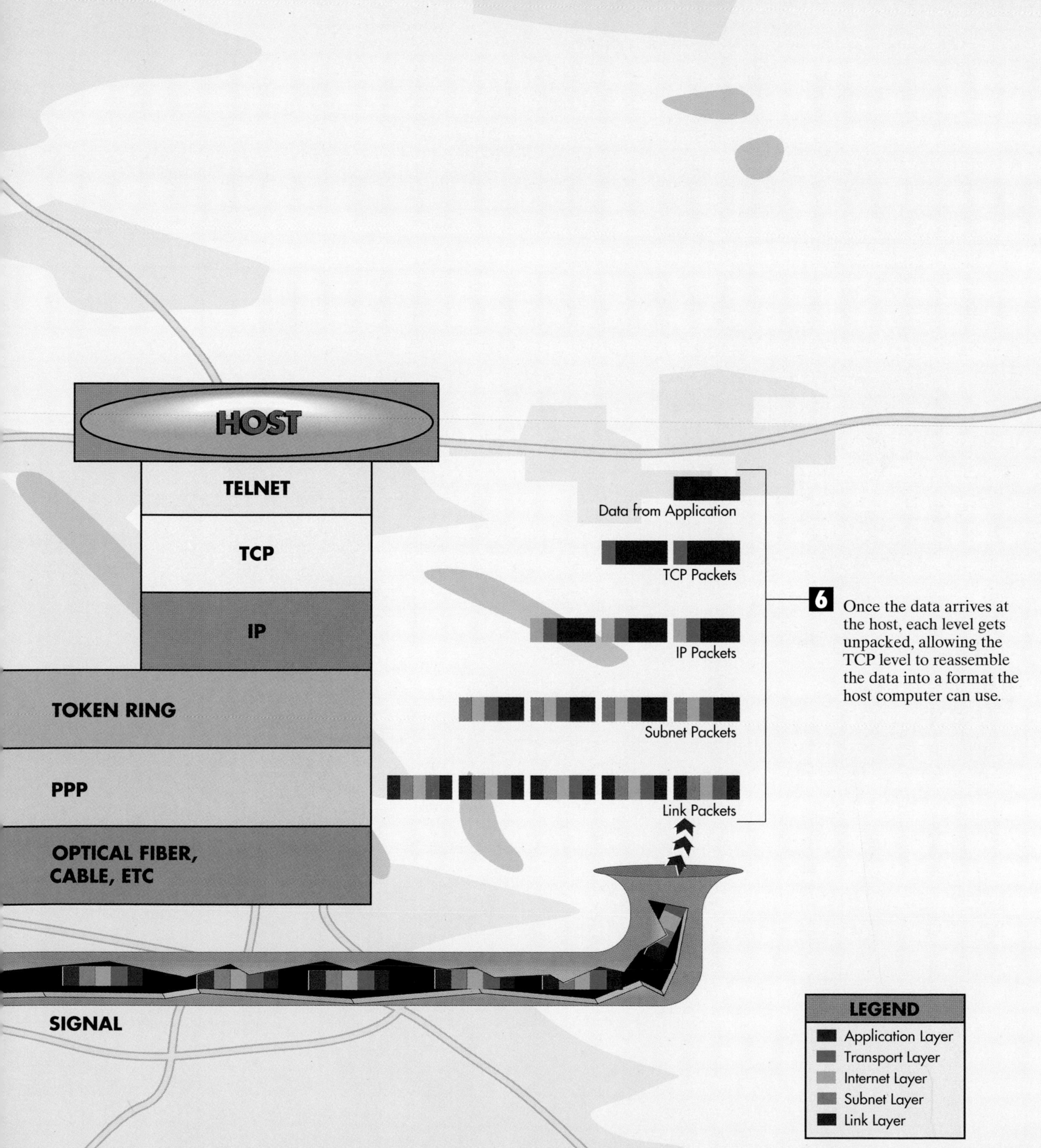
HOST
TELNET
TCP
IP
TOKEN RING
PPP
OPTICAL FIBER, CABLE, ETC
SIGNAL
Data from Application
TCP Packets
IP Packets
Subnet Packets
Link Packets
LEGEND
Application Layer
Transport Layer
Internet Layer
Subnet Layer
Link Layer

6 Once the data arrives at the host, each level gets unpacked, allowing the TCP level to reassemble the data into a format the host computer can use.

CHAPTER
5

Connecting Your Computer

HOW DOES A personal computer—whether it's an Apple Macintosh, an IBM PC-compatible, or even a UNIX workstation—connect to the Internet? Let's take a look at the range of possible connections.

If your computer is connected to a LAN or a campus network, you may be connected to the Internet already. A router or bridge extends the Internet to your computer over the network wiring already in place. This is a good way to gain access—the only limitations are the number of users on the system at any one time, and the speed of the links your network manager has put in place.

Your school or company may have a central computer. If so, you can use a *dumb terminal* (keyboard and a monitor) connected to the central computer. Dumb terminals use the computing resources of the central computer. You won't have any local disk access, and must rely on the central computer for storage space and processing power. If the central computer has a direct connection to the Internet, you can use that connection through your terminal.

The surest connection to the Internet is a direct connection. A direct connection wires your computer directly to a router over a special phone line, making it an official Internet computer. A direct connection is very expensive, and usually is used to connect larger networks and big computer systems to the Internet.

So what happens if you have a small LAN or single computer at home or at the office, and you can't afford a direct connection? There are a variety of dial-in options, all using modems over the general telephone system.

The simplest option is finding a network that supports dial-in connections with *terminal emulation software*. This special software makes the system you're calling think your computer (whether a Mac, a PC, or a UNIX workstation) is a dumb terminal calling in over regular phone lines. You don't actually run any of the Internet software on your computer, but on the computer you've connected with, and your screen "echoes" what's happening at the other end. You can use your computer to "capture" data coming over the line, and then work with that data off-line. A limitation of this type of connection, and of all dumb terminal connections, is that you can't use the processing power of your computer to run programs on the Internet. The choice of what you can run is limited by what the system administrator chooses to put on the system into which you are dialing.

A more flexible but less widespread variation of the dumb terminal is the *client/server* model. Client software running on your computer talks with a server over the phone line on the host computer, which is connected to the Internet. The client sends requests to the server, who then executes them and sends back the appropriate data or results.

A dial-in terminal emulation connection, even a client/server program, doesn't tap the full power of the Internet. You're only working remotely with another computer that is on the Internet. But there are ways to get a full Internet connection over phone lines.

SLIP (*Serial Line Internet Protocol*) and PPP (*Point to Point Protocol*) connections use a high-speed modem to connect a computer to the Internet over phone lines.

You dial in, connect, and your computer becomes part of the Internet. You have full access, up to the power and storage capacity of your computer. PPP is a newer protocol, and is able to "watch" the stream of data moving over the phone line. PPP can automatically have packets retransmitted if they get garbled, something that happens frequently on regular phone lines. Because SLIP doesn't check the packets being sent, it's faster than PPP, but not as reliable.

There are all kinds of connections available to the Internet, ranging from free dial-up terminal access to local systems such as the Cleveland Free-Net and local library systems, to expensive connections for the hard-core computer user. Start at your local college or library when looking for your own connection. Contact a *service provider* (a commercial company that provides network services as part of its business) for either direct connections or SLIP and PPP links. You may also want to check your local yellow pages under Telecommunications for the phone number of a local service provider, or check magazines about on-line computing for the number of a national service provider.

Connecting Your Computer

As long as you have access to a phone line, a modem, and a computer, you can connect to the Internet. There is a range of connections possible, from making a direct connection over special communications lines, to using a terminal emulation program and a modem on your computer to connect to a school or library system over the phone lines. Factors that determine the type of connection you can get include the types of networks that are already located in your building, your relationship to an institution that has an Internet network, and how much money you want to spend. Service providers can get you a SLIP or PPP connetion over any phone line. You can also check with commercial information systems to see if they offer Internet connections.

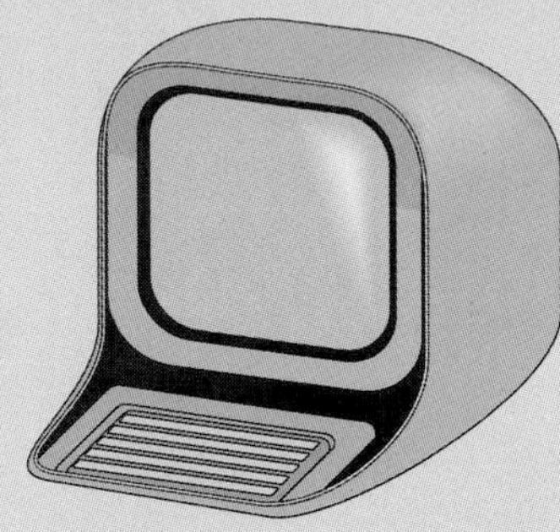

Dumb terminal A terminal that attaches directly to a mainframe or other large computer system. Usually found on campuses or in libraries.

Terminal emulation A personal computer can run a terminal emulation program, which communictes via a modem over a phone line to a central computer. The PC appears as a remote terminal to the host computer. A VT-100 is the most common terminal to emulate. This type of access to the Internet is limited to what the host computer system allows you to do.

Client/server software A personal computer becomes a client of a bigger computer running special server software. The PC can then use a more powerful graphical interface.

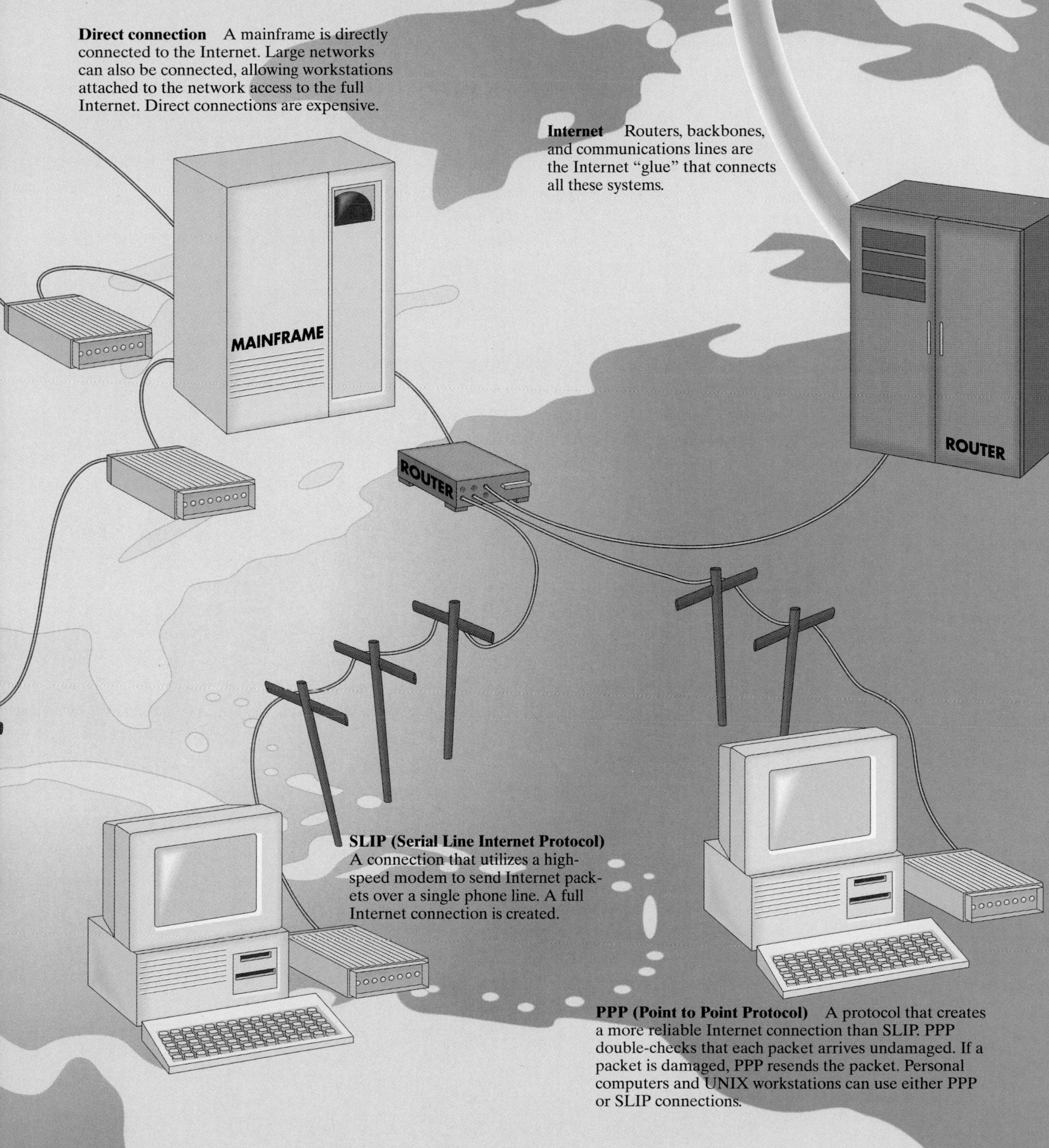
MAINFRAME
ROUTER
ROUTER

Direct connection A mainframe is directly connected to the Internet. Large networks can also be connected, allowing workstations attached to the network access to the full Internet. Direct connections are expensive.

Internet Routers, backbones, and communications lines are the Internet "glue" that connects all these systems.

SLIP (Serial Line Internet Protocol) A connection that utilizes a high-speed modem to send Internet packets over a single phone line. A full Internet connection is created.

PPP (Point to Point Protocol) A protocol that creates a more reliable Internet connection than SLIP. PPP double-checks that each packet arrives undamaged. If a packet is damaged, PPP resends the packet. Personal computers and UNIX workstations can use either PPP or SLIP connections.

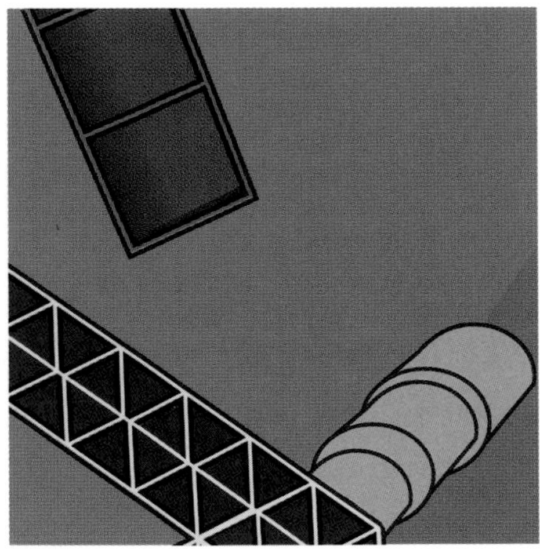

Telnet and NASA SPACElink

YOU CAN USE Telnet software when you want to log on to a host such as NASA SPACElink. NASA SPACElink, started in 1988, is a computer system run by the Public Services and Education Branch of the Marshall Space Flight Center Public Affairs Office, in Huntsville, Alabama. Telnet uses Transmission Contol Protocol (TCP) to send Internet Protocol (IP) packets between your computer and the host, creating a communications link across the Internet. Once Telnet connects your computer to NASA SPACElink, you can access the host system as if you were at a terminal in the next room.

SPACElink is a science teacher's dream come true. SPACElink's mission is to provide teachers and students electronic access to the vast amount of educational material available from NASA. In addition, NASA education specialists provide lesson plans, activities, programs, and other information that helps teachers use NASA's resources to teach science, physics, and aeronautics, from grade school all the way to the university level.

SPACElink contains information about NASA itself, and about the history and future of space exploration, as well as educational services and instructional materials. Under instructional materials you can find computer files such as animated clips of the Galileo flyby of Earth and Venus, periodic tables, and clip art. There are even plans for a paper shuttle glider kit. You can find electronic copies of NASA's Educators Newsletter, information on space program spinoffs and technology transfers, daily schedules for NASA Select TV, and much more.

At first, SPACElink was only available by modem and dial-up telephone lines. Now anyone can log on to NASA SPACElink from a personal computer by using a modem and calling (205) 895-0028. Outside Alabama, you have to pay some hefty long-distance charges, especially if you want to spend any time researching what's available.

The command telnet spacelink.msfc.nasa.gov connects your computer to NASA SPACElink. (If your version of Telnet won't accept spacelink.msfc.nasa.gov, try xsl.msfc.nasa.gov instead.) Spacelink.msfc.nasa.gov is the domain name, the Internet equivalent to the telephone number of NASA SPACElink. The domain name gets translated into a computer-readable Internet Protocol address, which is used by TCP/IP to find and connect with the host computer. (We'll take a closer look at domain names and Internet Protocol addresses in Chapter 13.)

Once Telnet connects your computer to NASA SPACElink, you log on to the system. You are then presented with the SPACElink menu. Under the current system you can poke around several levels of menus and view text files that interest you. Simply turn on the text capture mode of the software on your computer. You can also use Kermit, a file transfer protocol, to download large text files and program files to your computer.When you are finished with NASA SPACElink, choose the menu option to log out. This automatically closes your Telnet session, and takes you back home.

NASA connected NASA SPACElink to the Internet in 1991, allowing Telnet access to the system from any computer on the net. Now teachers and others have cheap or even free access to SPACElink, depending on what type of Internet access their school has. NASA continues to upgrade the hardware, software, and resources of SPACElink. By the summer of 1994, SPACElink should be running on a UNIX computer four times as powerful as the Data General computer it runs on now. The new computer will allow services such as e-mail for teachers, and a fuller implementation of File Transfer Protocol (FTP) to search for and download files. Storage space for scanned images and other files will also be greatly increased.

Telnet to NASA SPACElink

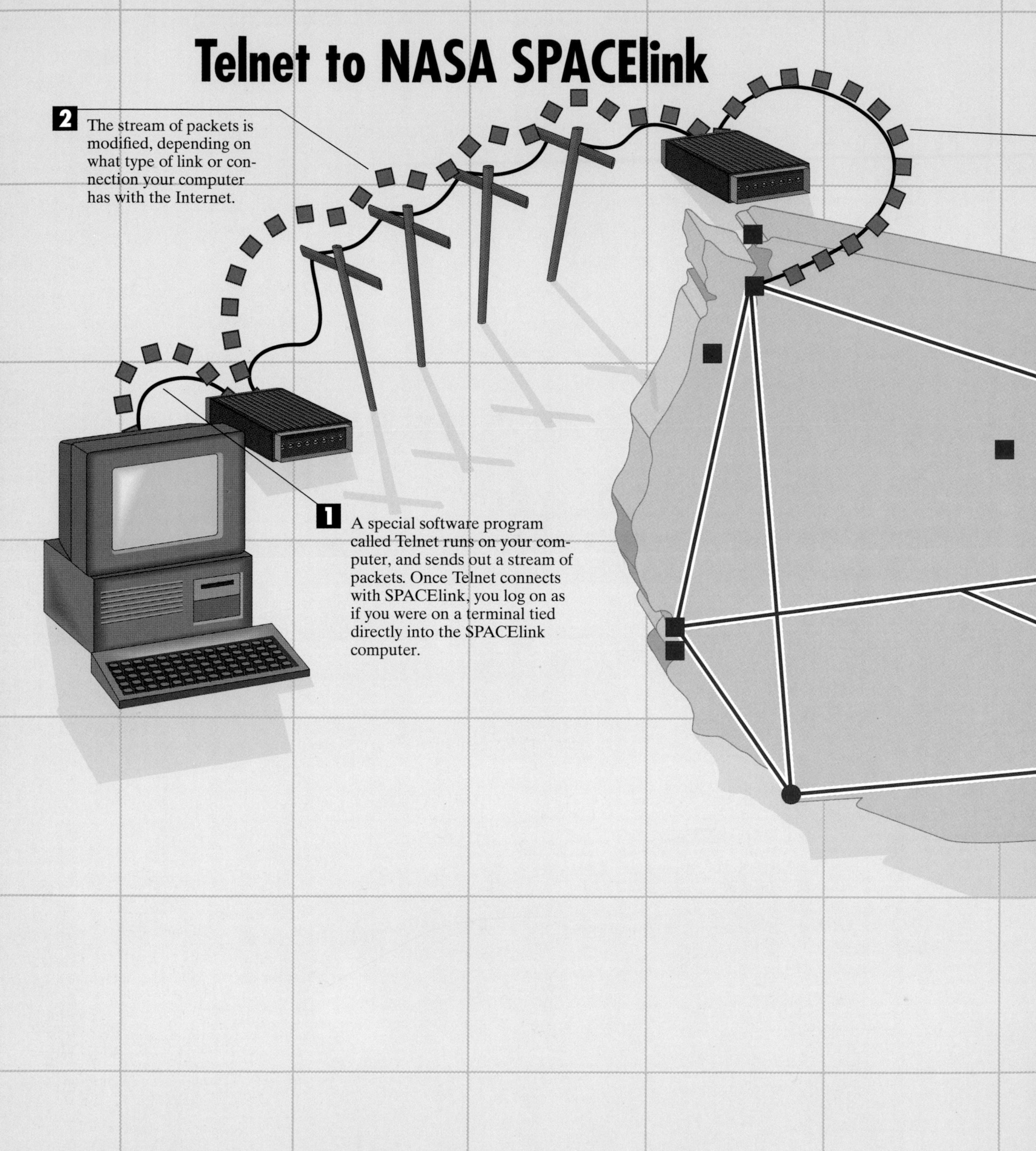
2 The stream of packets is modified, depending on what type of link or connection your computer has with the Internet.
1 A special software program called Telnet runs on your computer, and sends out a stream of packets. Once Telnet connects with SPACElink, you log on as if you were on a terminal tied directly into the SPACElink computer.

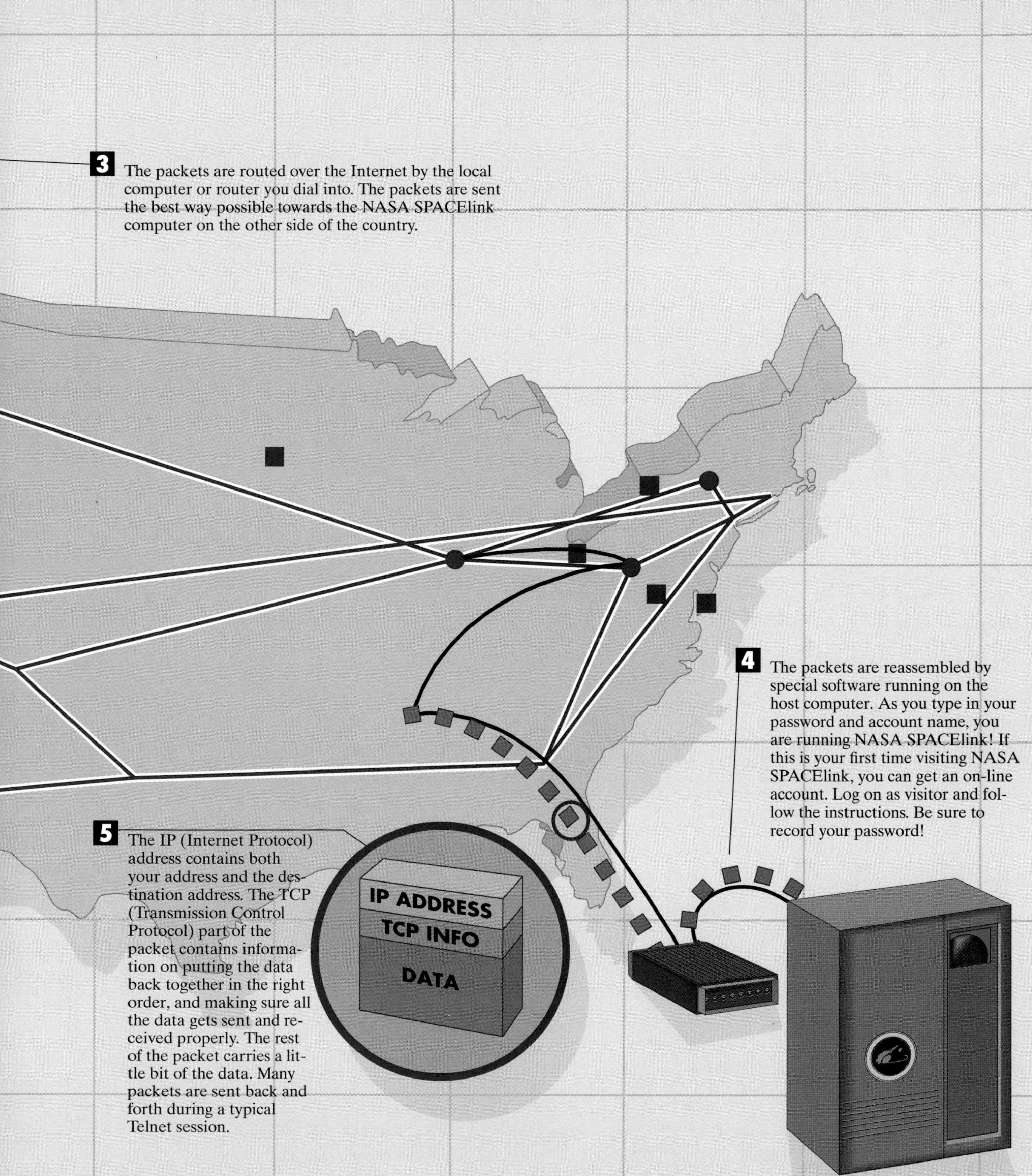
IP ADDRESS
TCP INFO
DATA

3 The packets are routed over the Internet by the local computer or router you dial into. The packets are sent the best way possible towards the NASA SPACElink computer on the other side of the country.

4 The packets are reassembled by special software running on the host computer. As you type in your password and account name, you are running NASA SPACElink! If this is your first time visiting NASA SPACElink, you can get an on-line account. Log on as visitor and follow the instructions. Be sure to record your password!

5 The IP (Internet Protocol) address contains both your address and the destination address. The TCP (Transmission Control Protocol) part of the packet contains information on putting the data back together in the right order, and making sure all the data gets sent and received properly. The rest of the packet carries a little bit of the data. Many packets are sent back and forth during a typical Telnet session.

NASA SPACElink

Once you log on to NASA SPACElink, a universe of scientific resources is opened for you from your own computer. This information, which is always growing and changing, has been gathered onto SPACElink by educational specialists for the benefit of teachers and spans the breadth of what NASA does.

Learn about everything from the Osprey VTOL (Vertical Takeoff and Landing) airplane to earth science, wind tunnels, virtual reality, and physics. NASA scientists are engaged in a tremendous variety of scientific work from Antarctica all the way to Mars.

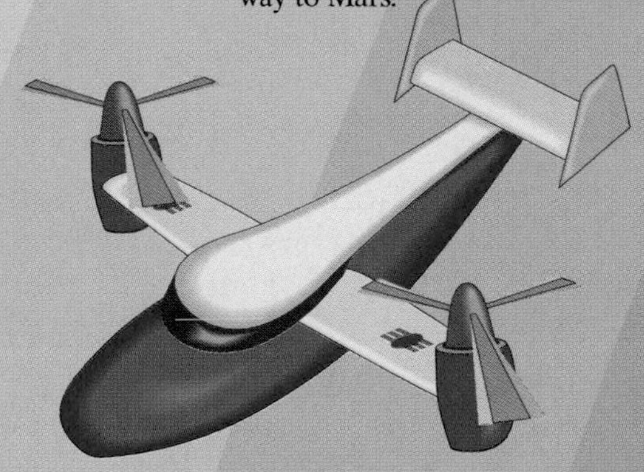

PASSWORD:
ACCOUNT NAME:

Get the latest schedules for NASA's own TV station, Select TV. Find out what's programmed for today. There's everything from live broadcasts from the space shuttle and historic documentaries on earlier missions, to science education specials and live press briefings. NASA Select TV is broadcast over a satellite, and is available free of charge to cable companies, schools, or anyone with a satellite TV system.

NATIONAL AERONAUTICS AND SPACE ADMINISTRATION
USA

Read about the history of the space program. Learn how rockets were first invented and used. Relive the Apollo missions to the moon and the Challenger disaster. Read about proposed trips to Mars and beyond. All this is stored electronically, waiting for you to read it—and share it with your students.

SPACE HISTORY
MISSION TO MARS

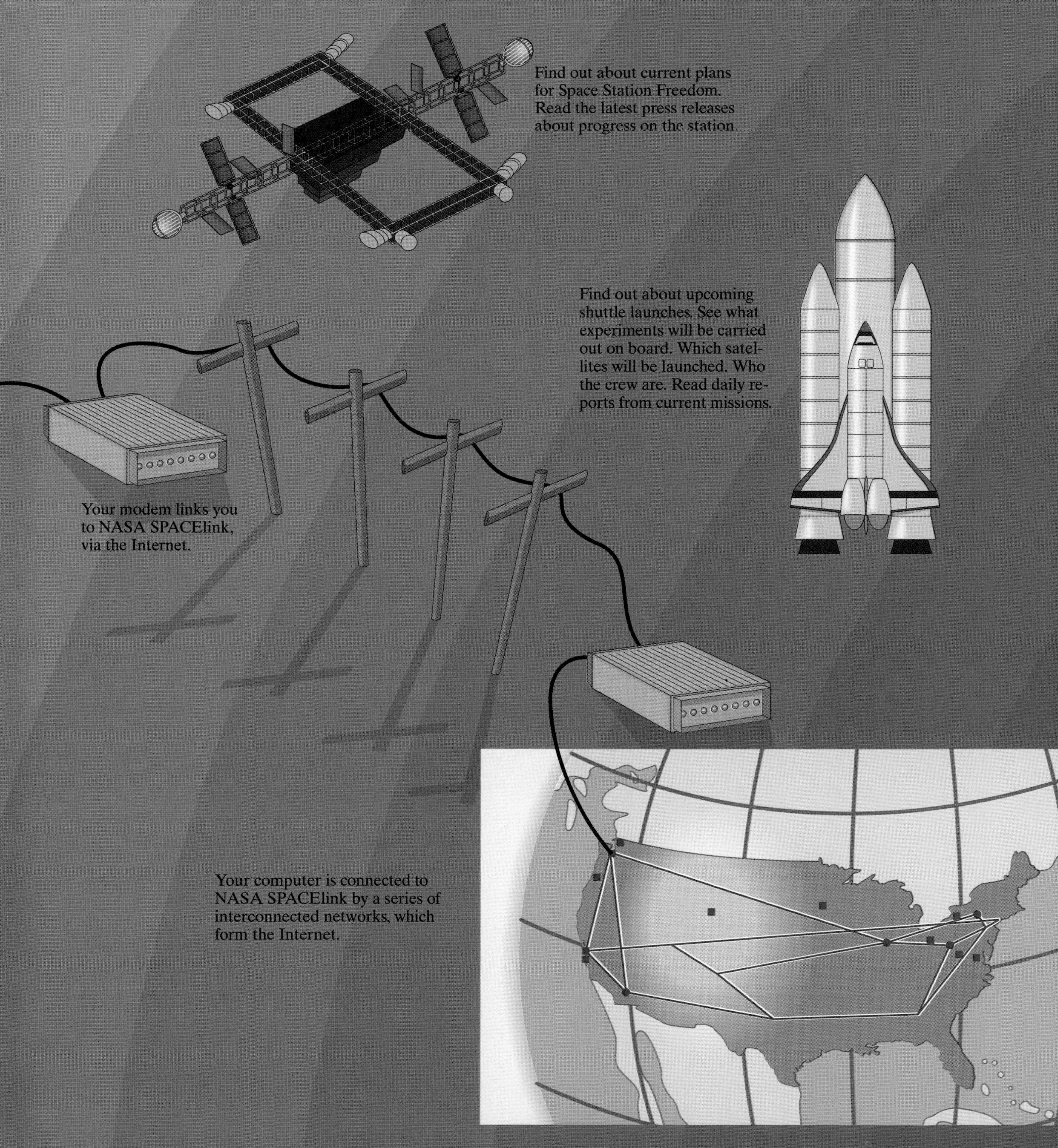
Find out about current plans for Space Station Freedom. Read the latest press releases about progress on the station.
Find out about upcoming shuttle launches. See what experiments will be carried out on board. Which satellites will be launched. Who the crew are. Read daily reports from current missions.
Your modem links you to NASA SPACElink, via the Internet.
Your computer is connected to NASA SPACElink by a series of interconnected networks, which form the Internet.

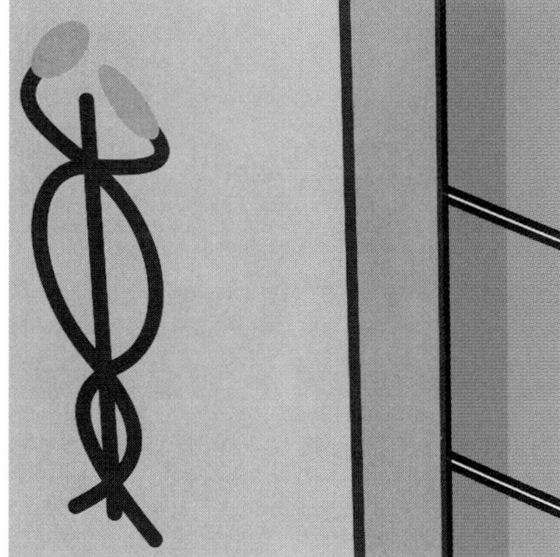

Telnet and Medline

MEDLINE IS THE National Library of Medicine (NLM) database. This database is an example of a useful resource you can reach via Telnet if you have an account and an Internet access. Medline on the Internet is not universally open to the public, but it is a good example of the specialized tools the Internet makes available. You can also reach a Medline database through CompuServe, a commercial on-line system, or by going directly to the National Library of Medicine.

The Medline database contains millions of articles from over 4,000 medical journals and publications. Often, abstracts of the article are also included. You can find complete bibliographic information, such as title, author, publication, date of publication, keywords, and much more. Medline pulls this data together, allowing researchers to look in just one place. For a price, anyone can access this database directly from the NLM. However, many university libraries license Medline and place copies on their own computer systems, allowing their researchers, teachers, and students to have unlimited access without an hourly or "per search" fee. Because of the cost of their license agreements and the cost of maintaining their hardware, most schools zealously guard accounts to "their" Medline. Many university libraries will tailor the Medline database to their own needs.

There are also different interfaces and application programs that provide access to the various Medline databases. For example, Medline at the University of California looks quite different from Medline at the University of Washington or the University of Michigan. Each uses a different computer system and software, although all Medlines provide the same sort of information.

The mechanics of using Telnet to access Medline are the same as using Telnet to access NASA SPACElink. If Medline@mymedschool.edu is the domain name of the Medline you want to use, the command telnet Medline@mymedschool.edu will connect you to it. Telnet turns your computer into a dumb terminal of the host computer running Medline.

After using Telnet to access a Medline system, you must log on with your account number and password. Accounts and passwords are usually obtained off line, directly from a medical school library. Once you've logged on, you can start your search.

Most Medlines offer a beginner-level search and an advanced, or expert mode. The beginner's search will lead you through the process, but is often rather limited in scope. In the advanced mode, a researcher has more control over the search parameters. With electronic researching, a researcher can sift through more material and search for keywords within abstracts and titles. You can search by word, or even partial word, within the title, abstract, author field, or subject and keyword fields. You can combine searches using the logical operators AND, OR, and NOT, as shown in the illustration for this chapter. You can also narrow a search by specifying the year or range of years of publication, or the type of publication. You can list your results or view complete bibliographic data for any or all of the results. Many libraries will fax you copies of the actual article (usually for a fee) if you request them.

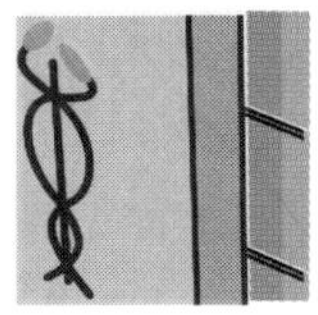

A Medline Search

Medline is just one of the many high-quality commercial databases available over the Internet. Access to such databases usually costs money because keeping a service like Medline current is expensive and requires a great amount of work.

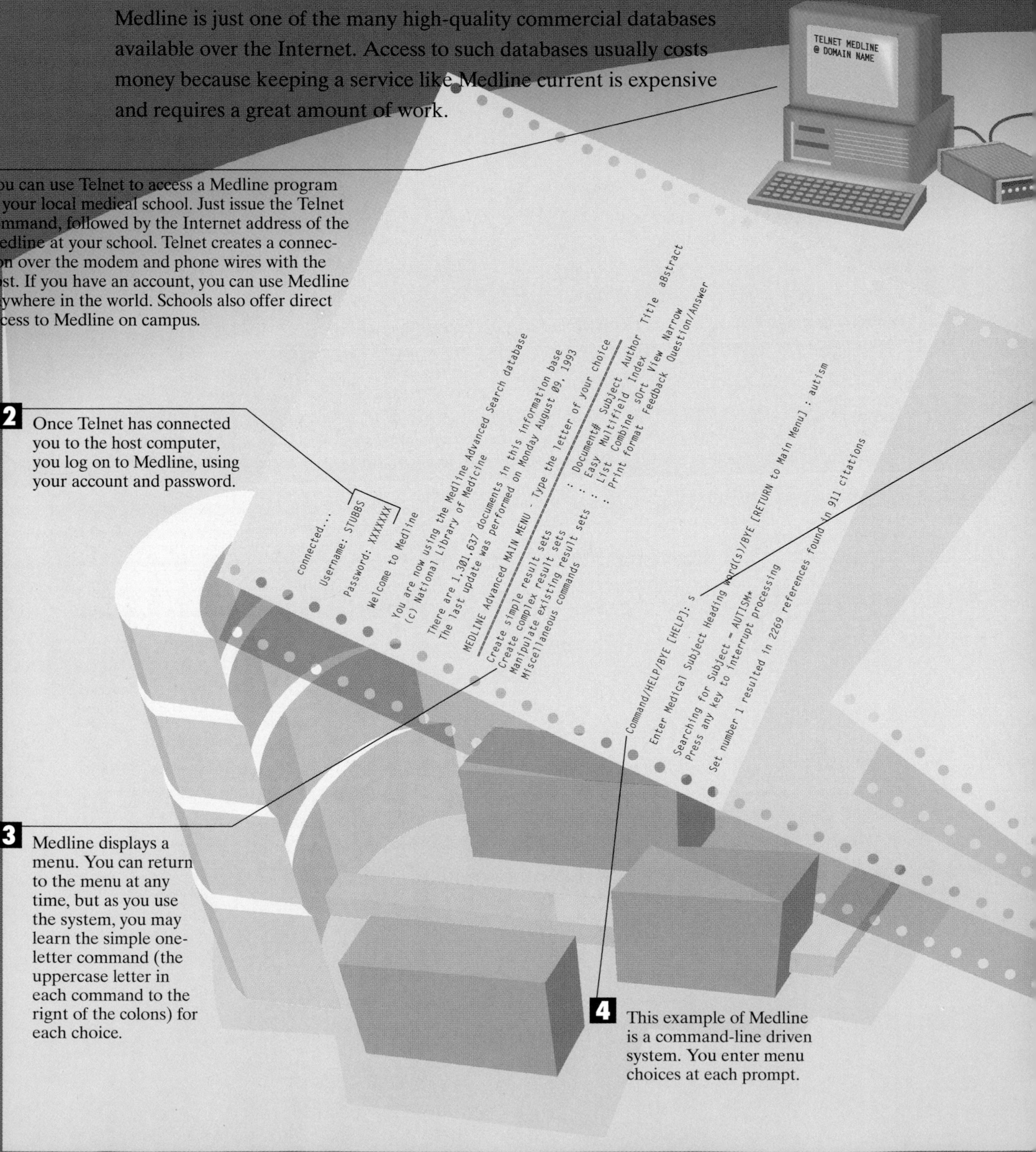

TELNET MEDLINE
@ DOMAIN NAME

1 You can use Telnet to access a Medline program at your local medical school. Just issue the Telnet command, followed by the Internet address of the Medline at your school. Telnet creates a connection over the modem and phone wires with the host. If you have an account, you can use Medline anywhere in the world. Schools also offer direct access to Medline on campus.

2 Once Telnet has connected you to the host computer, you log on to Medline, using your account and password.

```
connected...
Username: STUBBS
Password: XXXXXXX
Welcome to Medline
You are now using the Medline Advanced Search database
(c) National Library of Medicine
There are 1,301,637 documents in this information base
The last update was performed on Monday August 09, 1993
MEDLINE Advanced MAIN MENU - Type the letter of your choice
Create simple result sets        : Document# Subject Author Title aBstract
Create complex result sets       : Easy Multifield Index
Manipulate existing result sets  : List Combine sOrt View Narrow
Miscellaneous commands           : Print format Feedback Question/Answer
Command/HELP/BYE [HELP]: s
Enter Medical Subject Heading word(s)/BYE [RETURN to Main Menu] : autism
Searching for Subject = AUTISM*
Press any key to interrupt processing
Set number 1 resulted in 2269 references found in 911 citations
```

3 Medline displays a menu. You can return to the menu at any time, but as you use the system, you may learn the simple one-letter command (the uppercase letter in each command to the rignt of the colons) for each choice.

4 This example of Medline is a command-line driven system. You enter menu choices at each prompt.

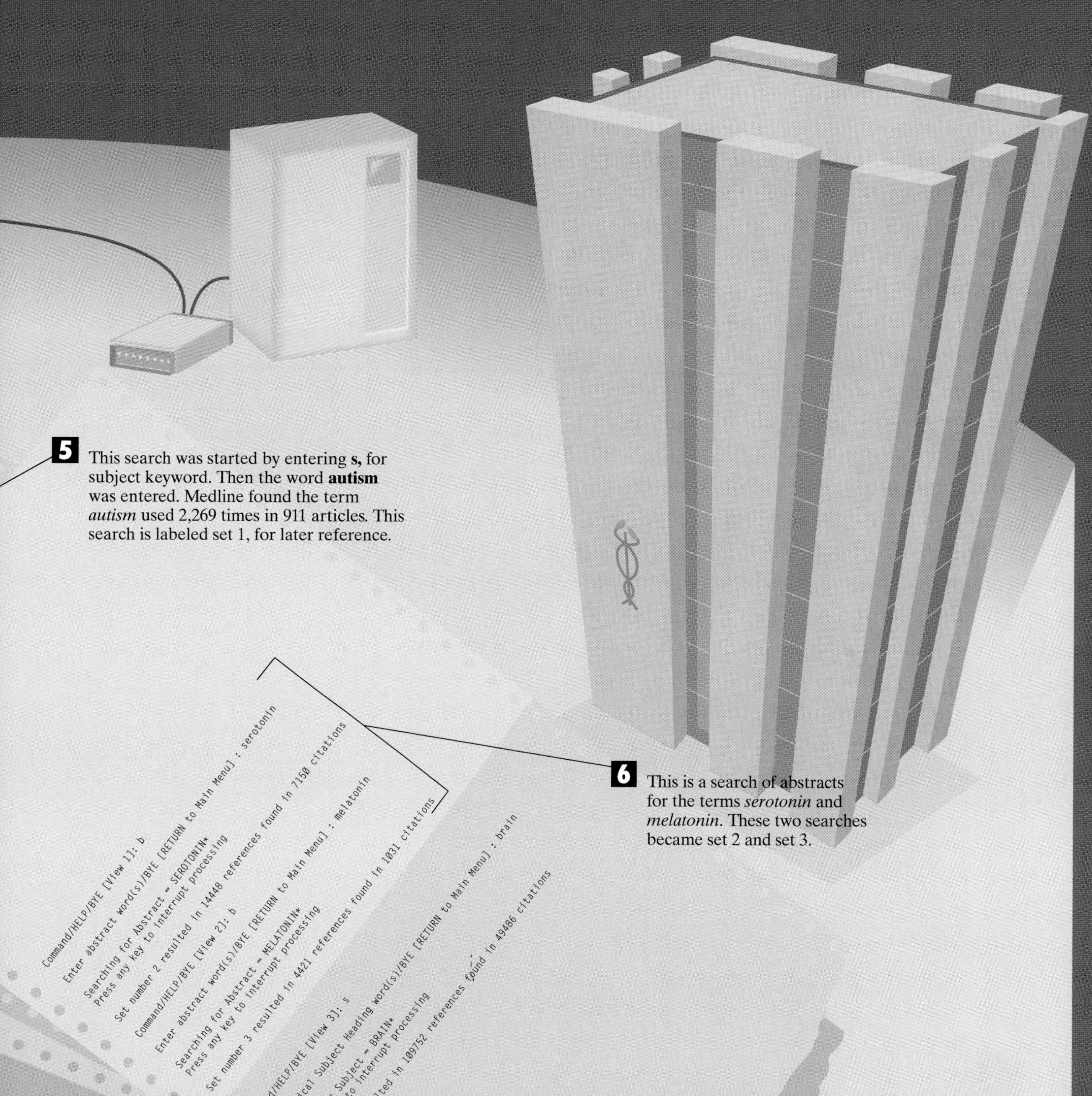

Command/HELP/BYE [View 1]: b
Enter abstract word(s)/BYE [RETURN to Main Menu] : serotonin
Searching for Abstract = SEROTONIN*
Press any key to interrupt processing
Set number 2 resulted in 14448 references found in 7150 citations
Command/HELP/BYE [View 2]: b
Enter abstract word(s)/BYE [RETURN to Main Menu] : melatonin
Searching for Abstract = MELATONIN*
Press any key to interrupt processing
Set number 3 resulted in 4421 references found in 1031 citations
Command/HELP/BYE [View 3]: s
Enter Medical Subject Heading word(s)/BYE [RETURN to Main Menu] : brain
Searching for Subject = BRAIN*
Press any key to interrupt processing
Set number 4 resulted in 109752 references found in 49486 citations

5 This search was started by entering **s,** for subject keyword. Then the word **autism** was entered. Medline found the term *autism* used 2,269 times in 911 articles. This search is labeled set 1, for later reference.

6 This is a search of abstracts for the terms *serotonin* and *melatonin*. These two searches became set 2 and set 3.

7 This is another subject heading search, this time on the term *brain*. This became set 4. [*Continued on next page.*]

Medline provides a good example of comprehensive search tools and shows how these tools can help you quickly sort through a massive amount of data to find what you really want.

8 The logical operators AND and OR were used to combine previous sets of searches into a single search. *Logical operators* allow the computer to make simple decisions. An English translation of this search would be, "Show me which articles are about autism *and* talk about serotonin *or* are about the brain *and* talk about melatonin."

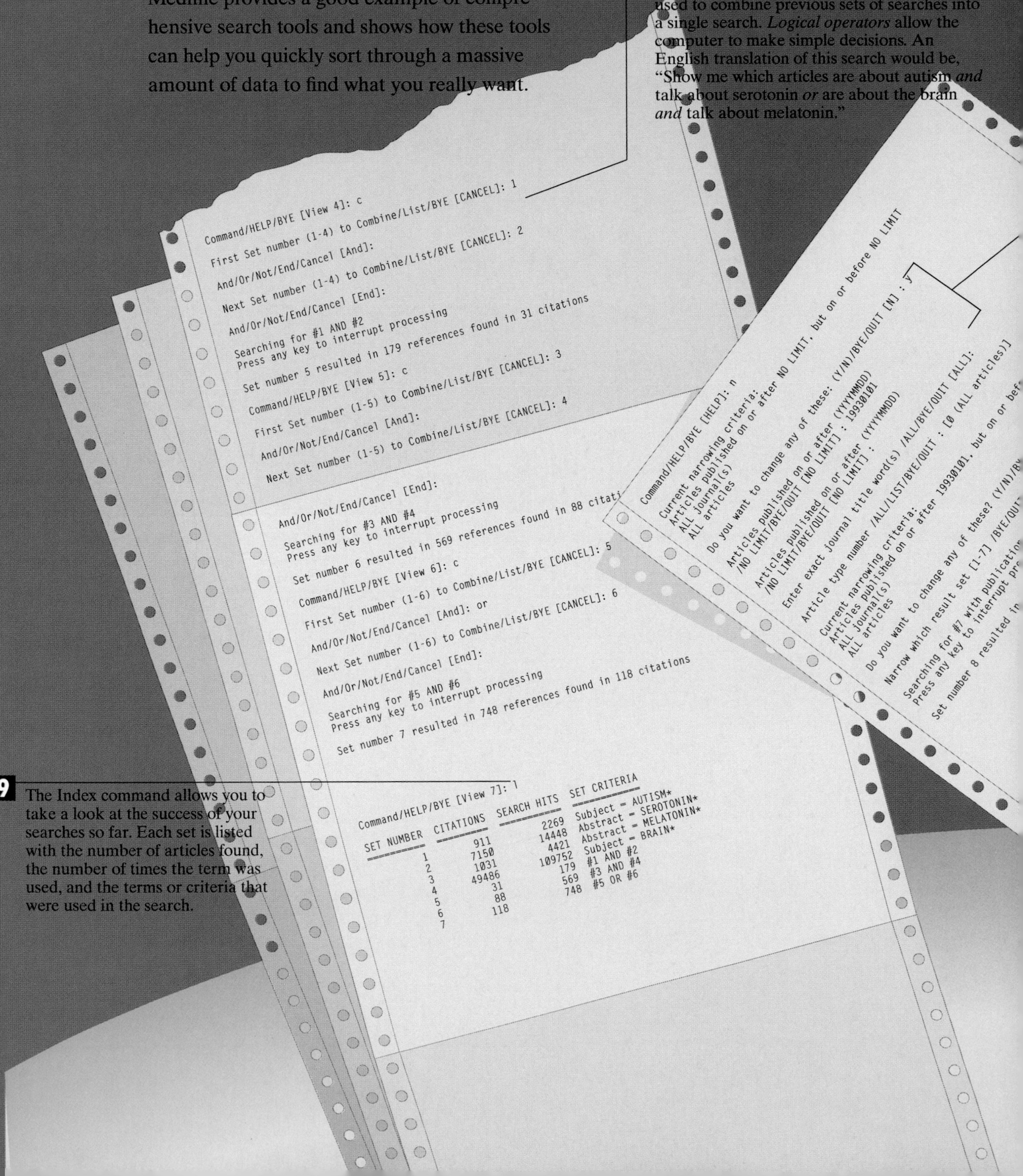

```
Command/HELP/BYE [View 4]: c
First Set number (1-4) to Combine/List/BYE [CANCEL]: 1
And/Or/Not/End/Cancel [And]:
Next Set number (1-4) to Combine/List/BYE [CANCEL]: 2
And/Or/Not/End/Cancel [End]:
Searching for #1 AND #2
Press any key to interrupt processing
Set number 5 resulted in 179 references found in 31 citations
Command/HELP/BYE [View 5]: c
First Set number (1-5) to Combine/List/BYE [CANCEL]: 3
And/Or/Not/End/Cancel [And]:
Next Set number (1-5) to Combine/List/BYE [CANCEL]: 4
And/Or/Not/End/Cancel [End]:
Searching for #3 AND #4
Press any key to interrupt processing
Set number 6 resulted in 569 references found in 88 citati
Command/HELP/BYE [View 6]: c
First Set number (1-6) to Combine/List/BYE [CANCEL]: 5
And/Or/Not/End/Cancel [And]: or
Next Set number (1-6) to Combine/List/BYE [CANCEL]: 6
And/Or/Not/End/Cancel [End]:
Searching for #5 AND #6
Press any key to interrupt processing
Set number 7 resulted in 748 references found in 118 citations

Command/HELP/BYE [View 7]: i

SET NUMBER  CITATIONS  SEARCH HITS  SET CRITERIA
==========  =========  ===========  ============
    1          911         2269     Subject = AUTISM*
    2         7150        14448     Abstract = SEROTONIN*
    3         1031         4421     Abstract = MELATONIN*
    4        49486       109752     Subject = BRAIN*
    5           31          179     #1 AND #2
    6           88          569     #3 AND #4
    7          118          748     #5 OR #6
```

```
Command/HELP/BYE [HELP]: n
Current narrowing criteria:
  Articles published on or after NO LIMIT, but on or before NO LIMIT
  ALL journal(s)
  ALL articles
Do you want to change any of these: (Y/N)/BYE/QUIT [N] : y
Articles published on or after (YYYYMMDD)
/NO LIMIT/BYE/QUIT [NO LIMIT] : 19930101
Articles published on or after (YYYYMMDD)
/NO LIMIT/BYE/QUIT [NO LIMIT] :
Enter exact journal title word(s) /ALL/LIST/BYE/QUIT [ALL]:
Article type number /ALL/BYE/QUIT : [0 (ALL articles)]
Current narrowing criteria:
  Articles published on or after 19930101, but on or bef
  ALL journal(s)
  ALL articles
Do you want to change any of these? (Y/N)/BYE/QUI
Narrow which result set [1-7] /BYE/QUI
Searching for #7 with publicatio
Press any key to interrupt pr
Set number 8 resulted in
```

9 The Index command allows you to take a look at the success of your searches so far. Each set is listed with the number of articles found, the number of times the term was used, and the terms or criteria that were used in the search.

10 Sometimes you may want to narrow a search. Search 7 found 118 articles that are about autism and serotonin or the brain and melatonin. That's too many to look at here! The search was narrowed down by limiting set 7 to articles published after January 1, 1993. This also produced the most current articles. The results of this narrowing process were stored in set 8.

11 Narrowing the search cut the number of articles down to 7. That's a manageable number. By pressing the Enter key at the command prompt, the default menu choice, View set 8, was chosen. The titles of the journal articles are listed on the screen.

```
Command/HELP/BYE [View 8]:
DOCUMENT 1 OF 7 - SET CRITERIA #7 with publications after 19930101
1. Autoradiographic localization of putative melatonin receptors in the brains
   of two Old World primates: Cercopithecus aethiops and Papio ursinus.
2. Distribution of melatonin receptors in the brain of the frog Rana pipiens as
   revealed by in vitro autoradiography.
3. Distribution and characterization of melatonin receptors in the brain of the
   Japanese quail, Coturnix japonica.
4. A double-blind comparison of clomipramine, desipramine, and placebo in the
   treatment of autistic disorder.
5. Platelet serotonin studies in hyperserotonemic relatives of childern with
   autistic disorder.
6. Serotonin and amino acid content in platelets of autistic children.
7. Melatonin Research in children with autism at Oregon Health Sciences University.
```

12 Suppose you decided to read article number 7. You would enter **7** at the prompt and press return. Medline would ask you if you wanted to view the document in the NLM (National Library of Medicine) format. *No* is entered in this example. The NLM format is a computer-style format, and you may simply want to read about the article. The citation is placed on the screen. Document number, title, authors, sources, keywords, and an abstract are contained in the citation.

```
Selection number(s)/Stop/BYE: [Stop] 7
Your selections have been noted. Choose READ to see them.
Selection number(s) /Read/All/Stop/BYE: [Read] a
NLM format? (Y/N) [N] :
Document 7 OF 7 - SET CRITERIA #7
Document No :
93XXXXXX
Title:
Melatonin Research in children with autism at Oregon Health Sciences University.
Author:
Stubbs G, Henley K; Eddings J
Source:
Rain Kids Newsletter
1993 August; 3(3): 4
MESH Headings:
Autism, Infantile!; child; Brain; Melatonin/urine;
Abstract:
Ten children with autism were tested for urinary levels of melatonin. Children
were prescreened for existence of sleep disorders. Medication contraindicated
for childrens' inclusion in the study were Inderol and Propanolol. A 24 hour
urine sample was taken and tested to detect whether levels of melatonin were
high, normal, or low.
```

13 Typing **bye** gets you out of Medline, and turns off the Telnet connection.

```
Titles/Stop/BYE [Titles]: bye
No more selections to display - Titles/Stop/BYE [Titles]
Thank you for using the MEDLINE Advanced Search Facility
```

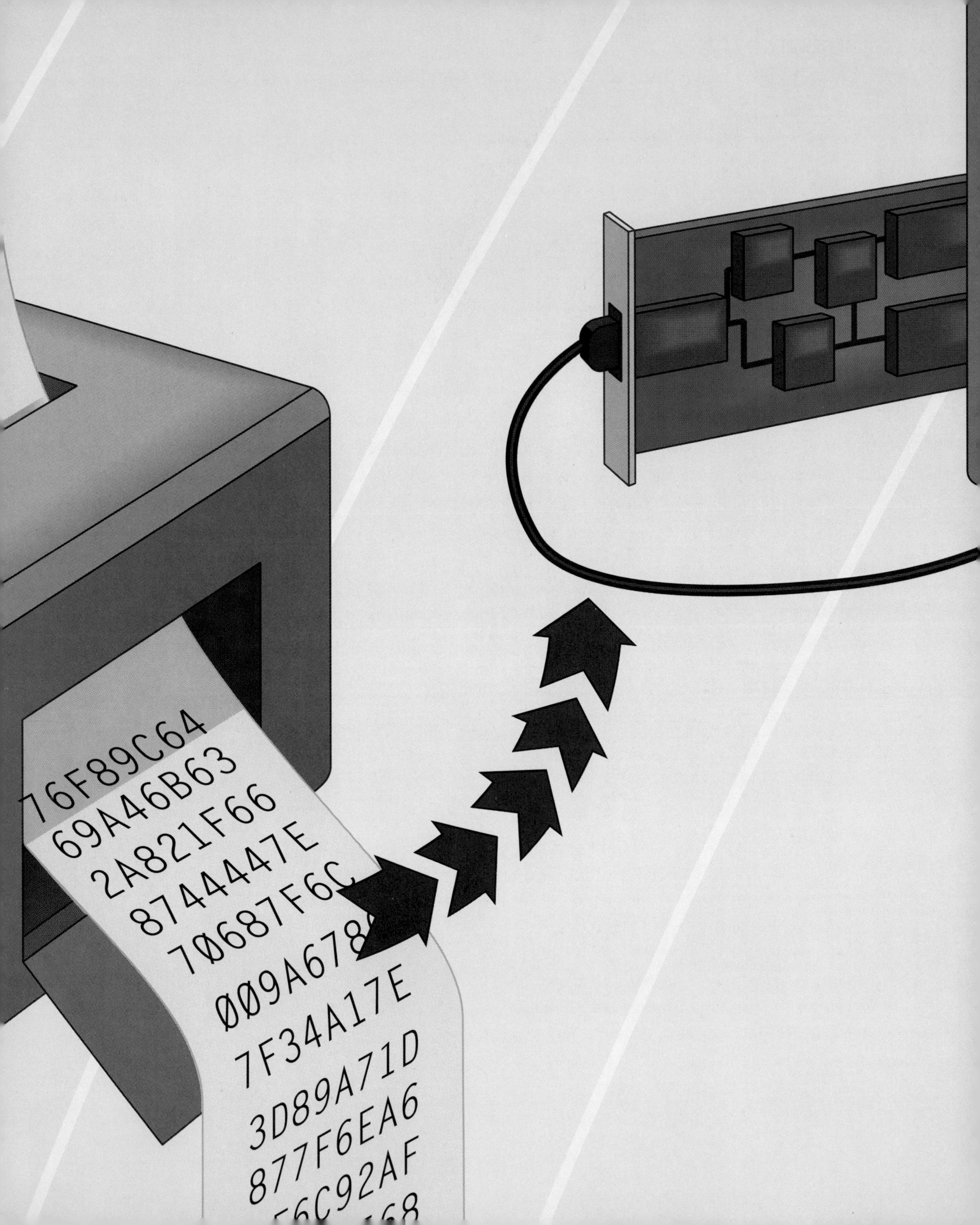
76F89C64
69A46B63
2A821F66
8744447E
7Ø687F6C
7F34A17E
3D89A71D
877F6EA6

DOWNLOADING FILES

CONTENTS

OVERVIEW

THERE ARE ALL kinds of resources available on the Internet. Much of this information is free; you just have to find the files you want and then *download* or transfer the files to your computer. Chapter 8 starts our exploration of downloading files by looking at archie. Archie is a robotlike program that checks over 1,500 FTP (File Transfer Protocol) sites about once a month to see what files are publicly available at each site. *FTP sites* are computers that store millions of files and data sets (collections of computerized data) on the Internet. The files at the FTP sites that archie checks occupy over 200 gigabytes of storage space (the average CD-ROM contains just over ½ gigabyte), and files are constantly being added and removed. Archie makes notes about each of the files it finds at these FTP repositories every month. These notes consist of the name of the file, the file's location—both the address of the FTP site and the location of the file within the site—and a description of the file, if archie finds one. You can use FTP to check each of these sites individually for files, but it's easier to use Telnet to access an archie server that contains information on files all over the world.

PART THREE

When you look for files on the Internet, you'll find software and data for all kinds of computers. For example, there are programs for Commodore 64s and Cray supercomputers, as well as ASCII text files, GIF (Graphics Interchange Format) images, and sound files. Program files are usually in binary code, and require special handling to send across the Internet. In this part, we'll take a close look at file types (Chapter 9) and file compression (Chapter 10). *File compression* shrinks files into smaller packages, so that the files take less time to send over the Internet. When you receive the file, you must *decompress* or expand the file into its original format. When you use a telephone connection that you pay for by the minute, the savings from file compression are obvious. On a packet-switched network such as the Internet, file compression allows more users to access the system at the same time.

We'll also take a close look at FTP in Chapter 11. FTP, along with Telnet and e-mail (the topic of Part 4 of this book), was one of the first tools developed for the Internet. FTP provides a simple way to move files across the Internet. You can use FTP to access an Internet address you found with archie—just give a password, and you're there! Anonymous FTP lets you find files on systems where you don't have a password. You can browse through the names and descriptions of files at an FTP site. You can download the files back to your computer. However, you can't run programs at the site—that's what Telnet is for.

Whether you're using FTP, archie, or a more advanced program that combines the two, a world of information that you can download is out there, waiting for you.

CHAPTER
8

Finding Files with Archie

THERE ARE OVER 30 archie servers in the world that let you look for files at FTP sites all over the Internet. An archie server is a computer, connected to the Internet that runs archie software. As of summer, 1993, there were approximately 12 archie servers in the United States alone. Some archie servers gather files from all over the globe. Others gather files from just the country or region in which the archie server is located. Limiting the geographic area an archie server gathers files from helps keep down the traffic on the transoceanic links of the Internet backbone. You should always choose the archie server that is closest to you. Otherwise, you waste Internet resources, tying up communication lines that could be used by others.

There are a couple of ways to use archie servers. The most basic way is to use Telnet to connect with an archie site, and log on using archie as the account name. This method does not require a password. You can then search for files within the archie database by name, by type of file, or by using wildcard characters, such as * and $. *Wildcard characters* are often used in UNIX and MS-DOS operating systems to do file searches when the full name of a file is not known. You can even search through any file descriptions that the archie server might contain. The archie server can give you a list of matching files, along with the names of the FTP sites that store the files. If you don't have full access to the Internet, you can send a search within an e-mail letter (see Part 4) to an archie server. The archie server searches its databases, then sends a reply to you via electronic mail.

You can also use client software to streamline and automate archie searches between your computer and the archie server. A full Telnet connection is not required, since the client software manages the communications. Client software is available from archie sites.

About once a month an archie server logs on to every file server it can access with FTP, and automatically asks for information on all files at that site. The archie server can update its own database, dropping files that are no longer at an FTP site, and adding new files. The archie server also reads any descriptions that may be with the files at the site.

Finding Files with Archie

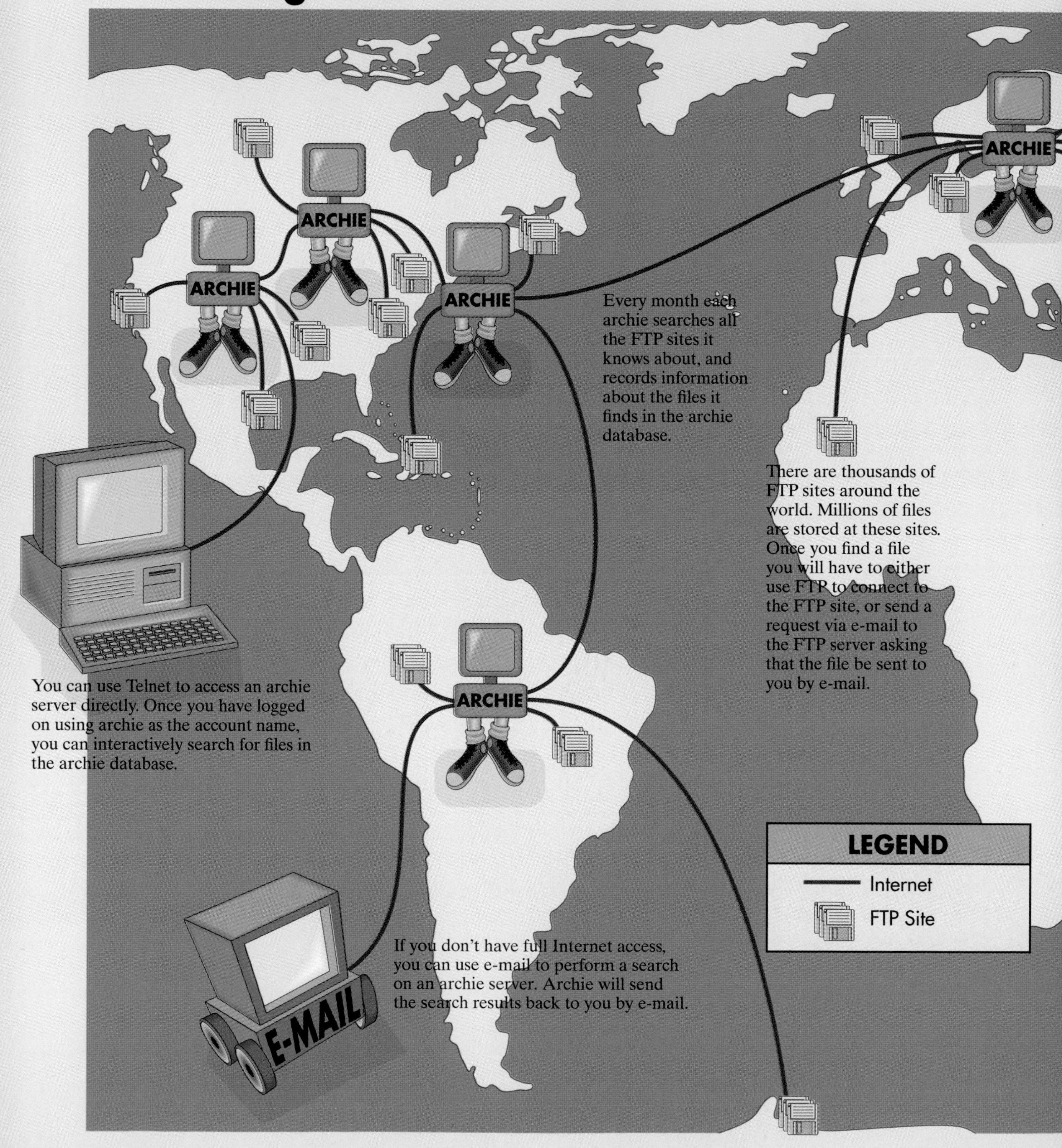
ARCHIE
ARCHIE
ARCHIE
ARCHIE
ARCHIE
E-MAIL
LEGEND
Internet
FTP Site

Every month each archie searches all the FTP sites it knows about, and records information about the files it finds in the archie database.

There are thousands of FTP sites around the world. Millions of files are stored at these sites. Once you find a file you will have to either use FTP to connect to the FTP site, or send a request via e-mail to the FTP server asking that the file be sent to you by e-mail.

You can use Telnet to access an archie server directly. Once you have logged on using archie as the account name, you can interactively search for files in the archie database.

If you don't have full Internet access, you can use e-mail to perform a search on an archie server. Archie will send the search results back to you by e-mail.

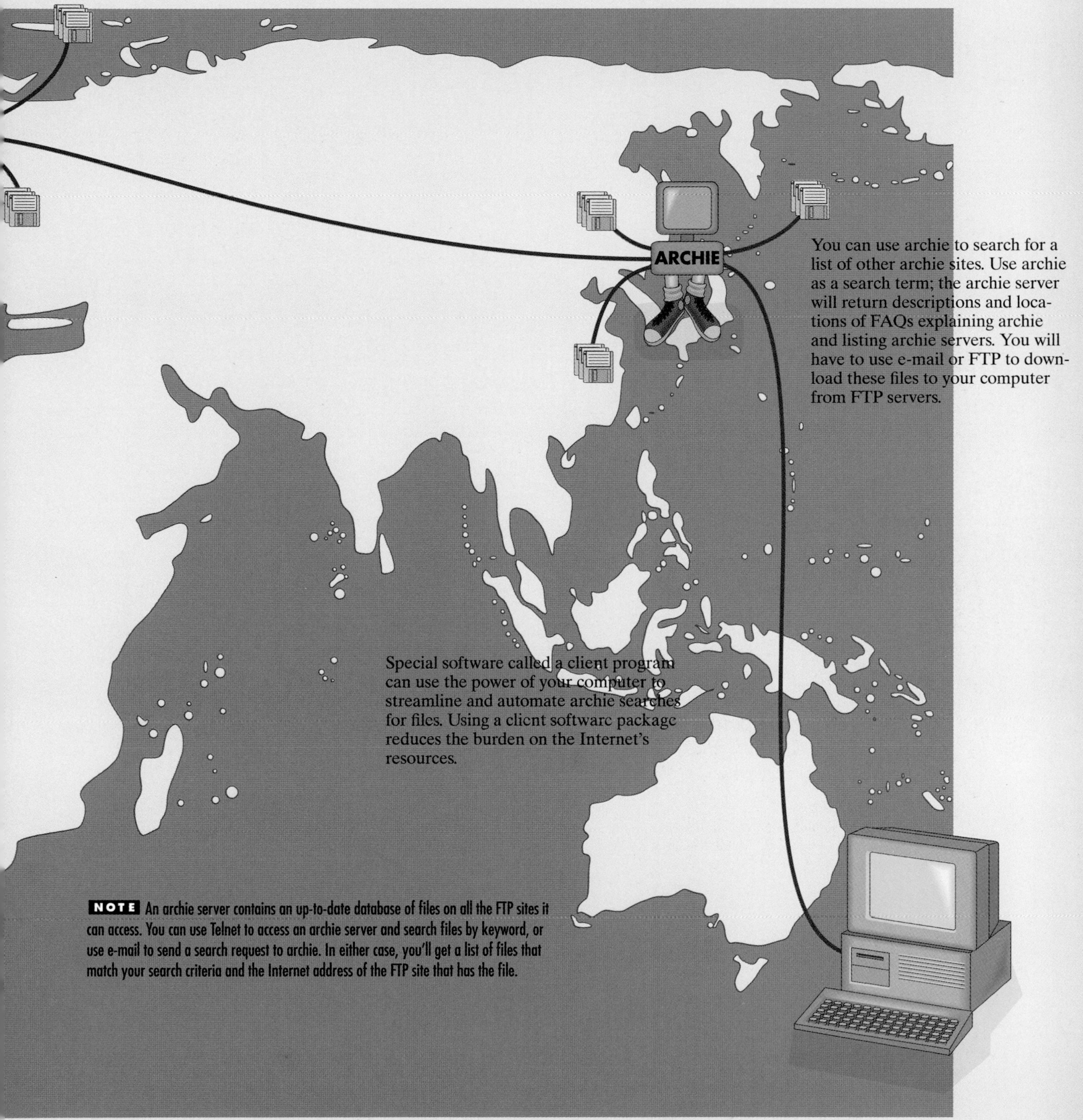
ARCHIE

You can use archie to search for a list of other archie sites. Use archie as a search term; the archie server will return descriptions and locations of FAQs explaining archie and listing archie servers. You will have to use e-mail or FTP to download these files to your computer from FTP servers.

Special software called a client program can use the power of your computer to streamline and automate archie searches for files. Using a client software package reduces the burden on the Internet's resources.

NOTE An archie server contains an up-to-date database of files on all the FTP sites it can access. You can use Telnet to access an archie server and search files by keyword, or use e-mail to send a search request to archie. In either case, you'll get a list of files that match your search criteria and the Internet address of the FTP site that has the file.

76F89
69A4
2A

File Types

THERE ARE MILLIONS of files on the Internet. In order for different computer systems, such as Macs and IBM-compatibles, to exchange various types of files over the Internet, they must have the right software. Some files even require special hardware.

As far as the Internet is concerned, there are three basic types of files: ASCII (American Standard Code for Information Interchange), EBCDIC (Extended Binary Coded Decimal Interchange Code), and binary. ASCII and EBCDIC are nothing more than protocols, or standard ways to organize bits of data into something that humans can understand. ASCII is the common denominator for character-based computing. ASCII codes within your computer represent the characters you see on your screen. EBCDIC works like ASCII, but is only used between certain types of mainframe computers, and isn't something you'll normally run into.

As far as computers are concerned, everything is *binary*—a stream of bits of 1s and 0s. Binary files can be *executable program files*, which contain instructions for a specific kind of computer. For example, a Mac program will not run on an IBM-compatible computer. Sometimes you may be able to translate instructions for your computer. To do this, you need a compiler and a copy of the programmer's original code, both of which are often not available. (A *compiler* is a program designed for translating computer-specific instructions into machine code.) As an alternative, you may be able to get your computer to emulate another type of computer. But getting a computer to *emulate*, or pretend it's another type of computer, requires special hardware, and it can be impractical. It's usually easier to run program files that were written for your computer.

You will find many ASCII text files on the Internet that contain nothing but simple character data. These files lack the sophisticated formatting commands word processing or desktop publishing can apply to a document. These formatting commands are stored in binary files. Word processing and desktop publishing programs from WordStar to PageMaker have each created their own binary file standard. You can always view ASCII files, but binary files may not always be compatible with your computer or software.

In contrast to word processing files, the *PostScript page description language* uses ASCII characters to tell a printer how to "draw" a page. PostScript printers are very popular and you'll find quite a few PostScript files out on the Internet. Don't bother downloading PostScript files unless you have a PostScript printer or software that can translate PostScript files into graphics your computer can handle. If you ever accidentally try to print a PostScript file on a non-PostScript printer, you'll get miles of description on just how that file would look on a PostScript printer!

Sound and visual images can be created from binary files that contain the appropriate data. You can find *sound clips* on the Internet, which are short recorded sounds for Macs and PCs. These files are fairly large, and usually need special hardware and software. We'll take a closer look at how sound files are used when we look at Internet Talk Radio in Chapter 24.

Although visual images are very complex, much work has gone into creating software that translates images between different file formats. GIF, or *Graphics Interchange Format*, is a standard that has emerged in the personal computer world. CompuServe, a commercial on-line service, created this standard and GIF files are common on the Internet, and have become a standard way to store pictures that are computer generated or scanned into computer files. Computer images also require high-resolution monitors and the appropriate hardware and software to drive them.

How File Types Work

You can find all sorts of file types on the Internet. Let's take a look at how some of the common file types work on your computer. If you understand how files work you have a better chance at deciphering what a file does and whether you can use it on your computer.

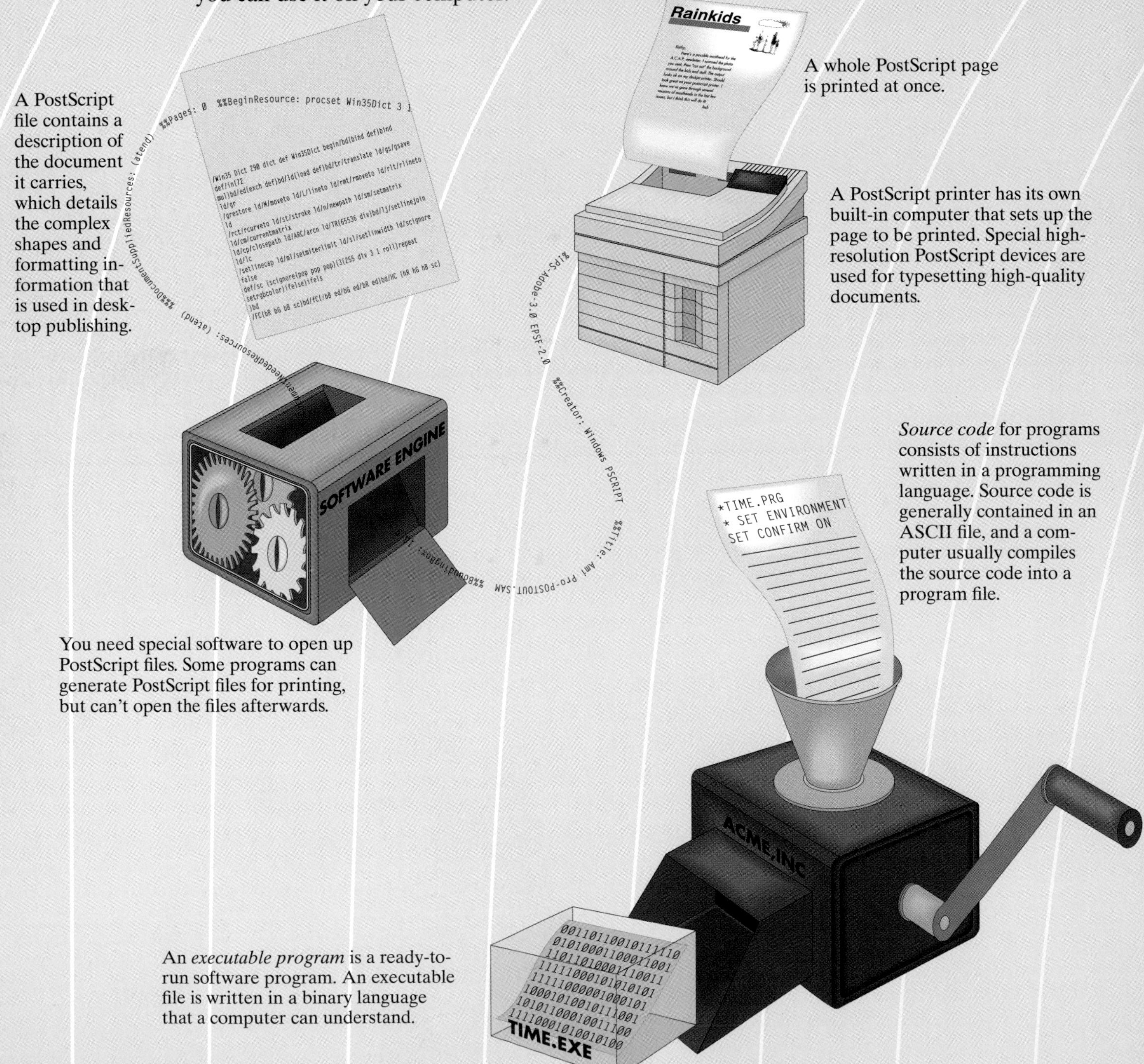
Rainkids
%%Pages: 0 %%BeginResource: procset Win35Dict 3 1
%%DocumentSuppliedResources: (atend)
%%DocumentNeededResources: (atend)
%!PS-Adobe-3.0 EPSF-2.0
%%Creator: Windows PSCRIPT
%%Title: Ami Pro-POSTOUT.SAM
SOFTWARE ENGINE
*TIME.PRG
* SET ENVIRONMENT
SET CONFIRM ON
ACME,INC
TIME.EXE

A PostScript file contains a description of the document it carries, which details the complex shapes and formatting information that is used in desktop publishing.

A whole PostScript page is printed at once.

A PostScript printer has its own built-in computer that sets up the page to be printed. Special high-resolution PostScript devices are used for typesetting high-quality documents.

You need special software to open up PostScript files. Some programs can generate PostScript files for printing, but can't open the files afterwards.

Source code for programs consists of instructions written in a programming language. Source code is generally contained in an ASCII file, and a computer usually compiles the source code into a program file.

An *executable program* is a ready-to-run software program. An executable file is written in a binary language that a computer can understand.

A GIF file allows the exchange of many types of image files between different kinds of computers. GIF files can also be downloaded quickly.

Your computer will need a video monitor that is advanced enough to display GIF images. The video display card helps translate the data into the signals that display the image on your monitor.

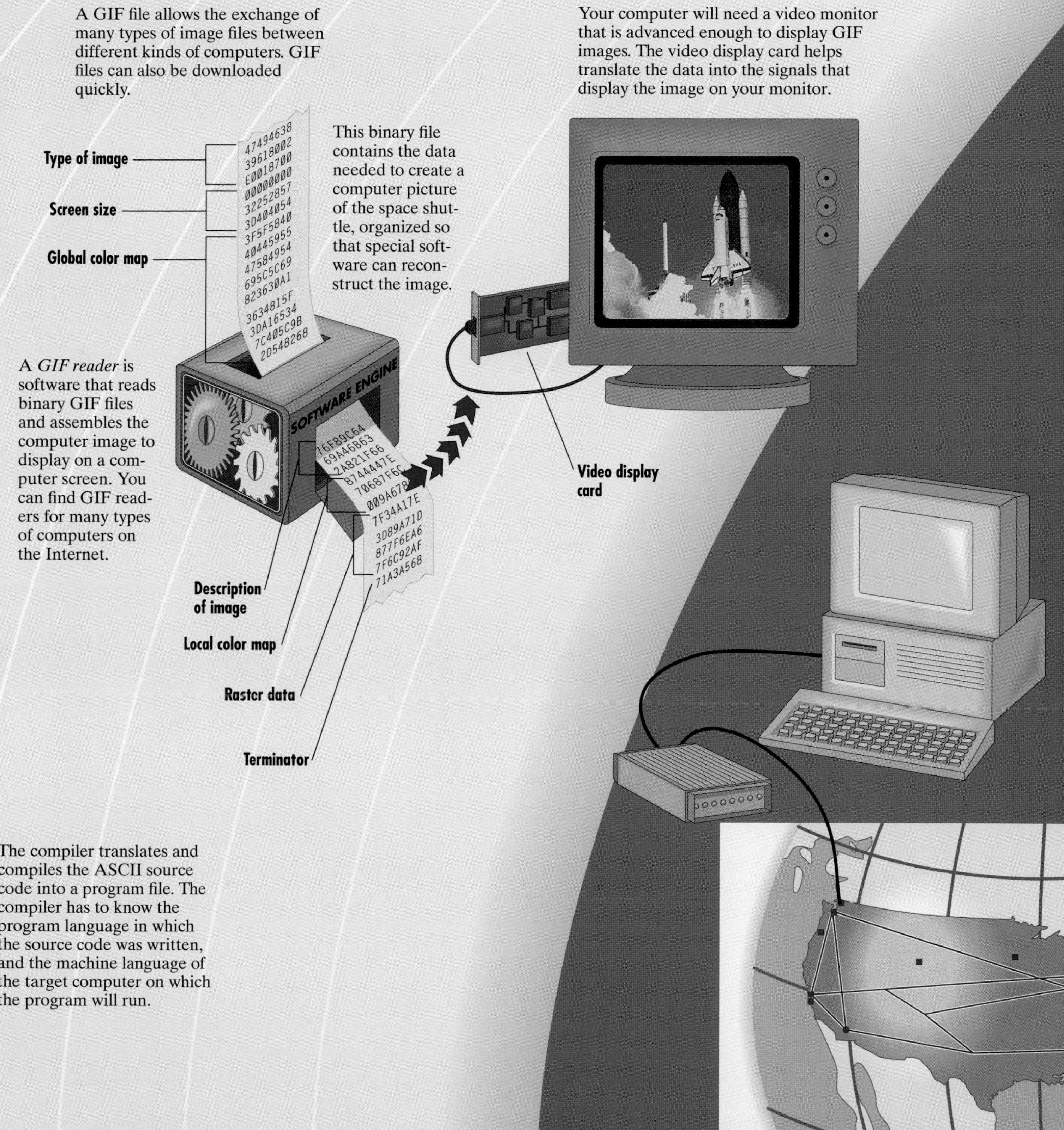
Type of image
Screen size
Global color map
SOFTWARE ENGINE
Description of image
Local color map
Raster data
Terminator
Video display card

This binary file contains the data needed to create a computer picture of the space shuttle, organized so that special software can reconstruct the image.

A *GIF reader* is software that reads binary GIF files and assembles the computer image to display on a computer screen. You can find GIF readers for many types of computers on the Internet.

The compiler translates and compiles the ASCII source code into a program file. The compiler has to know the program language in which the source code was written, and the machine language of the target computer on which the program will run.

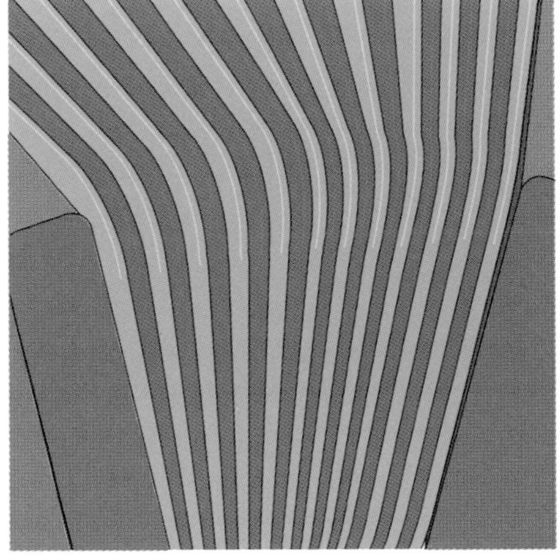

CHAPTER
10

File Compression

FILE COMPRESSION SIMPLY squeezes a file down into the smallest size possible. It takes less disk space to store a compressed file, and the file can be sent over the Internet faster. The methods used to compress files can be very sophisticated. A *compression program* replaces frequently occurring words or data with smaller, symbolic tokens that expand back to full words or data when the program is decompressed. Some compression programs, such as UNIX's TAR, will combine a group of files before compression takes place. Once you download the compressed file, you can decompress it on your computer. A compression protocol can be added to a file of any type, and there is a wide variety of compression programs, many of which are computer specific.

Once you get the compressed file to your computer, you'll need to use the proper decompression program to pop the file back to its original size. Decompression programs for different computer platforms are usually available from the same source from which you transferred the file. If you don't already have the right decompression program, you should download the correct program when you download the file. A *self-extracting* program automatically restores the original file once the file is in your computer. Of course, self-extracting files only work on the type of computer they were compressed for; decompression programs are available for extracting files that were compressed for different computer platforms, such as Macs and PCs.

When you look for files on the Internet you should be familiar with the different file types and compression methods used on these files. You should know how to identify file extensions—the three-letter suffixes that often follow the period after a file name. The extension often identifies the file type, the computer or software type, as well as the decompression method required. This is very handy information when you decide what files you want to download with FTP.

File Compression

Many files you will find on the Internet are compressed to save space on the FTP server and to save time when the files travel across the Internet.

3 The file is sent over the Internet.

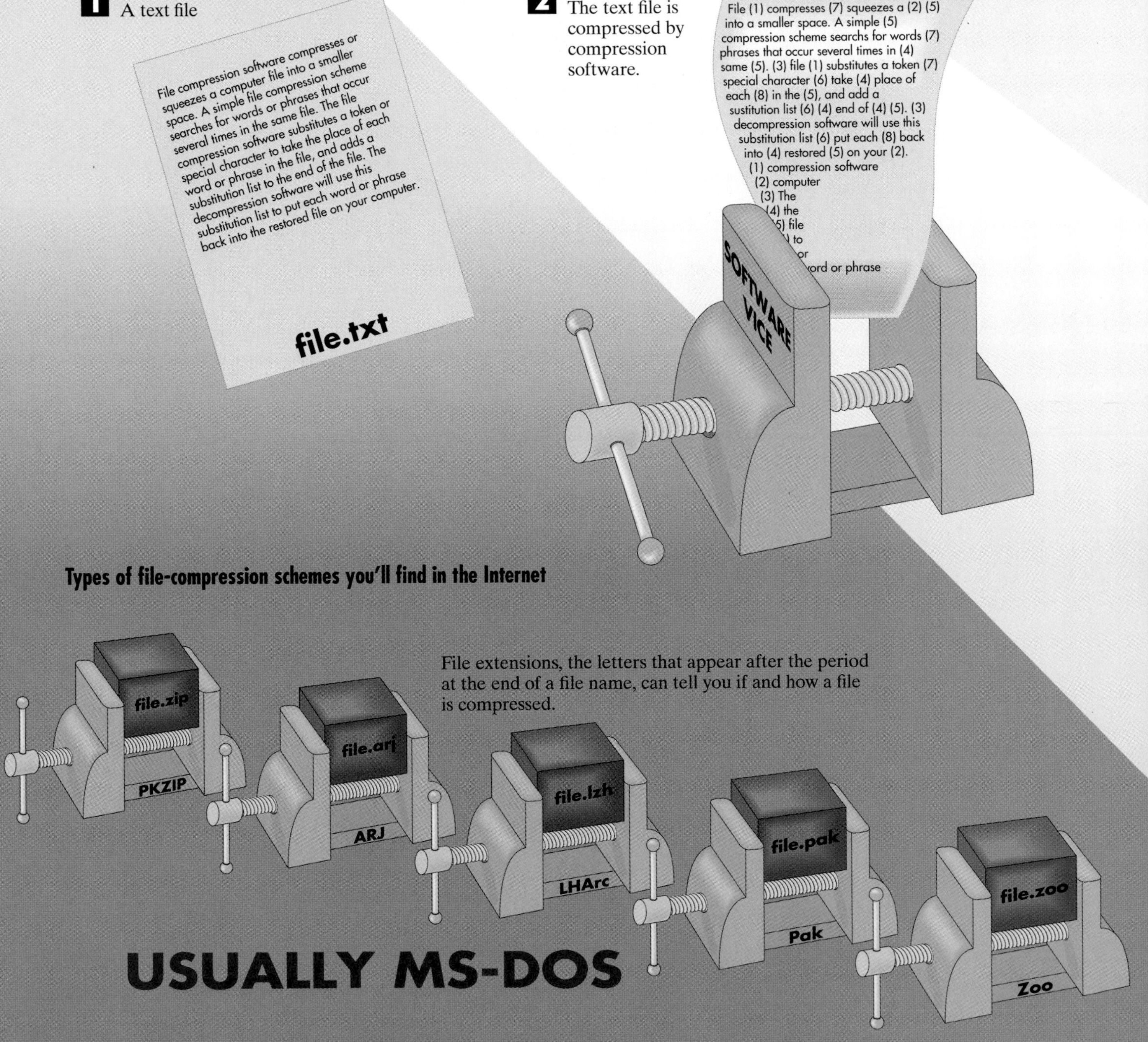

1 A text file
File compression software compresses or squeezes a computer file into a smaller space. A simple file compression scheme searches for words or phrases that occur several times in the same file. The file compression software substitutes a token or special character to take the place of each word or phrase in the file, and adds a substitution list to the end of the file. The decompression software will use this substitution list to put each word or phrase back into the restored file on your computer.
file.txt
2 The text file is compressed by compression software.
File (1) compresses (7) squeezes a (2) (5) into a smaller space. A simple (5) compression scheme searchs for words (7) phrases that occur several times in (4) same (5). (3) file (1) substitutes a token (7) special character (6) take (4) place of each (8) in the (5), and add a sustitution list (6) (4) end of (4) (5). (3) decompression software will use this substitution list (6) put each (8) back into (4) restored (5) on your (2).
(1) compression software
(2) computer
(3) The
(4) the
5) file
to
or
ord or phrase
SOFTWARE VICE
Types of file-compression schemes you'll find in the Internet
File extensions, the letters that appear after the period at the end of a file name, can tell you if and how a file is compressed.
file.zip
PKZIP
file.arj
ARJ
file.lzh
LHArc
file.pak
Pak
file.zoo
Zoo
USUALLY MS-DOS

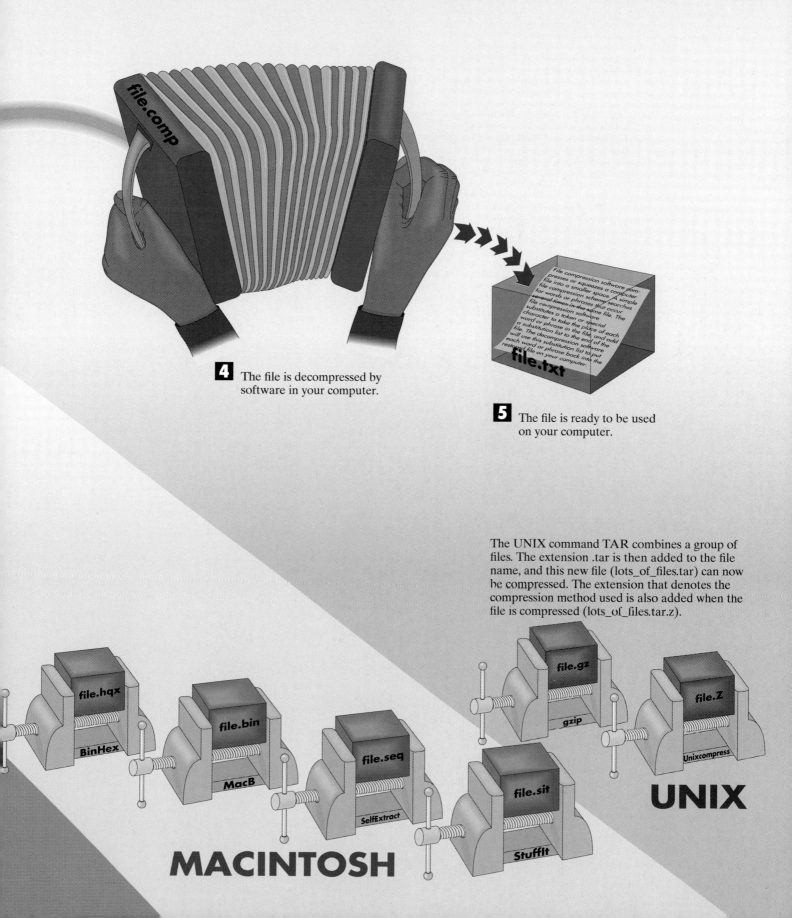

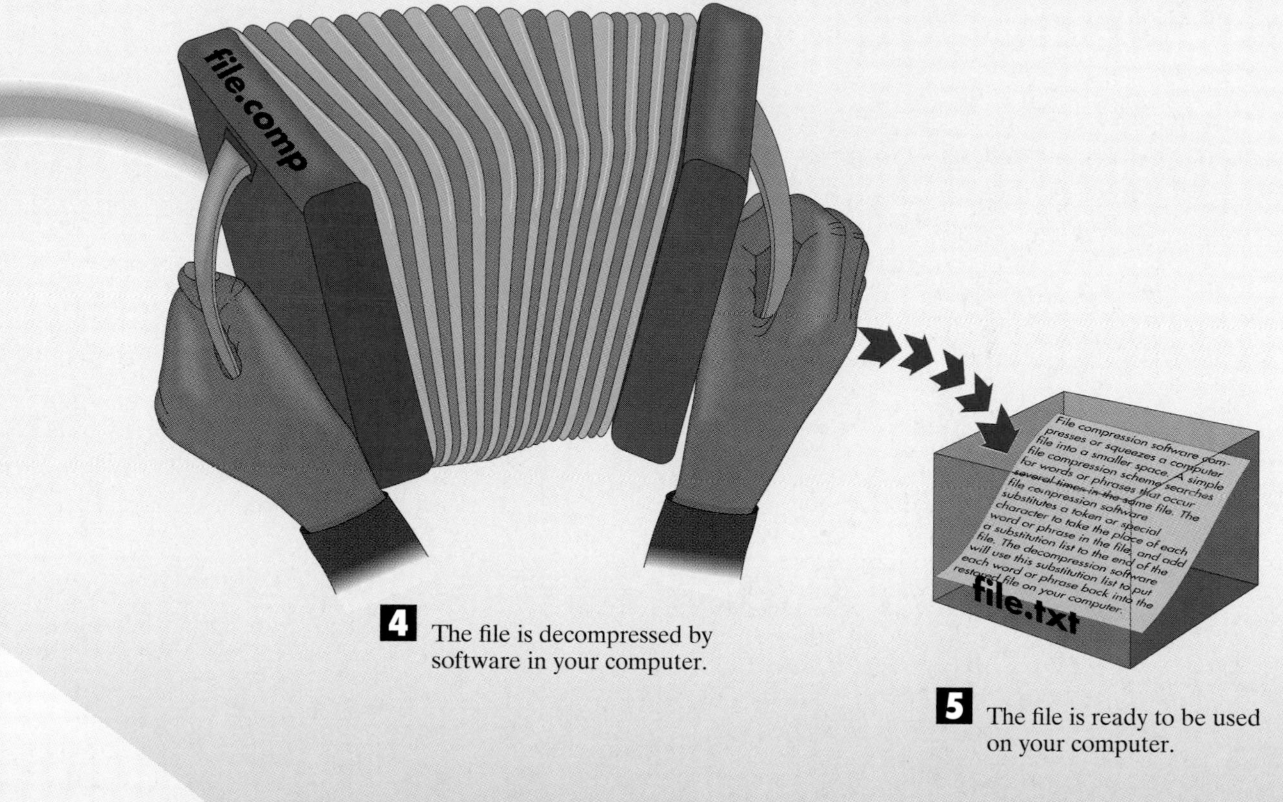
file.comp
file.txt

4 The file is decompressed by software in your computer.

5 The file is ready to be used on your computer.

The UNIX command TAR combines a group of files. The extension .tar is then added to the file name, and this new file (lots_of_files.tar) can now be compressed. The extension that denotes the compression method used is also added when the file is compressed (lots_of_files.tar.z).

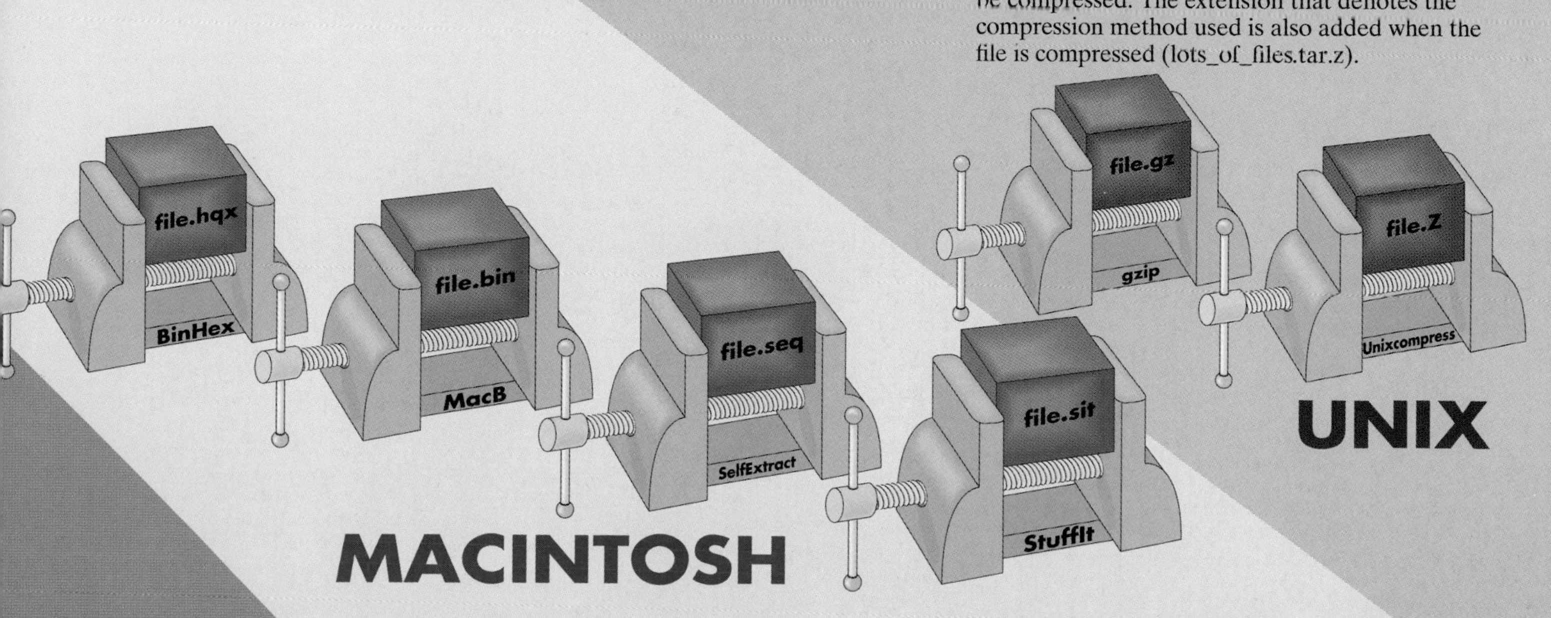
file.hqx
BinHex
file.bin
MacB
file.seq
SelfExtract
file.sit
StuffIt
MACINTOSH
file.gz
gzip
file.Z
Unixcompress
UNIX

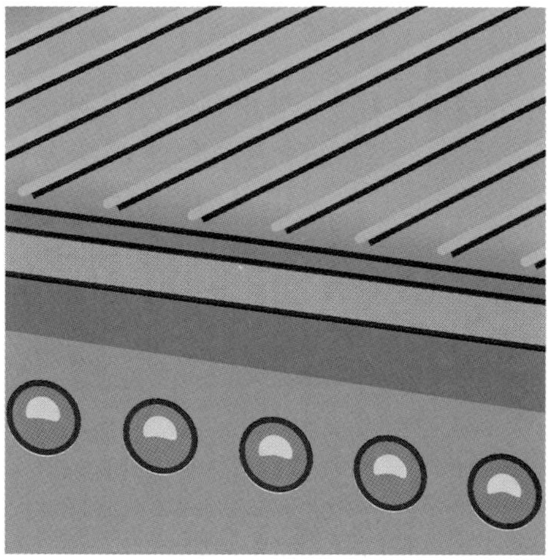

Downloading Files

FTP (FILE TRANSFER PROTOCOL) is the traditional Internet application for receiving or *downloading* files from the Internet to your computer. You can also use FTP to send or *upload* files from your computer to another computer.

As with Telnet, a version of FTP running on your computer allows you to create a connection and log on to a remote host computer. However, while Telnet makes your computer a terminal of the remote host, FTP only allows you to look at the names of files on the remote computer, and to download files from or upload files to that computer.

FTP needs both client and server software. An FTP client program runs on your computer, and an FTP *daemon,* or server program, runs on the host computer. When you log on to an FTP site or server by giving your account number and password, a command link is established across the Internet. The client sends commands such as list files or change directory to the FTP server, which sends status messages back. Once you are connected and ready to download a file, FTP opens a second data connection. This connection is in either binary or ASCII mode, depending on the type of file you want to transfer. Once the file is transferred the data connection is closed, and the FTP server sends an acknowledgment via the control connection, which remains open. You can then do more searching on that server, open another data connection to download more files, or just log off with the command bye or quit.

Many FTP sites or servers allow you to log on as anonymous, but anonymous FTP usually asks you for your e-mail address as the password. Remember, most computers on the Internet are there for the convenience of the people who own or use them on a regular basis. The owner may be a university and its students and teachers, a company and its employees, or a government agency and the clients it serves. Don't expect that everyone is going to invite you in to roam all through their computer. That's why passwords and accounts were set up!

An FTP daemon that allows anonymous visitors usually sets aside a special directory for them. To the visitors, this directory appears complete. However, only the files the sysops want publicly available are seen. For example, licensed software or data files are kept out of public view. An anonymous FTP site may also provide disk space to upload files. These files become part of the resource the FTP server offers.

There are a few other file transfer protocols you may run across. The Kermit protocol is used to transfer files between two computers connected by Telnet, but doesn't have the speed or flexibility of FTP. The Xmodem, Ymodem, and Zmodem protocols are used to transfer binary files via regular phone lines and modems, but these protocols don't work over the Internet.

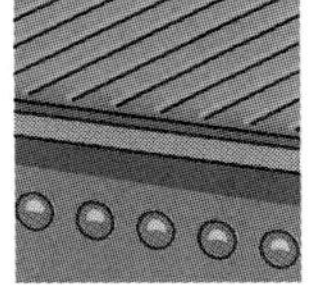

An FTP Session

You can use FTP to connect your computer to an FTP server at a remote site in the Internet. Once you've logged on, you can perform various functions on the server, including downloading files to your computer. You can run an FTP client on your machine. Look at your manual or check with your system administrator for instructions on how to make FTP work on your computer.

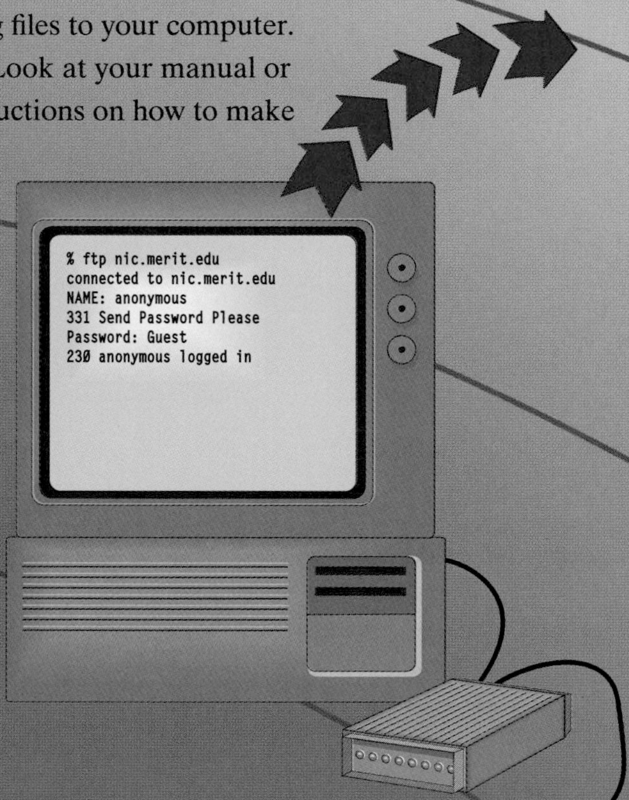

1 Start FTP on your computer by entering **ftp** at the command prompt (% is the UNIX command prompt, just as C is the standard DOS prompt). Enter on the same line the name of the FTP host you want to connect with. FTP opens a command connection through the Internet to the host computer, through which your FTP client program tells the FTP server what to do.
You can log on to many FTP hosts with the account name anonymous. Use guest as a password if you are asked for one. You can also log on to an FTP server with a valid account name and password for that host computer.

% ftp nic.merit.edu
connected to nic.merit.edu
NAME: anonymous
331 Send Password Please
Password: Guest
230 anonymous logged in

5 FTP software creates a connection between your computer and a host computer running an FTP server program, with which you can explore the names and descriptions of any files available from the FTP host. You can copy these files to your computer, or send your own files to the host computer. You cannot run any program files or look into any data files over an FTP connection. You need to use Telnet to log on to a host computer as a remote terminal of that computer.

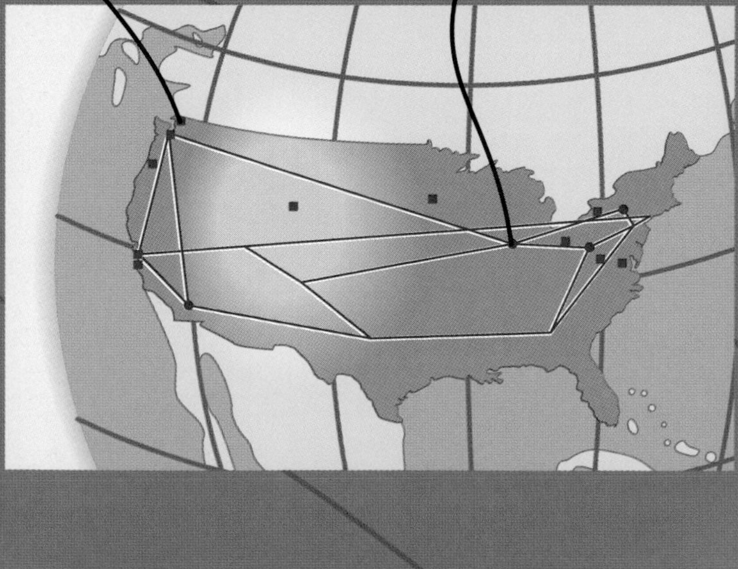

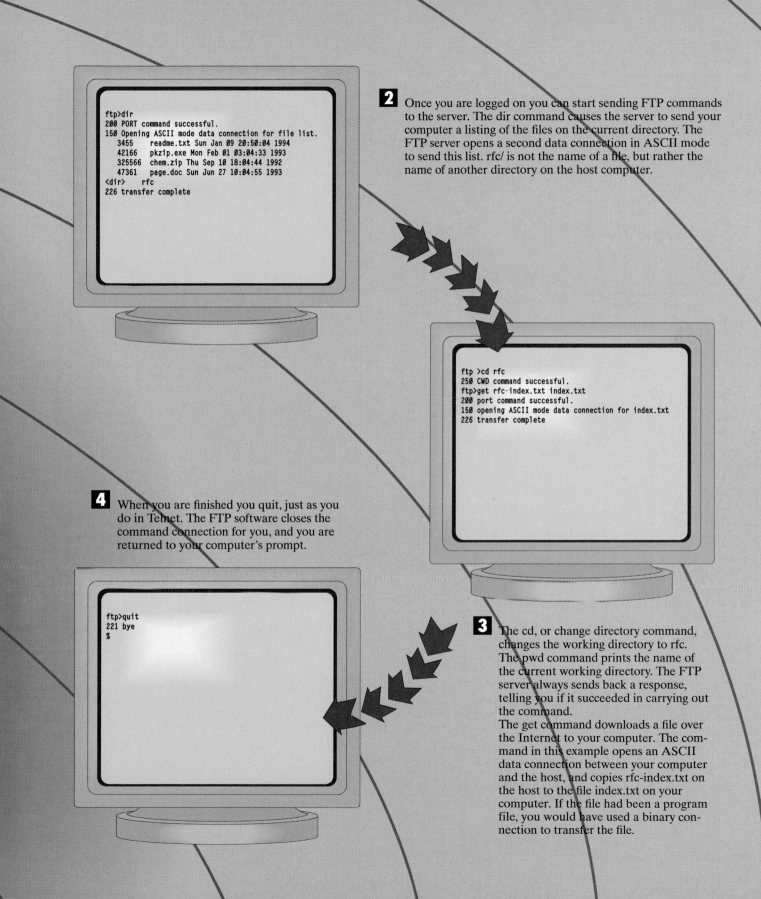

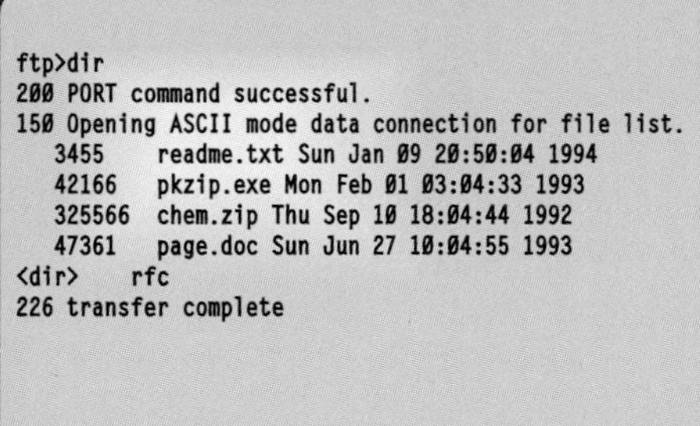
ftp>dir
200 PORT command successful.
150 Opening ASCII mode data connection for file list.
3455 readme.txt Sun Jan 09 20:50:04 1994
42166 pkzip.exe Mon Feb 01 03:04:33 1993
325566 chem.zip Thu Sep 10 18:04:44 1992
47361 page.doc Sun Jun 27 10:04:55 1993
<dir> rfc
226 transfer complete

2 Once you are logged on you can start sending FTP commands to the server. The dir command causes the server to send your computer a listing of the files on the current directory. The FTP server opens a second data connection in ASCII mode to send this list. rfc/ is not the name of a file, but rather the name of another directory on the host computer.

```
ftp >cd rfc
250 CWD command successful.
ftp>get rfc-index.txt index.txt
200 port command successful.
150 opening ASCII mode data connection for index.txt
226 transfer complete
```

3 The cd, or change directory command, changes the working directory to rfc. The pwd command prints the name of the current working directory. The FTP server always sends back a response, telling you if it succeeded in carrying out the command.
The get command downloads a file over the Internet to your computer. The command in this example opens an ASCII data connection between your computer and the host, and copies rfc-index.txt on the host to the file index.txt on your computer. If the file had been a program file, you would have used a binary connection to transfer the file.

4 When you are finished you quit, just as you do in Telnet. The FTP software closes the command connection for you, and you are returned to your computer's prompt.

```
ftp>quit
221 bye
%
```

PART 4

E-MAIL

CONTENTS

OVERVIEW

ELECTRONIC MAIL, OR e-mail, is a way of sending an electronic letter or messages between individuals or computers. E-mail travels through the systems and networks that make up the Internet, and even outside the Internet through other networks to deliver electronic messages. E-mail is the most popular of the three traditional Internet applications; FTP and Telnet are the other two traditional applications. Unlike Telnet and FTP, e-mail is not limited to the Internet—e-mail messages can be translated through gateways to other networks and systems.

In this part, you'll see the anatomy of an e-mail message. You'll see how the address, the return address, and the message itself are put into an envelope, and how that envelope is broken into TCP/IP packets and zapped over the Internet. You'll also learn how the Internet address system works. You'll learn about domain names, which identify the networks or computers an address is connected to. You'll also see how the domain name is translated into a numeric IP address that Internet computers and routers can understand.

PART FOUR

This part covers how software programs that run on your computer or workstation can manage your e-mail for you by creating mail off-line, filing incoming mail, forwarding mail to others, and otherwise automating routine e-mail tasks. You'll also see how mail servers on Internet host computers maintain special mailing lists.

UseNet is a system closely allied with the Internet that uses e-mail to provide a centralized news service. In the UseNet system, e-mail messages are sent to a host computer that acts as a UseNet server. This server gathers into a central place messages about a single topic. People send e-mail to the server, which stores the messages. You can then log on to the server to read these messages, or you can have software on your computer log on and automatically download the latest messages so you can read them at your leisure.

We'll end this part with a look at *netiquette*, the type of behavior that is normally expected of people on the Internet. Here we'll concentrate on the etiquette that has evolved in the Internet community for communicating through e-mail and UseNet.

E-mail

E-MAIL, OR ELECTRONIC mail, facilitates sending messages between computers that are electrically connected. Here's how it works: You type up a message on your computer and connect to the Internet or another on-line service. Then you drop the message into an electronic mailbox just as you would mail a letter. Like little electronic mail trucks, packets carry the message to the destination mailbox. When the recipient checks his or her mailbox and sees the message, that person can download the electronic message from the host computer their mail account is on. The recipient of your message can respond to you with a few keystrokes, forward the message to someone else, file the message in the computer, or just delete the message.

The range of e-mail packets extends far beyond the Internet world, if we define the Internet as any group of networks that communicate via the TCP/IP protocol. There are many other types of extensive networks, some almost as far ranging as the Internet. Many of these other networks have agreements with the Internet and with each other to exchange e-mail back and forth, just as countries exchange regular post across their borders. Often, an e-mail message may have to pass through a series of intermediate networks to reach the destination address. Since not all networks use the same e-mail format, a *gateway* translates the format of an e-mail message into one that the next network can understand.

You can ultimately send e-mail in the following ways: between two computers connected by modems, across a local-area network in your office, across the Internet, to any commercial network, and to other systems that have gateways to the Internet.

Each gateway reads the To line of the e-mail message and routes the envelope closer to the destination mail box. You can send electronic messages to anyone in the world if you know that person's e-mail address, and if you have access to the Internet or another system that can send e-mail. Addresses and gateways are the topics of Chapter 14 and 17, respectively.

When you send e-mail to another computer on the network, for example, a request with keywords to an archie server, the archie server checks its database to see if there are any files that contain the keywords. Then the archie server sends you via e-mail a list of these files to the address in the From line of your request. Some FTP hosts will also let you query their files in this manner. An FTP host can even send a file back to you via e-mail.

E-mail is no longer limited to simple text messages. Depending upon your hardware and software, and, of course, the hardware and software of the recipient of your e-mail message, you can embed sound and images in your message, or even attach binary files that contain executable programs. Such advanced uses of e-mail are not yet standardized, and they are also limited by the networks your e-mail may have to cross to get to the destination mailbox.

E-mail is changing the way people communicate. The parties on the receiving end don't have to be present at their computer when you send e-mail to them. (This is like an answering machine that picks up a telephone message you leave for someone else when they're not home.) Your message travels to the destination mailbox at the speed of light, making e-mail much faster than old-fashioned mail. But the person at the other end still has to check the mailbox to read your message!

How E-mail Works

You can send e-mail from your computer to anyone who has an Internet address, or to anyone who has an e-mail address on a system that the Internet can reach. You can also send instructions by e-mail to a variety of computers on the Internet. Such a computer carries out your instructions and mails the results back to you.

MAIL
MAIL

Whether you are connected directly to the Internet or use a telephone line to dial in for your access, you can send an electronic message over the Internet. All you need to do is address your message correctly and be sure that the message is properly transmitted to an Internet mailbox. The Internet will take care of the rest.

To the Internet, your e-mail message is a stream of packets, each bearing the address of the destination. In a process known as packet switching, the Internet sends the packets on the best path from your computer to the destination address. This path may not be the shortest, but takes into account factors such as the amount of mail on different backbones or lines and the quality of transmission.

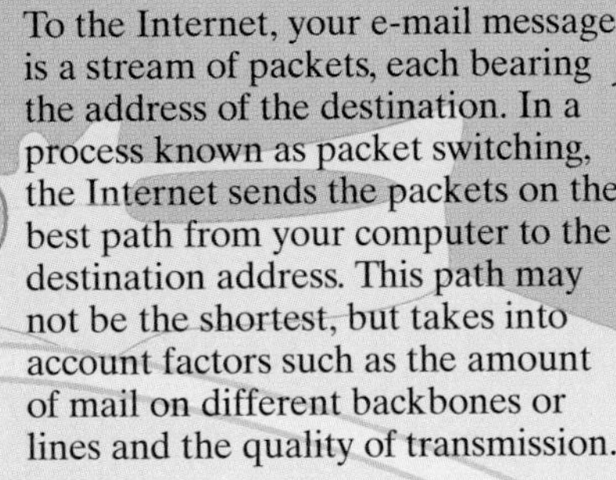
MAIL

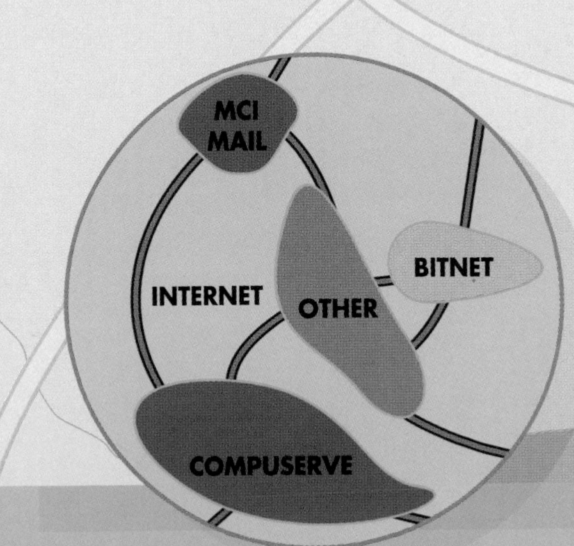
MCI MAIL
INTERNET
OTHER
BITNET
COMPUSERVE

Although the Internet spans the world as the largest network in existence, it only consists of smaller networks communicating with TCP/IP. E-mail can travel to networks and systems outside the Internet through gateways that translate the messages into other network languages.

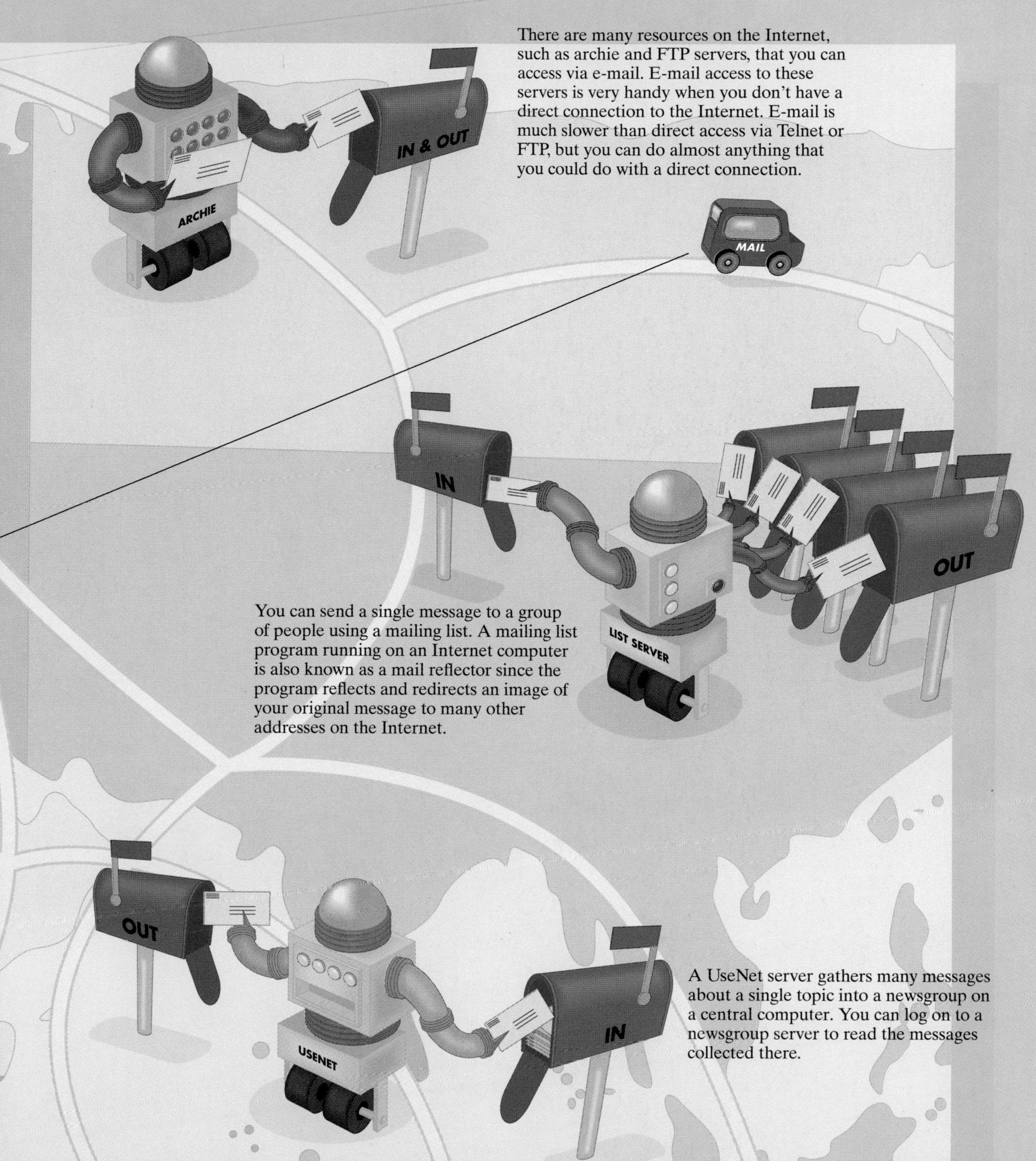
IN & OUT
ARCHIE
MAIL
IN
OUT
LIST SERVER
OUT
USENET
IN

There are many resources on the Internet, such as archie and FTP servers, that you can access via e-mail. E-mail access to these servers is very handy when you don't have a direct connection to the Internet. E-mail is much slower than direct access via Telnet or FTP, but you can do almost anything that you could do with a direct connection.

You can send a single message to a group of people using a mailing list. A mailing list program running on an Internet computer is also known as a mail reflector since the program reflects and redirects an image of your original message to many other addresses on the Internet.

A UseNet server gathers many messages about a single topic into a newsgroup on a central computer. You can log on to a newsgroup server to read the messages collected there.

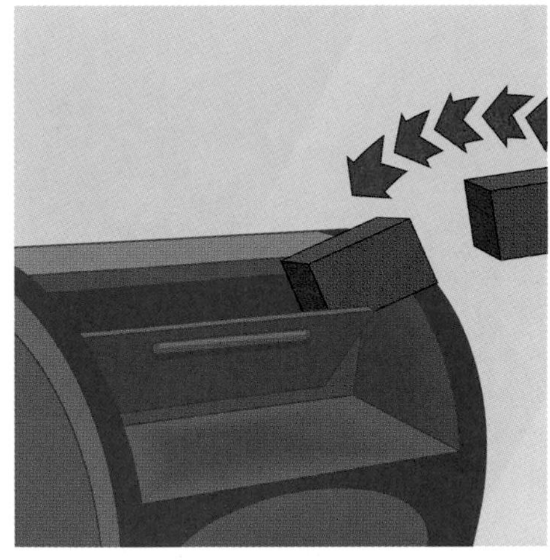

Anatomy of a Message

LET'S TAKE A close look at an electronic message. There are many programs that can create e-mail, but typical e-mail messages will always have certain features in common. These common features facilitate the translation of e-mail between different types of systems to get the mail through to the recipient.

A typical e-mail message includes the From line (the sender's address), the To line (the recipient's address), a Subject line, and the body of the message. The To and From lines are just like the addresses you put on a paper envelope, except that the electronic postmaster is much stricter about the format of the address. All the spelling and punctuation must be correct, or the message will be sent right back to you from the electronic mailbox. The Subject line is a convenient place to give a one-line description of your message. This description is really handy for giving people an idea of what your message is about, since the Subject line is almost always displayed when someone checks his or her mailbox.

Often a mailer program will automatically attach a signature line to the end of the body of an e-mail message. The signature line can even include the sender's phone number and old-fashioned address. Many senders also include some information about themselves, or a one-line joke or saying drawn from a list of sayings. These are ways to personalize an otherwise stark medium.

An e-mail message is usually written into an ASCII file. However, some computer systems can integrate e-mail with binary files that might contain graphics, sound, or application programs. You should only use this option if the network over which you are sending the mail and the person to whom you are sending it have equipment and software that can handle binary files.

You can create the text of an e-mail message on your word processor; or, you can run a mailer program on your machine or on the host computer to which you're logged on. A mailer program deposits the e-mail message into an electronic mailbox. If you are sending the message over the Internet, the program first converts an ASCII file into TCP packets and then converts TCP packets into IP packets and sends them off across the network.

At each stage of the journey that an e-mail message makes, routers or gateways open each packet and read just enough to determine the destination address; then the router or gateway sends the packet off in the direction of its final destination. When an e-mail message arrives at the host computer for the recipient, the e-mail is stored in an electronic mailbox if the recipient's computer is not turned on. Along each step of the way, the electronic message is stored until it can be forwarded to the next computer. For this reason, e-mail is often called a "store and forward" system. The final stop is the recipient's host computer, where the IP packets are reassembled by TCP into an ASCII file or message. The type of Internet connection the recipient has determines where the final opening of the message takes place. The reassembly takes place on the recipient's computer if there is a direct connection. If the recipient is using terminal emulation software and a modem to connect his or her computer to a campuswide system as a dumb terminal, the message is reassembled on the large system, and transmitted in ASCII to the computer over the telephone line.

A full Internet connection is not necessary for e-mail. All you need is an e-mail address that the Internet can understand, and a way to connect your computer to an e-mail system.

Anatomy of an E-mail Message

No matter what type of computer you are using or how your message gets to the Internet, all e-mail messages will have certain features in common. E-mail can be sent over all kinds of systems and networks, regardless of the type of file that contains the message.

E-mail, like all computer data, ultimately consists of binary data, which is expressed in 0s and 1s.

MAIL

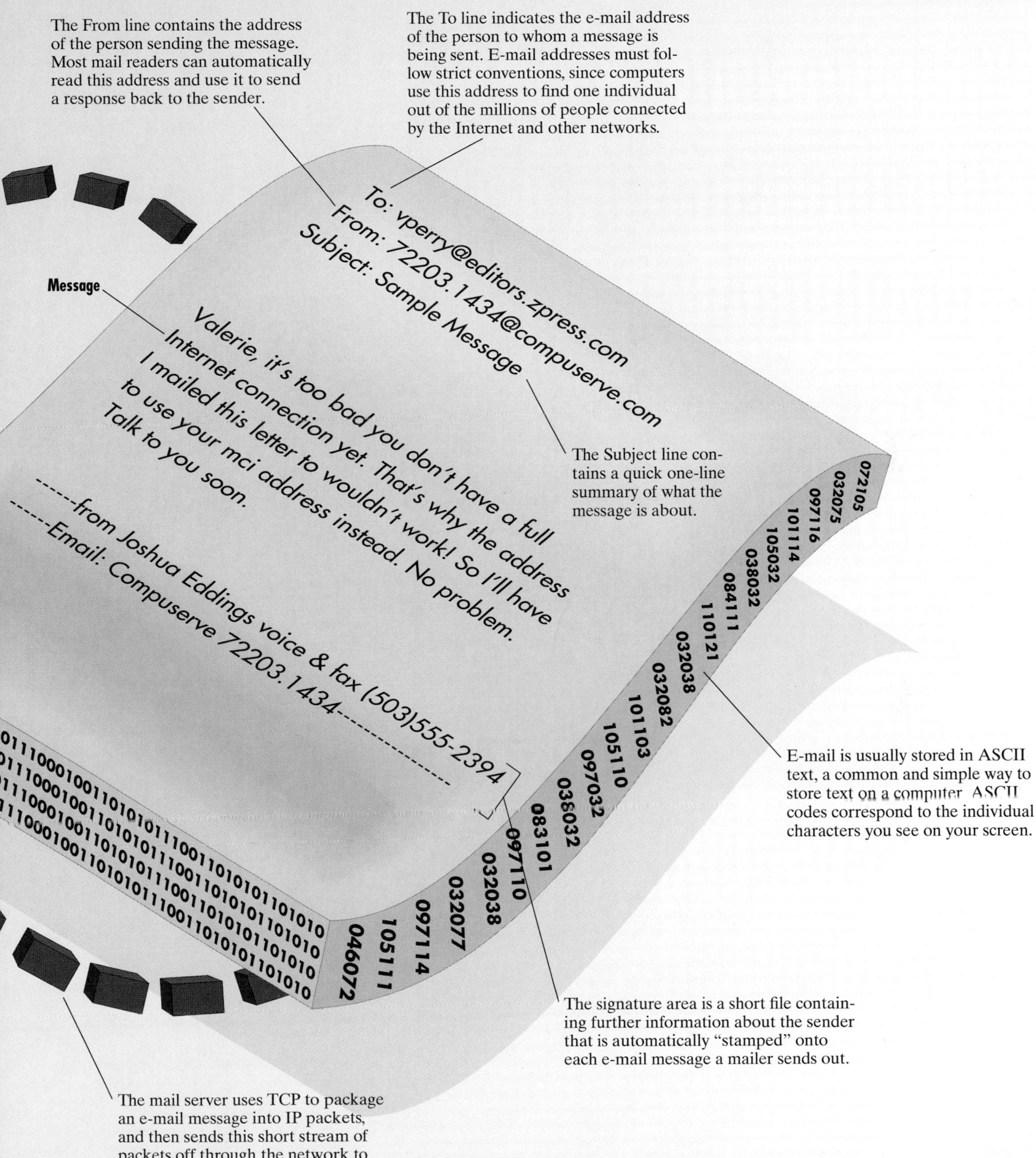
The From line contains the address of the person sending the message. Most mail readers can automatically read this address and use it to send a response back to the sender.
The To line indicates the e-mail address of the person to whom a message is being sent. E-mail addresses must follow strict conventions, since computers use this address to find one individual out of the millions of people connected by the Internet and other networks.
To: vperry@editors.zpress.com
From: 72203.1434@compuserve.com
Subject: Sample Message
Message
Valerie, it's too bad you don't have a full
Internet connection yet. That's why the address
I mailed this letter to wouldn't work! So I'll have
to use your mci address instead. No problem.
Talk to you soon.
-----from Joshua Eddings voice & fax (503)555-2394
-----Email: Compuserve 72203.1434-----------------
The Subject line contains a quick one-line summary of what the message is about.
072105 032075 097116 101114 105032 038032 084111 110121 032038 032082 101103 105110 097032 038032 083101 097110 032038 032077 097114 105111 046072
E-mail is usually stored in ASCII text, a common and simple way to store text on a computer. ASCII codes correspond to the individual characters you see on your screen.
The signature area is a short file containing further information about the sender that is automatically "stamped" onto each e-mail message a mailer sends out.
The mail server uses TCP to package an e-mail message into IP packets, and then sends this short stream of packets off through the network to the destination.

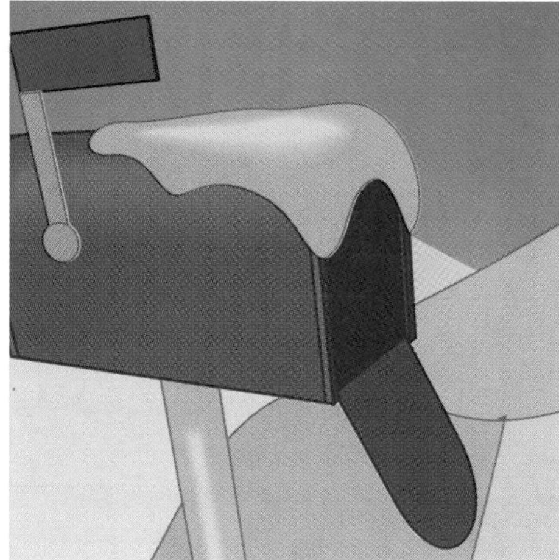

Internet Addresses

AT ONE POINT the Internet tried to maintain a complete list of all its computers and networks. As the Internet grew, this list became unmanageable, because of both the size of the list and the number of changes made to the list daily. The Domain Name System evolved as a way to manage these lists.

The *Domain Name System* (DNS) does several things. It creates a hierarchy of *domains*, or groups, of computers. It establishes a *domain name* (also known as an Internet *address*) for each computer on the Internet. Major domains have responsibility for maintaining lists and addresses of other domains on the next lower level of domains within each group. That next level of domains is responsible for the following level and so on down to the end user, or end computer. The DNS also provides a way for Internet computers to translate e-mail and data between an Internet address and an IP (Internet Protocol) address. An *IP address* is the numeric address the Internet needs to send streams of packets that carry e-mail and other data between computers.

To see how the DNS works, let's look at the Internet address for NASA's SPACElink: spacelink.msfc.nasa.gov. The major domain responsible for this name is *gov*, or government. The next domain is *nasa*. The domain Marshall Space Center (msfc), is one of the many networks that NASA maintains. The space center itself is the home of the computer that runs SPACElink.

The IP address 192.149.89.69 refers to the actual computer and network addresses that connect SPACElink to the Internet. As you can see, the IP address is not quite as informative as the Internet address, and IP addresses often change. For example, SPACElink's IP address will change in 1994 when NASA upgrades its computer system. However, the Internet address will remain the same. Administrators of the various domains keep track of these changes. That way, when you access the Internet, the DNS can translate any Internet address you enter into the most current IP address. This ensures that the right connections are made to send data between your computer and the host.

You can use the @ sign to add non-Internet information to an Internet address. For example, if the SPACElink computer allows you to send e-mail to users of that system, you could send Tom Jones e-mail at tjones@spacelink.msfc.nasa.gov or tom@spacelink.msfc.nasa.gov, depending on

The @ sign also facilitates using the Internet address for systems outside the Internet. For example, my CompuServe address is 72203,1434. You can turn this into an Internet address by writing it as 72203.1434@compuserve.com. CompuServe has a connection to the Internet under the domain *com*, or commercial. The DNS translates the compuserve.com part of the address into an IP address so the Internet can forward the e-mail to the CompuServe computer. The CompuServe computer sends the message to my CompuServe mailbox, 72203,1434, where I can pick it up the next time I check in.

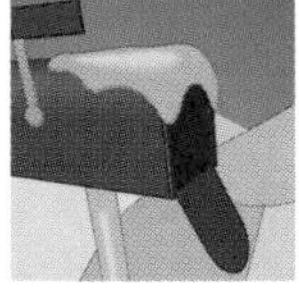

Domain Name System

The Domain Name System is a way of dividing the Internet into understandable groups, or domains. The name of each domain is tacked on the Internet address, starting from the right with the largest domain. End users at the end computer are often hooked on to the domain name by an @ sign.

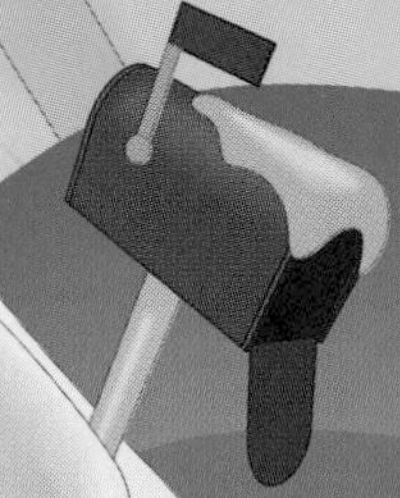

72203.1434@
compuserve.com

mil (Military): parts of the U.S. Military, such as the Army, connected to the Internet.

MILITARY

MIL

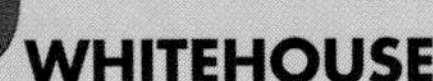
pres.Whitehouse.gov

spacelink.msfc.nasa.gov

WHITEHOUSE

MSFC

gov (Government): U.S. government agencies connected to the Internet.

GOVERNMENT

GOV

APPLE

COMPUSERVE

SUN

com (Commercial): commercial companies that have computers connected to the Internet.

COMMERCIAL

COM

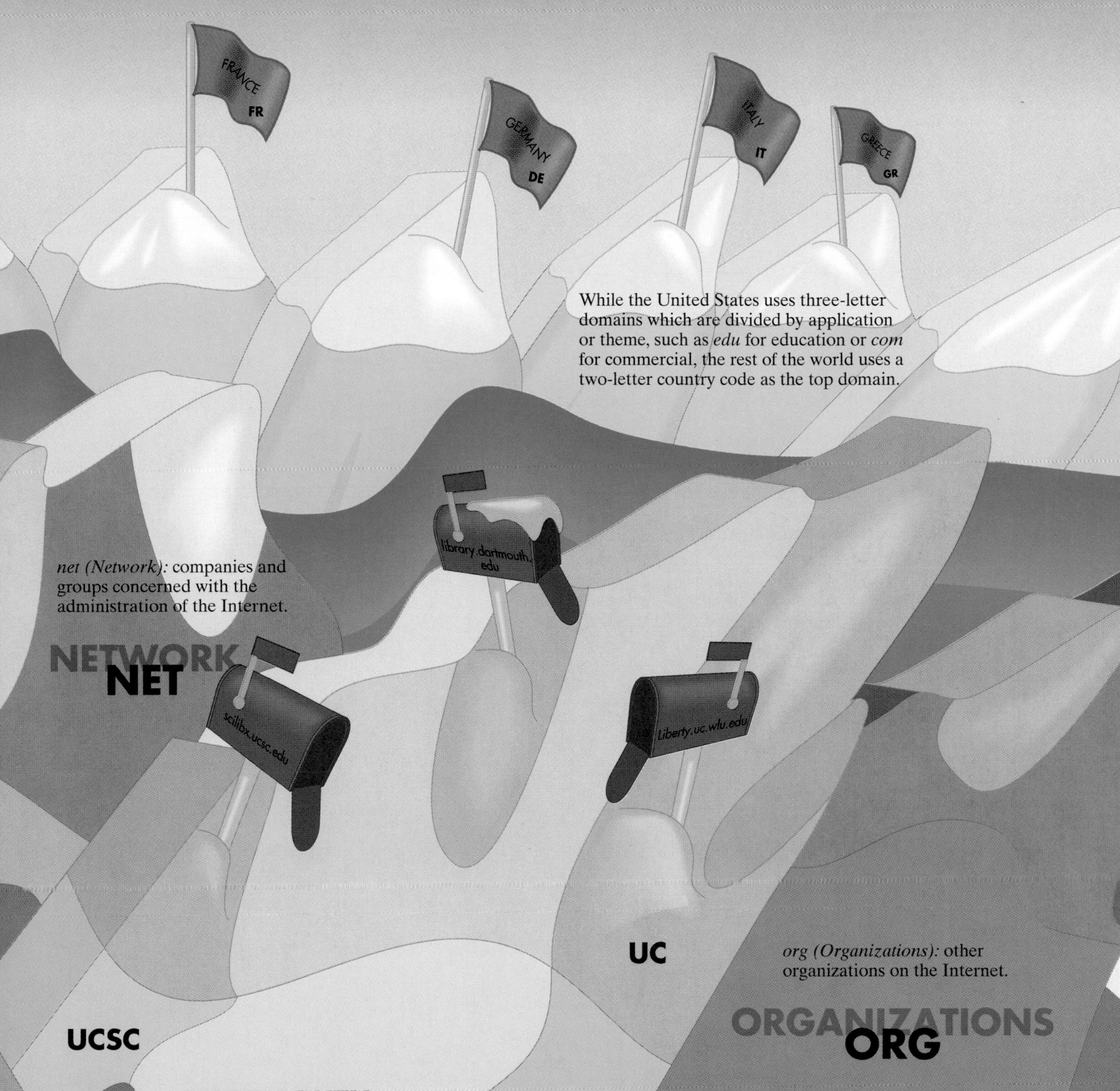
FRANCE
FR
GERMANY
DE
ITALY
IT
GREECE
GR
library.dartmouth.edu
NETWORK
NET
scilibx.ucsc.edu
Liberty.uc.wlu.edu
UC
ORGANIZATIONS
ORG
UCSC
DARTMOUTH
WLU
EDUCATION
EDU

While the United States uses three-letter domains which are divided by application or theme, such as *edu* for education or *com* for commercial, the rest of the world uses a two-letter country code as the top domain.

net (Network): companies and groups concerned with the administration of the Internet.

org (Organizations): other organizations on the Internet.

edu (Educational): schools and universities that are connected to the Internet.

Mailers and Readers

A *MAILER PROGRAM* LETS you create a message, usually on line or while connected to a remote network. Communications software connects your computer to the e-mail host computer. Depending on your communications software, your mailer program also might let you *upload*, or send, previously prepared text at a much faster rate than if you were typing it on line. Other options mailer programs provide are usually limited to sending mail, reading and deleting incoming mail, and sometimes sending a *carbon copy*, or a duplicate message, to a second or third address.

E-mail reader programs take advantage of your computer's processing power and storage space to streamline and automate the mailing process. Reader programs work with mailer programs, just as client software works with server software on a host computer, to give you a broad range of options with your mail.

In the next illustration you'll see a typical reader program, which uses a graphical interface to simplify the available operations. This kind of interface uses icons to represent tasks and e-mail messages. Reader programs are available for Macintosh computers, PCs running Windows, and computers running X-Windows, a graphical interface for UNIX.

The range of options that a sophisticated reader program offers includes off-line preparation of messages, automatic sending and receiving (to reduce the time you spend on line with an e-mail host), automatic filing of e-mail messages in separate files or folders, the use of an address book in which you can store frequently used e-mail addresses, and the ability to send carbon copies to a group of addresses.

Regardless of what type of e-mail program you use, check your mail frequently and remove mail from your mailbox after you have read it. Some systems will automatically purge or delete messages from your mailbox, usually after several months.

An E-Mail Reader

You can use a graphical e-mail software package on your computer to simplify many e-mail tasks and to maximize e-mail's capabilities.

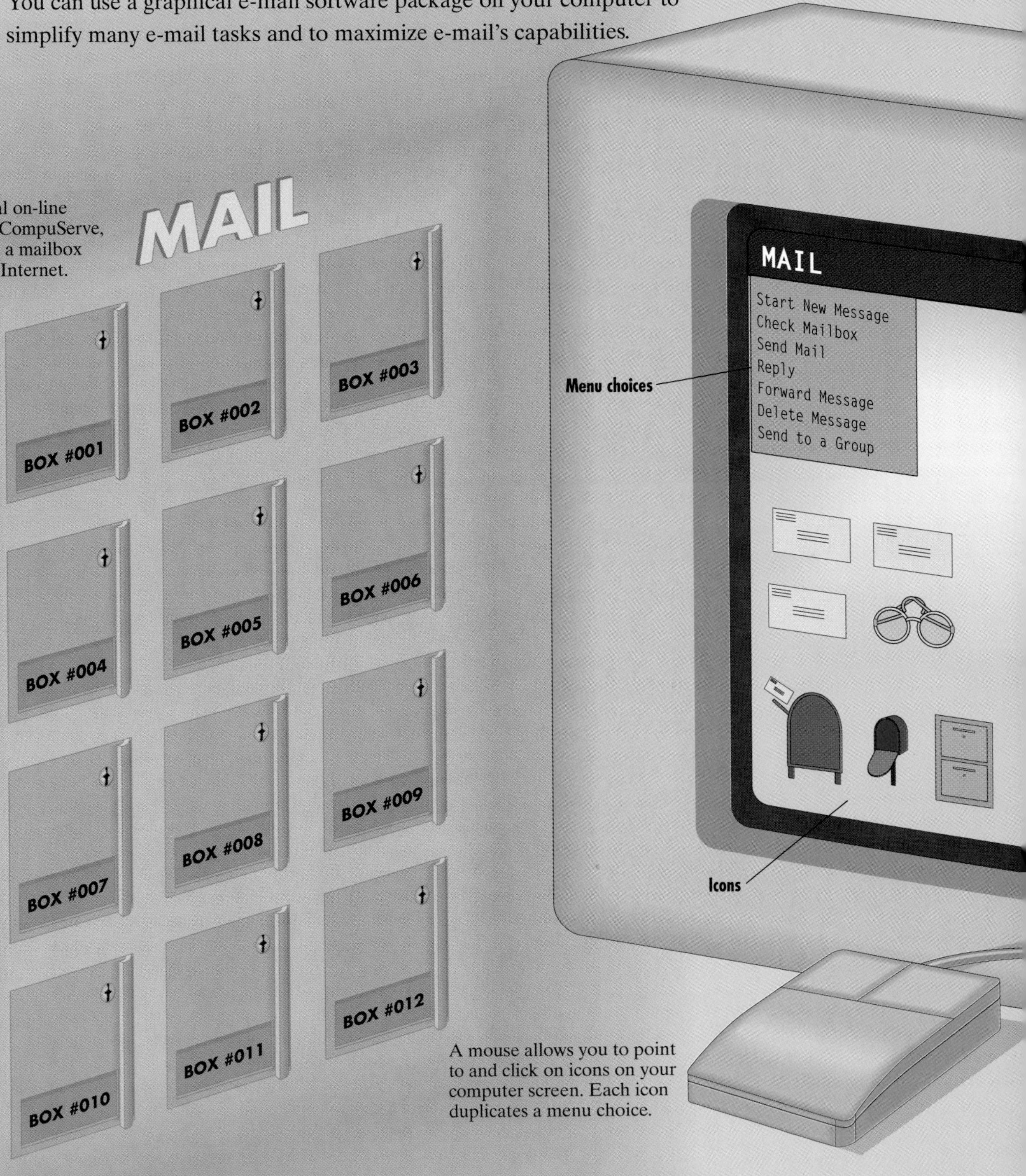

Many commercial on-line services, such as CompuServe, allow you to rent a mailbox accessible to the Internet.

Menu choices

Icons

A mouse allows you to point to and click on icons on your computer screen. Each icon duplicates a menu choice.

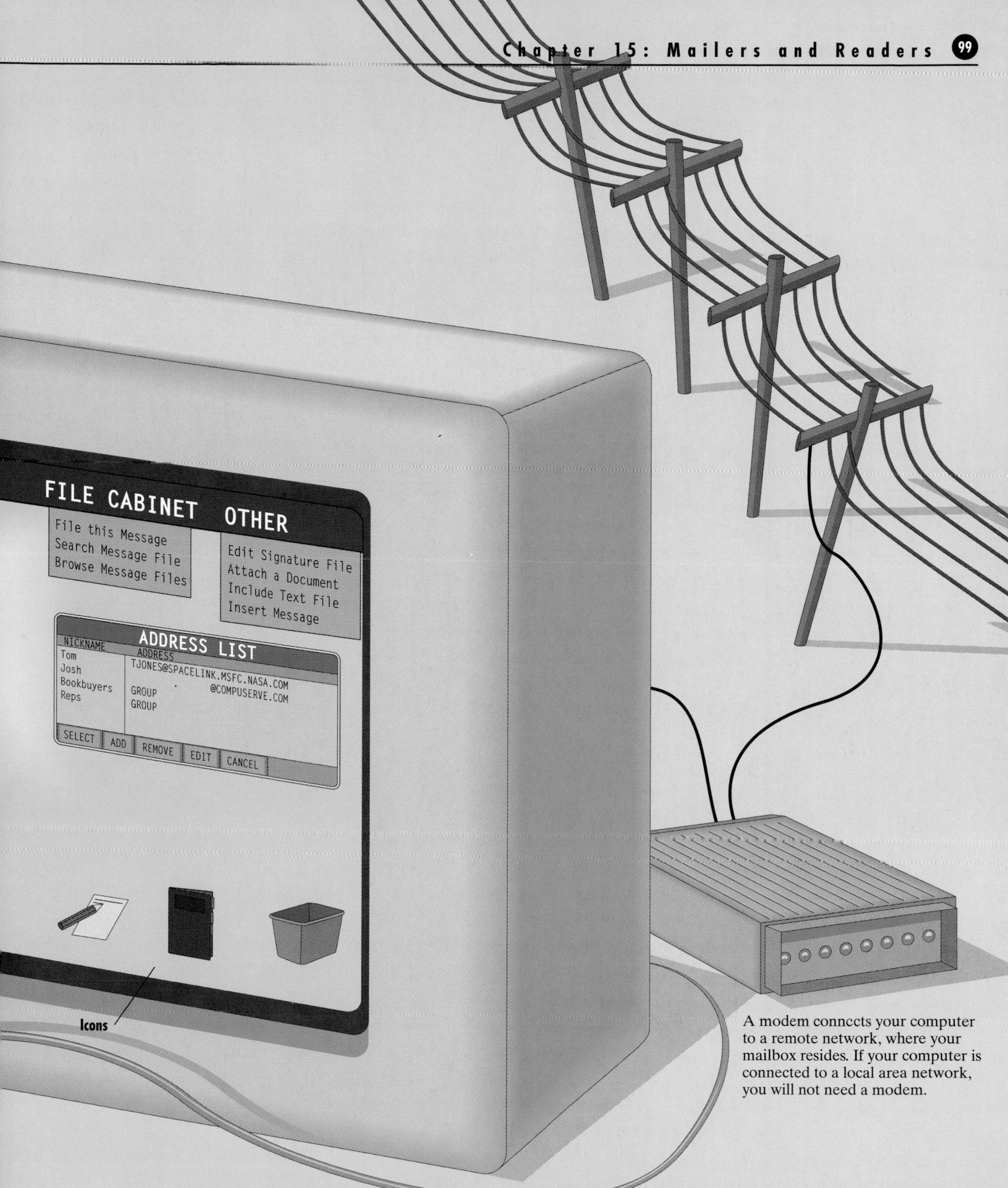
FILE CABINET
OTHER
File this Message
Search Message File
Browse Message Files
Edit Signature File
Attach a Document
Include Text File
Insert Message
ADDRESS LIST
NICKNAME
ADDRESS
Tom
Josh
Bookbuyers
Reps
TJONES@SPACELINK.MSFC.NASA.COM
@COMPUSERVE.COM
GROUP
GROUP
SELECT
ADD
REMOVE
EDIT
CANCEL
Icons

A modem connects your computer to a remote network, where your mailbox resides. If your computer is connected to a local area network, you will not need a modem.

Mailing Lists

A *MAILING LIST* on the Internet is a database of people interested in a particular topic. Mailing lists can be created for any subject from autism to wine-tasting. Any e-mail sent to the mailing list is automatically resent to everyone in the database. Mailing lists that automatically resend e-mail are also known as *mail reflectors*.

To subscribe to a mailing list you use e-mail to send a request to the mailing list administrator. You must also include your Internet address. You don't need full access to the Internet to subscribe, as long as you have a mailbox and an address that can handle Internet e-mail. You can cancel a subscription to a mailing list the same way. Just send an e-mail message to the administrator of that list, asking that your address be taken off.

Where do you find out about different mailing lists? On the Internet, of course! Many Internet or host computers maintain various mailing lists. You can use FTP with these computers to download, or receive information about lists via e-mail. You may have to poke around a little to find a current list. You can also use *gophers*, highly automated software directories, to search for lists on Internet computers. You'll see how gophers work in Chapter 21.

Mailing lists are often referred to as moderated or unmoderated. A *moderated mailing list* is one that has been screened by the list administrator. For example, the administrator may weed out duplicate messages, or messages inappropriate to the theme of the mailing list. An *unmoderated list* contains all mail automatically re-sent by the mail reflector.

List servers are even more automated than reflectors. Bitnet, an academic network linking colleges and universities, uses list servers to manage mailing lists. Bitnet is closely allied with the Internet, and if you're on the Internet, you can use e-mail to access list servers on Bitnet. You can sometimes use a list server to automatically subscribe to a mailing list. This is accomplished by embedding your address in the e-mail message you send as your sign-up request. A list server can also read your e-mail request without a human administrator, and can add you to or remove you from the list.

A Mailing List

Mailing lists on the Internet send a single message to many subscribers. There are hundreds of mailing lists available, covering almost every topic under the sun. Anyone can send an e-mail message to the mailing list, but to receive messages sent to the mailing list you must be a subscriber.

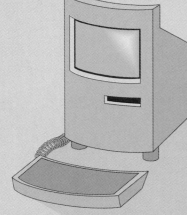

When you send a single e-mail message to a mailing list, copies of your message are sent to everyone who subscribes to that mailing list.

You send an e-mail message requesting that you be put on the mailing list to the mailing list administrator. Don't send such a request to the mailing list! Your request would automatically be sent to everyone on the list, and you still wouldn't be a subscriber! You can also cancel a subscription the same way, by sending a request to the administrator of that list.

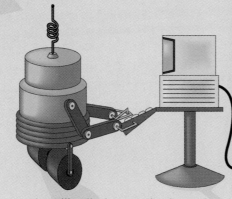

A mailing list keeps a database of everyone who has subscribed to that particular mailing list. When the mailing list computer receives a message, the computer mails the message to everyone on the mailing list.

If you subscribe to a mailing list, you should check your mailbox frequently because mail can build up quickly, sometimes dozens of messages in a few minutes. You don't want to overburden the computer your mailbox resides on.

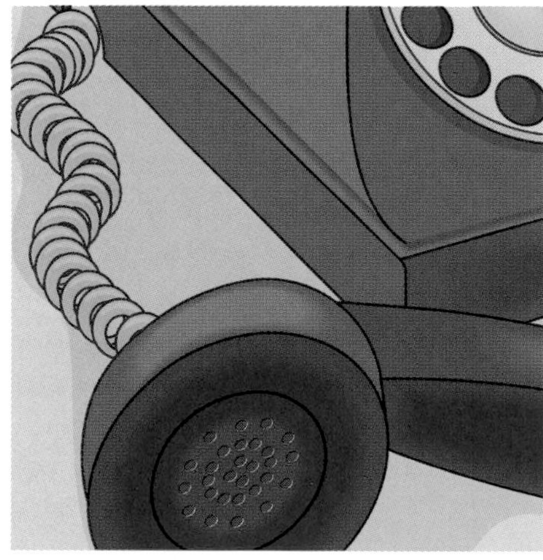

Finding People on the Internet

YOU NEED THE recipient's address before you can send them e-mail on the Internet. You may have already obtained this address from a business card or other correspondence. However, sometimes you will need to look up the address in an on-line directory. Like a printed telephone directory, this on-line directory is referred to as *white pages*.

When the Internet was small, you could use the Finger command to list everyone on a computer. The Finger command still works on many UNIX systems, but it is no longer a practical way to look someone up in the thousands of networks connected to the Internet today. As the Internet grew, maintaining a database of everyone on the net became impractical, because of both the size of the database and the amount of changes needed to keep it current. The WHOIS system was developed to gather names and addresses from all over the Internet into one computer. You use Telnet to connect to a WHOIS server, and then look up an address. WHOIS servers are still available but are limited in scope, and may even be limited to special types of addresses.

A Distributed Internet Directory (DID) is being developed using the X.500 protocol. The *X.500 protocol* is an international standard for directory services for all sorts of networks. Like the Domain Name System (DNS), it distributes the responsibility for maintaining lists of names and addresses across the Internet to different domains and computers. Each group that participates in the DID uses a Directory Server Agent (DSA) program to maintain its own directory, and can also use a Directory Client Agent (DCA) program to track down names and addresses. When you supply your DCA with some information about the recipient—for example, an address, a company name, the network they are connected to, or the city they're in—your DCA tries to find a DSA that meets your criteria. Your DCA then connects to the DSA you've located and lets you search for the recipient's address. (It's like knowing the area code of the city a person lives in before you can call that city's directory assistance.) The Fred program is a DCA that automates some of the guesswork needed to figure out which DSA to search.

The Internet is always changing, and X.500 is not the final word in finding addresses on the Internet. Other protocols are also being developed, such as WHOIS++, a distributed version of WHOIS. You will find services such as X.500 and WHOIS++ built into gophers and wide-area information servers (WAISs), as you will see in Chapters 20 and 22.

White Pages

Directory programs on the Internet are known collectively as *white pages*. No one directory contains every name and address.

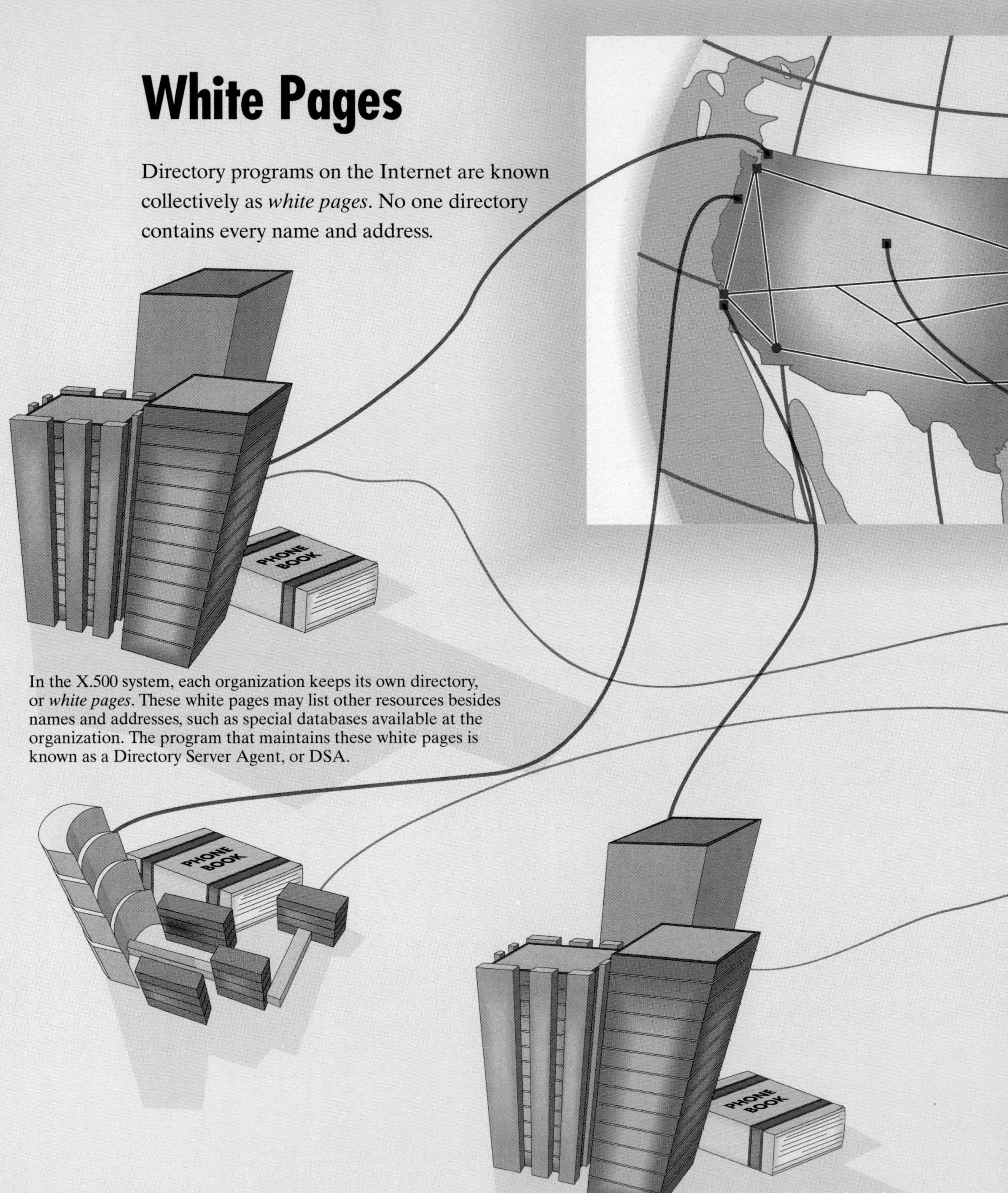
PHONE BOOK
PHONE BOOK
PHONE BOOK

In the X.500 system, each organization keeps its own directory, or *white pages*. These white pages may list other resources besides names and addresses, such as special databases available at the organization. The program that maintains these white pages is known as a Directory Server Agent, or DSA.

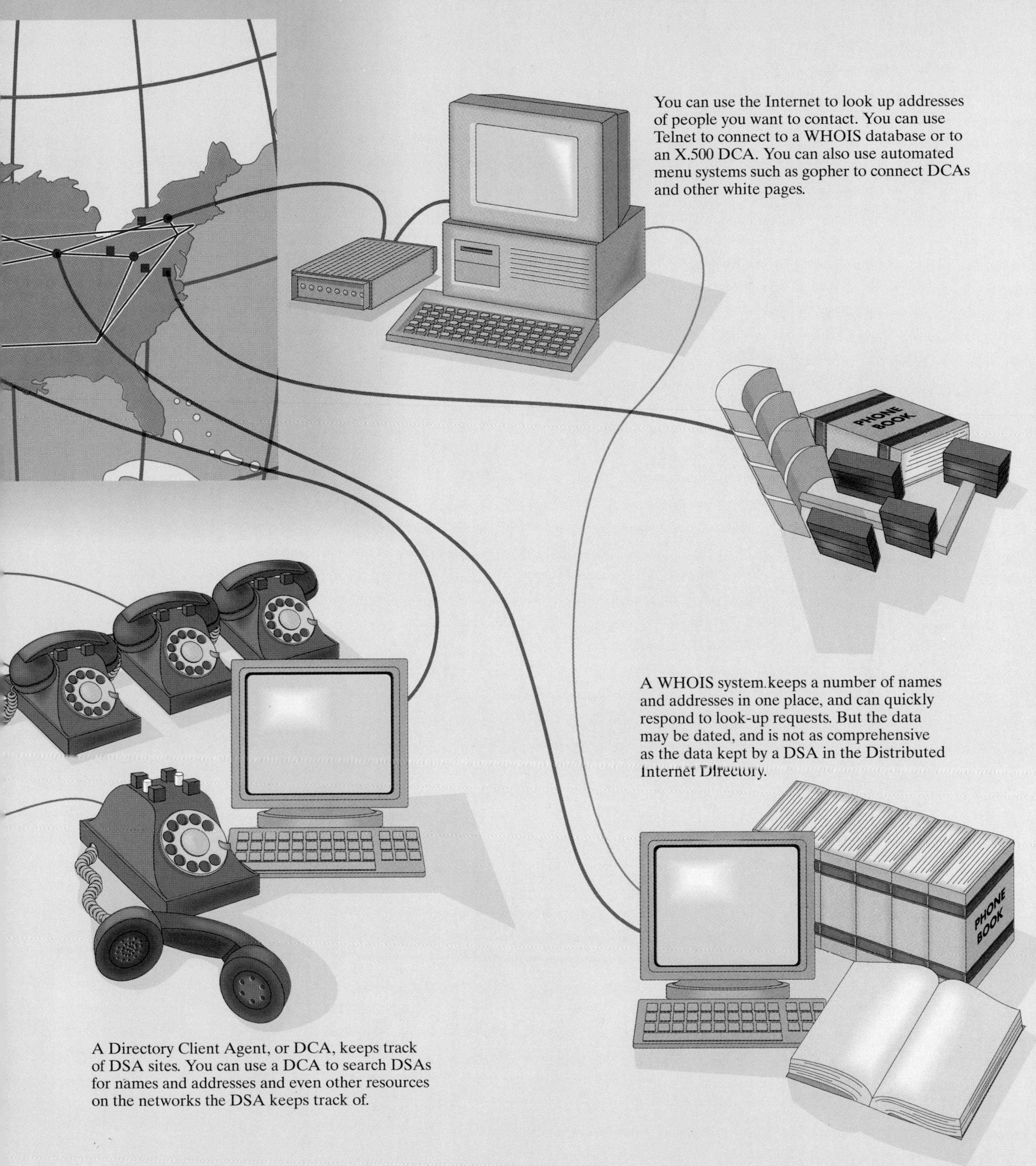
PHONE BOOK
PHONE BOOK

You can use the Internet to look up addresses of people you want to contact. You can use Telnet to connect to a WHOIS database or to an X.500 DCA. You can also use automated menu systems such as gopher to connect DCAs and other white pages.

A WHOIS system keeps a number of names and addresses in one place, and can quickly respond to look-up requests. But the data may be dated, and is not as comprehensive as the data kept by a DSA in the Distributed Internet Directory.

A Directory Client Agent, or DCA, keeps track of DSA sites. You can use a DCA to search DSAs for names and addresses and even other resources on the networks the DSA keeps track of.

IP
IP

Connecting with Other Networks and Commerial Services

WHILE THE INTERNET interconnects many networks, there are also other networks that are not part of the Internet. For example, Bitnet is an academic network that uses e-mail to link colleges and universities. The administrators of many of these other networks have set up agreements to send e-mail between their networks and the Internet. These interchanges of e-mail take place at gateways.

Gateways are specialized computers that translate e-mail from one network protocol to another. When a gateway receives an Internet e-mail message, the computer uses TCP to reassemble the stream of IP packets into a message, then breaks the message down into a format the other network understands. This process also involves stripping or reformatting the Internet address into the type of address that the other network uses. For example, when my e-mail messages arrive at the Internet/CompuServe gateway, they may be addressed to 72203.1434@compuserve.com; that's one of my Internet addresses. On the CompuServe side of the gateway, the address becomes 72203,1434—a format familiar to thousands of CompuServe users. If you use networks that are not part of the Internet, but that have gateways to the Internet, you can also send e-mail to anyone on the Internet.

CompuServe, America Online, Prodigy, Delphi, and GEnie are some of the larger commercial on-line services. Bulletin board systems (BBSs) are smaller on-line services that you can access or connect to with a simple phone call. Large and small on-line services offer all sorts of information resources, from stock market price quotes to discussion groups, on-line encyclopedias, and collections of computer files. Many of the resources that you can find on the Internet are also available on these commercial services. If you can't find local access to the Internet, you may want to check out one of these commercial services for a gateway to worldwide Internet e-mail. Keep in mind you must pay for all of the large services, and there is also a fee for most BBSs.

Fidonet is a worldwide network of bulletin board systems. Each BBS is a personal computer running Fido bulletin board software and is connected to a number of incoming phone lines. Fidonet BBSs are not connected directly to each other; information is sent over the network every night when each BBS calls several neighboring BBSs to trade messages. You can check with local computer groups to find local Fidonet BBSs or other BBSs that your computer can connect to via modem. You may also be able to find lists of BBSs by checking magazines about on-line computing.

E-mail networks like MCI Mail are set up to offer quick, inexpensive, and dependable e-mail service to customers. Many corporations use these services. If you work for a big company you might want to see if they use MCI Mail. You may be able to get an account that could double as an Internet e-mail address.

If you have access to networks like Bitnet and UUCP (UNIX to UNIX Copy Protocol), you are probably at a university or research company, and can most likely find an Internet connection at your institution.

Gateways

EMAIL
INTERNET

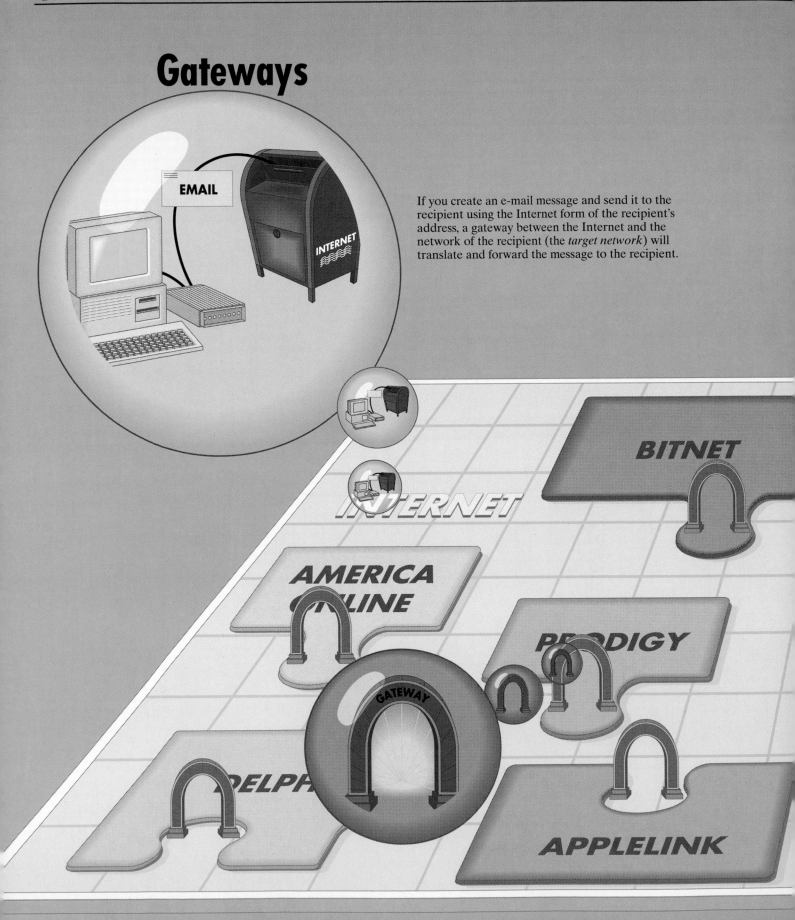

If you create an e-mail message and send it to the recipient using the Internet form of the recipient's address, a gateway between the Internet and the network of the recipient (the *target network*) will translate and forward the message to the recipient.

INTERNET
AMERICA
BITNET

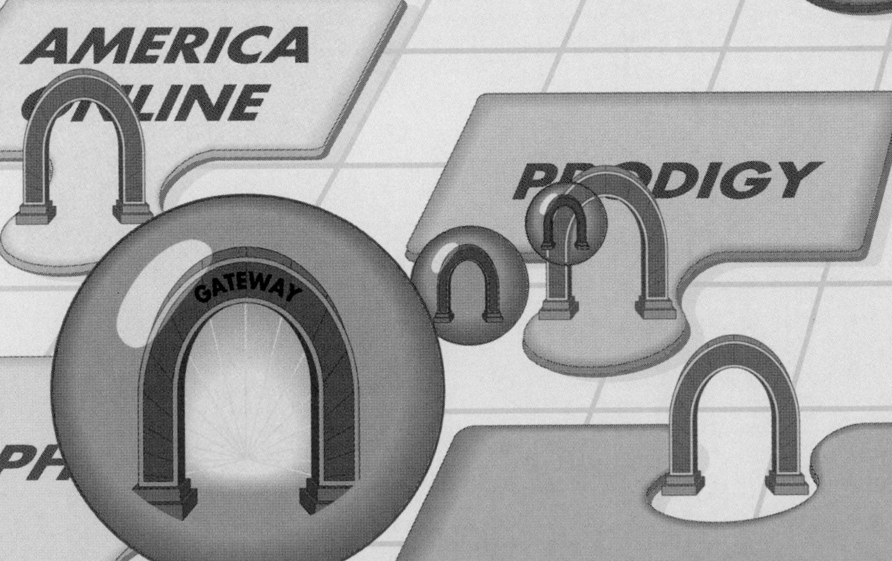
PRODIGY
GATEWAY
APPLELINK

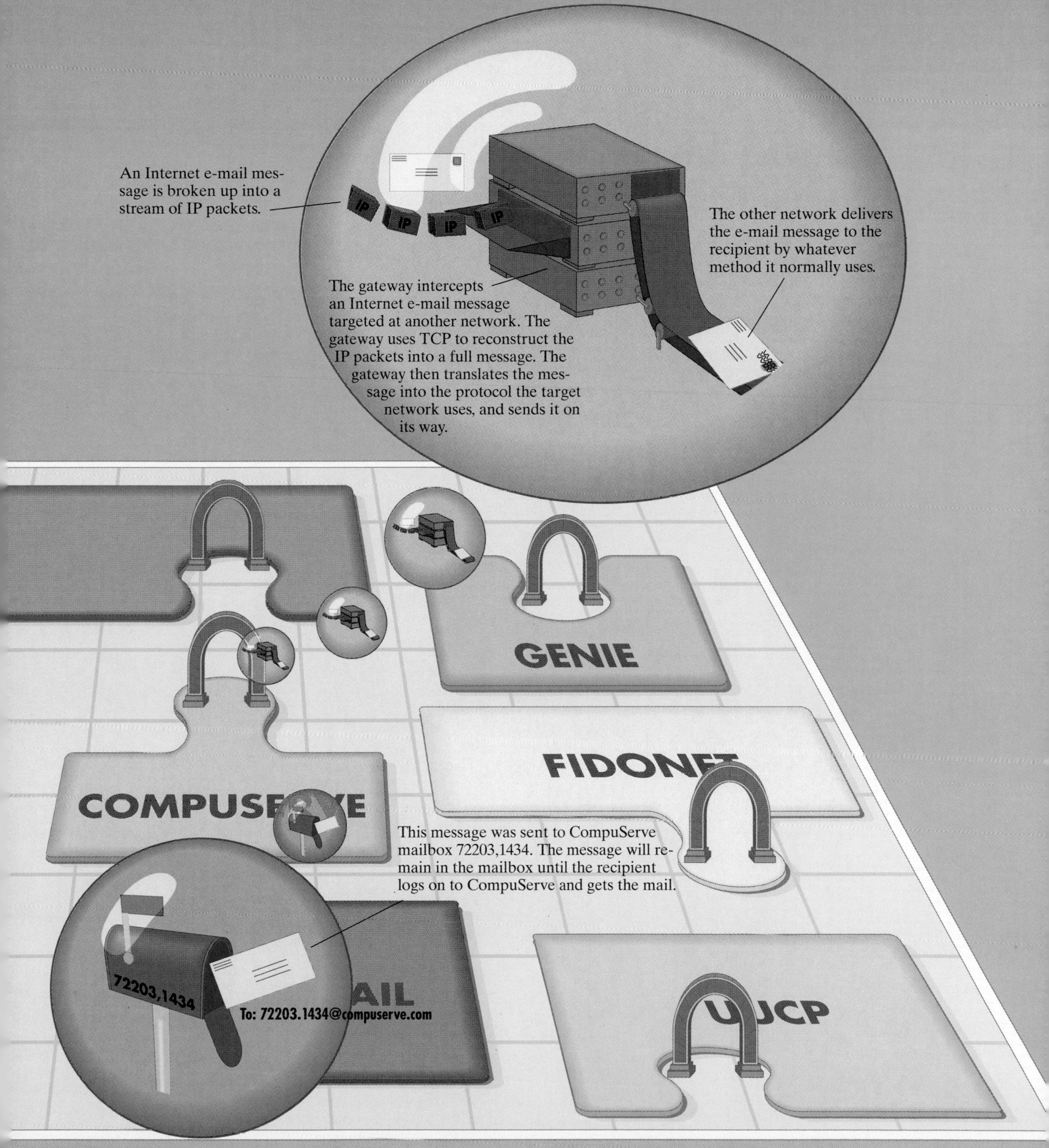

An Internet e-mail message is broken up into a stream of IP packets.

The gateway intercepts an Internet e-mail message targeted at another network. The gateway uses TCP to reconstruct the IP packets into a full message. The gateway then translates the message into the protocol the target network uses, and sends it on its way.

The other network delivers the e-mail message to the recipient by whatever method it normally uses.

GENIE

FIDONET

COMPUSERVE

This message was sent to CompuServe mailbox 72203,1434. The message will remain in the mailbox until the recipient logs on to CompuServe and gets the mail.

72203,1434

To: 72203.1434@compuserve.com

UUCP

On-line Services and Other Major Networks

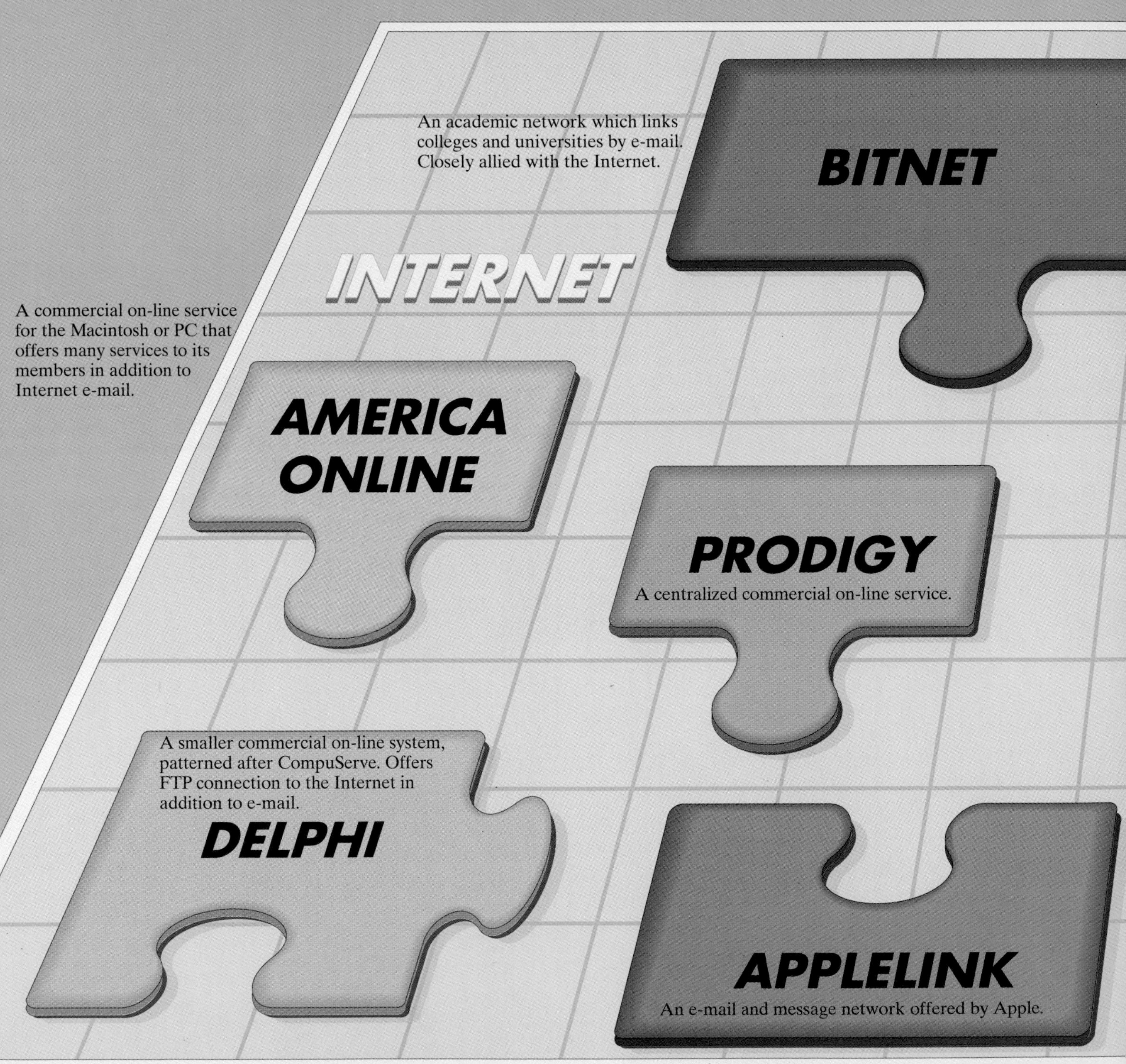
An academic network which links colleges and universities by e-mail. Closely allied with the Internet.
BITNET
INTERNET
A commercial on-line service for the Macintosh or PC that offers many services to its members in addition to Internet e-mail.
AMERICA ONLINE
PRODIGY
A centralized commercial on-line service.
A smaller commercial on-line system, patterned after CompuServe. Offers FTP connection to the Internet in addition to e-mail.
DELPHI
APPLELINK
An e-mail and message network offered by Apple.

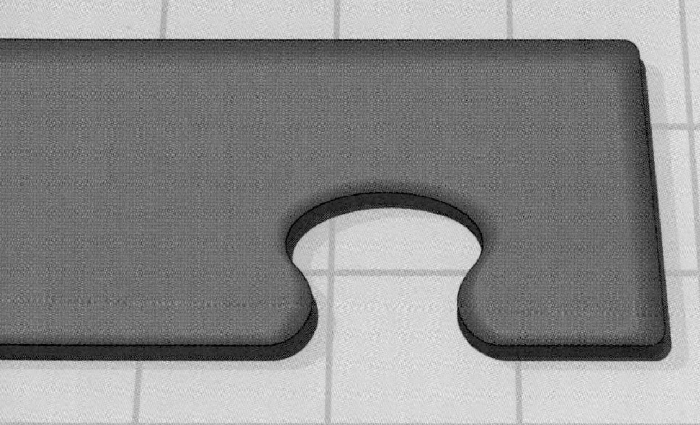

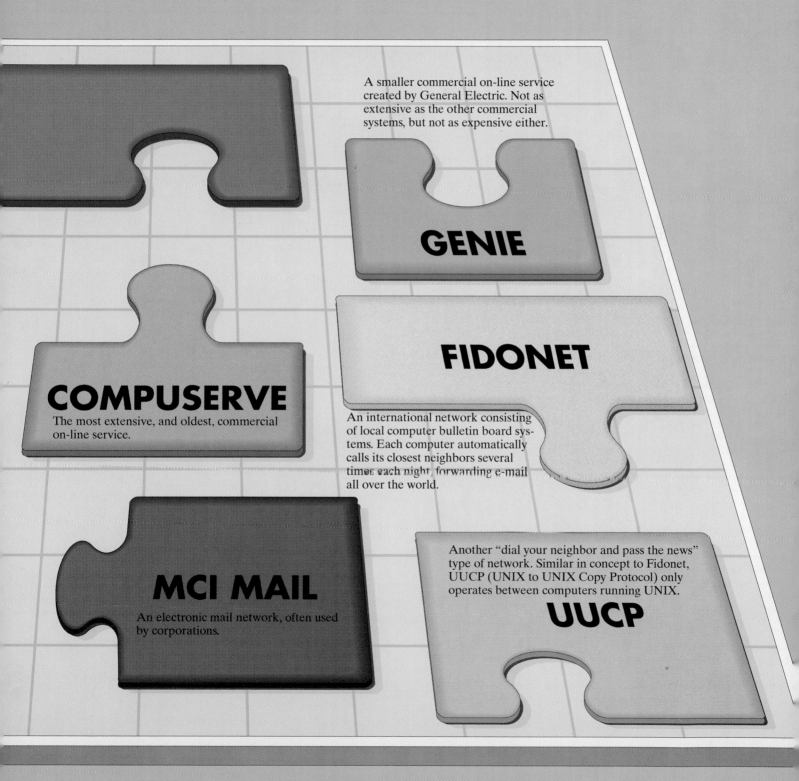

A smaller commercial on-line service created by General Electric. Not as extensive as the other commercial systems, but not as expensive either.

GENIE

FIDONET

COMPUSERVE

The most extensive, and oldest, commercial on-line service.

An international network consisting of local computer bulletin board systems. Each computer automatically calls its closest neighbors several times each night, forwarding e-mail all over the world.

Another "dial your neighbor and pass the news" type of network. Similar in concept to Fidonet, UUCP (UNIX to UNIX Copy Protocol) only operates between computers running UNIX.

MCI MAIL

An electronic mail network, often used by corporations.

UUCP

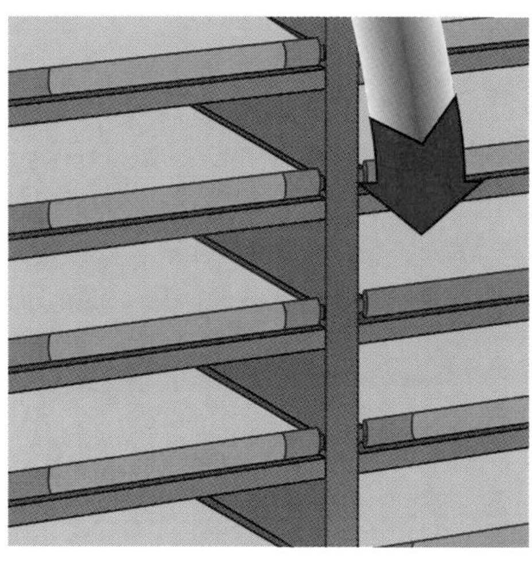

UseNet and Newsgroups

USENET IS A protocol that describes how groups of messages can be stored on and sent between computers, many of which lay outside the Internet. UseNet forms a virtual forum for the electronic community. This forum is divided into at least 20 major hierarchies of *newsgroups*, or varied areas of interest. Individual newsgroups can cover anything from news about UseNet or computers to cyberpunk, neuroscience, sociology, or comic books. The site administrator decides which newsgroups to carry.

The best way to access a newsgroup is with a UseNet reader software program. A good reader software package will support threads. A *thread* is a string of ongoing conversations. Use your reader to check its list of Frequently Asked Questions, or FAQs (pronounced "facks"), before you submit any questions to the newsgroup itself. This list will have answers to common questions about a certain newsgroup. It's considered impolite to waste computer resources by asking common questions when FAQs are available.

Discussions in virtual forums take place via e-mail, which is sent to a newsgroup's address. Like mailing lists on the Internet, a newsgroup may be moderated or unmoderated. If a newsgroup is moderated, e-mail is sent to the moderator, a person who screens all incoming e-mail to make sure it is appropriate before posting it to the newsgroup.

Any e-mail that is sent to an unmoderated newsgroup is automatically distributed to all UseNet servers that carry the newsgroup. The servers then distribute these messages to other UseNet sites that carry that particular newsgroup. A site will usually carry only the current portion of a newsgroup discussion on line, depending on the computer resources or space available at that site. Some sites *archive* old discussions, or store them off-line.

Once you start receiving e-mail from a UseNet newsgroup, you should *lurk*, or just read messages without responding at first. Many newsgroups are distributed throughout the world, and in the interest of courtesy, you should pick up some sense of the audience and its culture before jumping in with questions and opinions.

How UseNet Works

UseNet is a system for collecting into newsgroups messages about a single topic. Newsgroups are databases of these messages that are often duplicated on many computer systems.

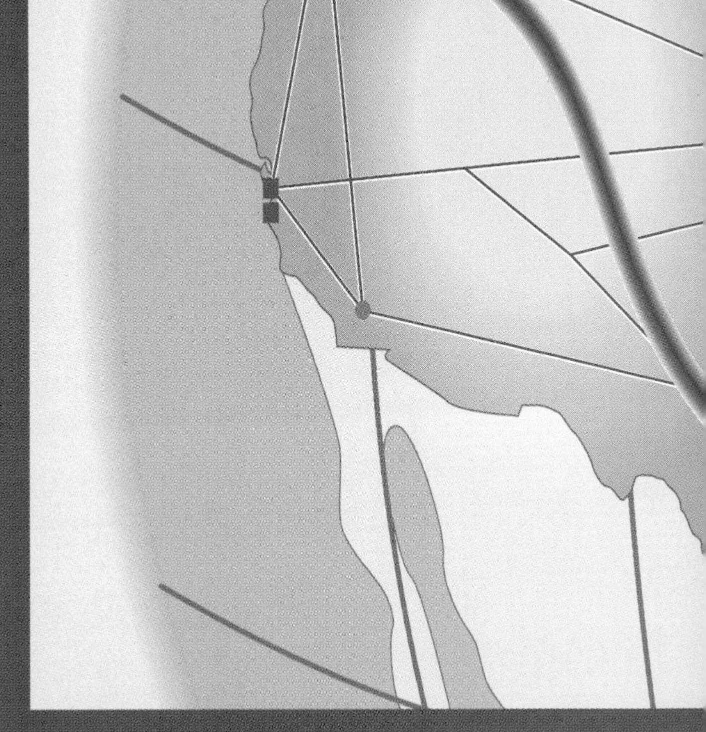

Reader software allows you to download newsgroups from a UseNet server. Some reader packages will help you respond, or send your own e-mail back to the newsgroup.

There are many UseNet servers—virtually any computer system that wants to carry newsgroups of interest to that site can be a UseNet server.

TALK
ALT
COM

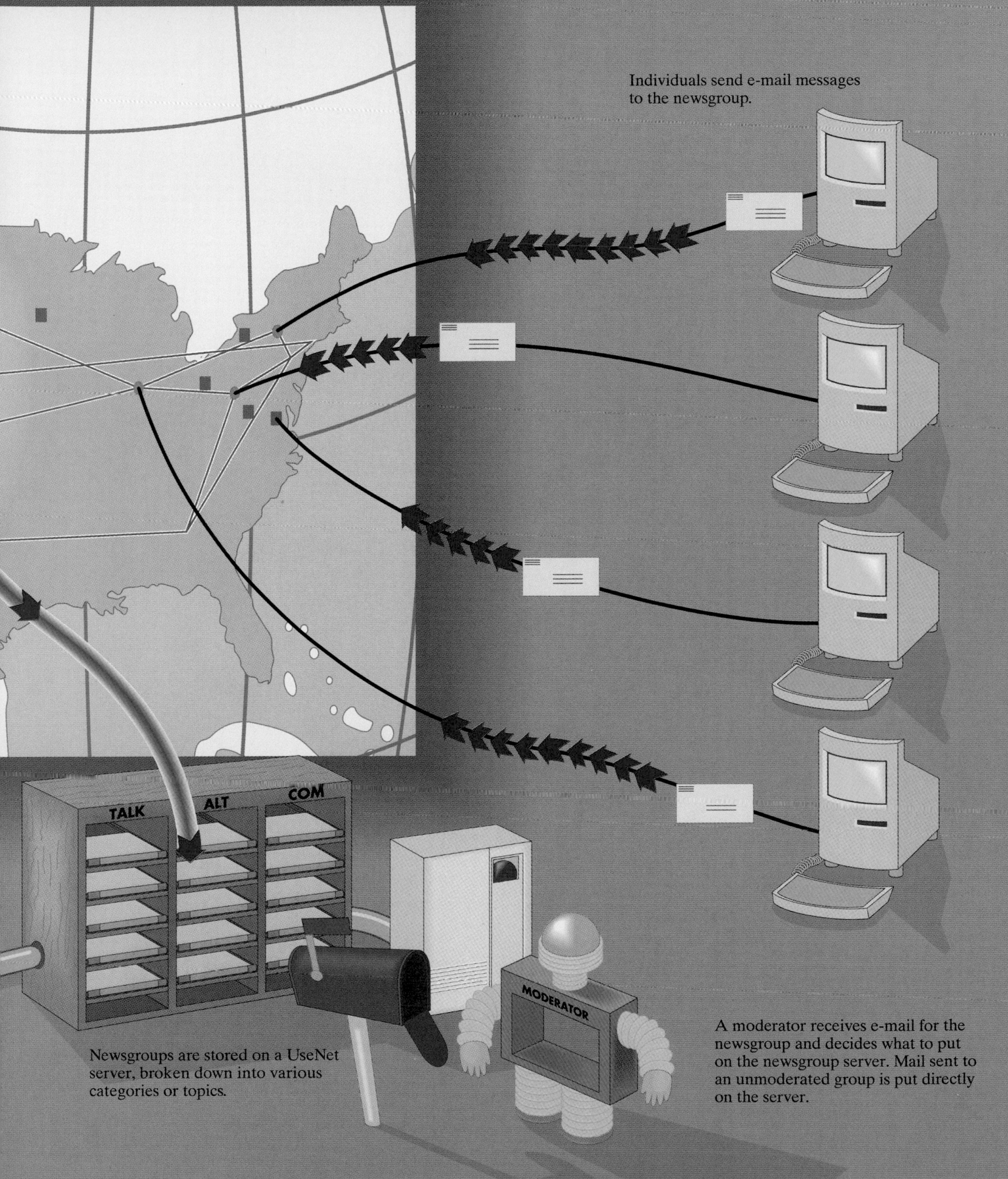
TALK
ALT
COM
MODERATOR

Individuals send e-mail messages to the newsgroup.

Newsgroups are stored on a UseNet server, broken down into various categories or topics.

A moderator receives e-mail for the newsgroup and decides what to put on the newsgroup server. Mail sent to an unmoderated group is put directly on the server.

UseNet Newsgroups

The electronic community uses UseNet as a virtual forum. When you locate a computer that offers UseNet, you will find the newsgroups divided into hierarchies of topics. System administrators can pick and choose individual newsgroups for their site.

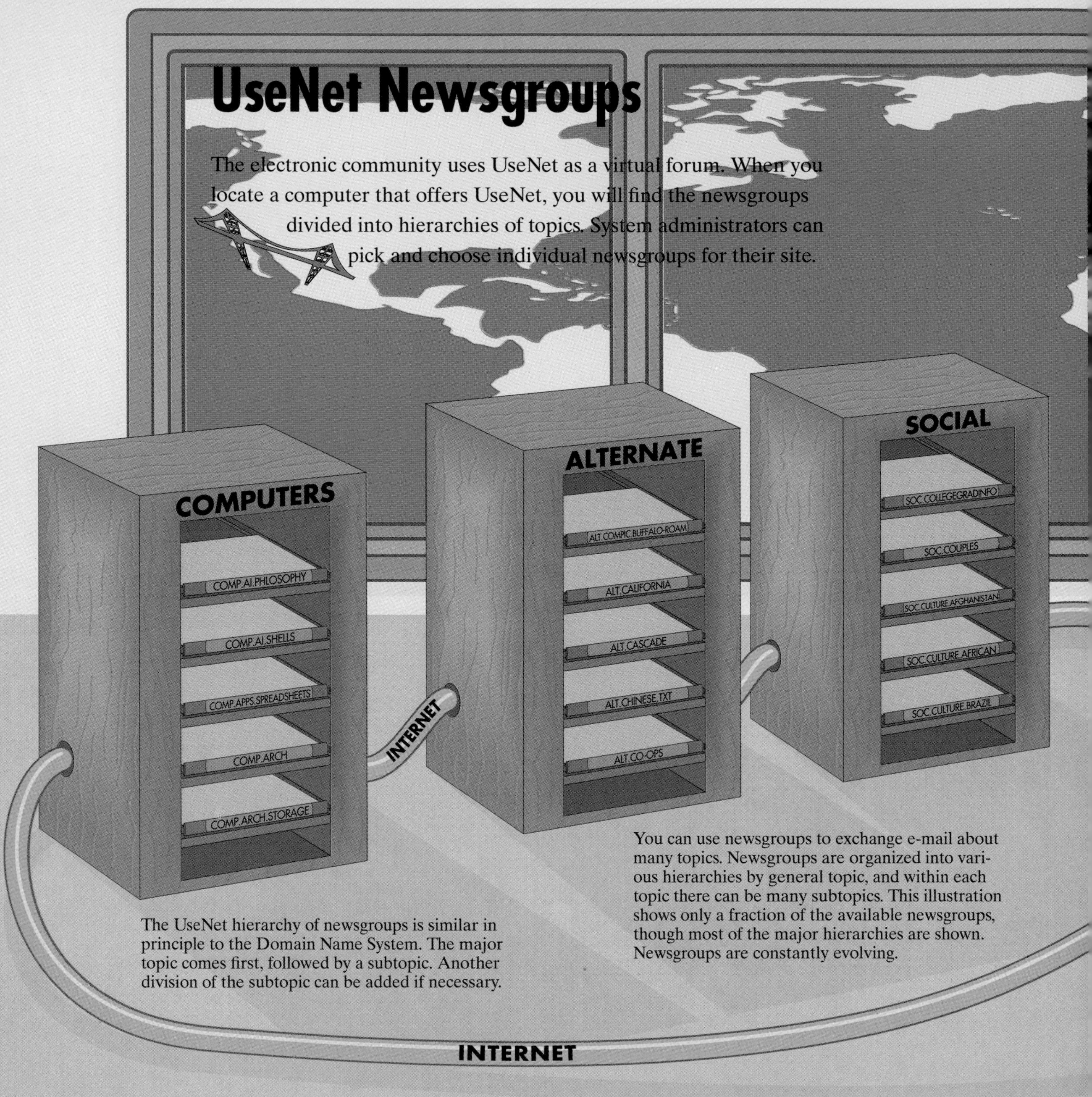

COMPUTERS
COMP.AI.PHILOSOPHY
COMP.AI.SHELLS
COMP.APPS.SPREADSHEETS
COMP.ARCH
COMP.ARCH.STORAGE
ALTERNATE
ALT.COMPIC.BUFFALO-ROAM
ALT.CALIFORNIA
ALT.CASCADE
ALT.CHINESE.TXT
ALT.CO-OPS
SOCIAL
SOC.COLLEGEGRADINFO
SOC.COUPLES
SOC.CULTURE.AFGHANISTAN
SOC.CULTURE.AFRICAN
SOC.CULTURE.BRAZIL
INTERNET
INTERNET

You can use newsgroups to exchange e-mail about many topics. Newsgroups are organized into various hierarchies by general topic, and within each topic there can be many subtopics. This illustration shows only a fraction of the available newsgroups, though most of the major hierarchies are shown. Newsgroups are constantly evolving.

The UseNet hierarchy of newsgroups is similar in principle to the Domain Name System. The major topic comes first, followed by a subtopic. Another division of the subtopic can be added if necessary.

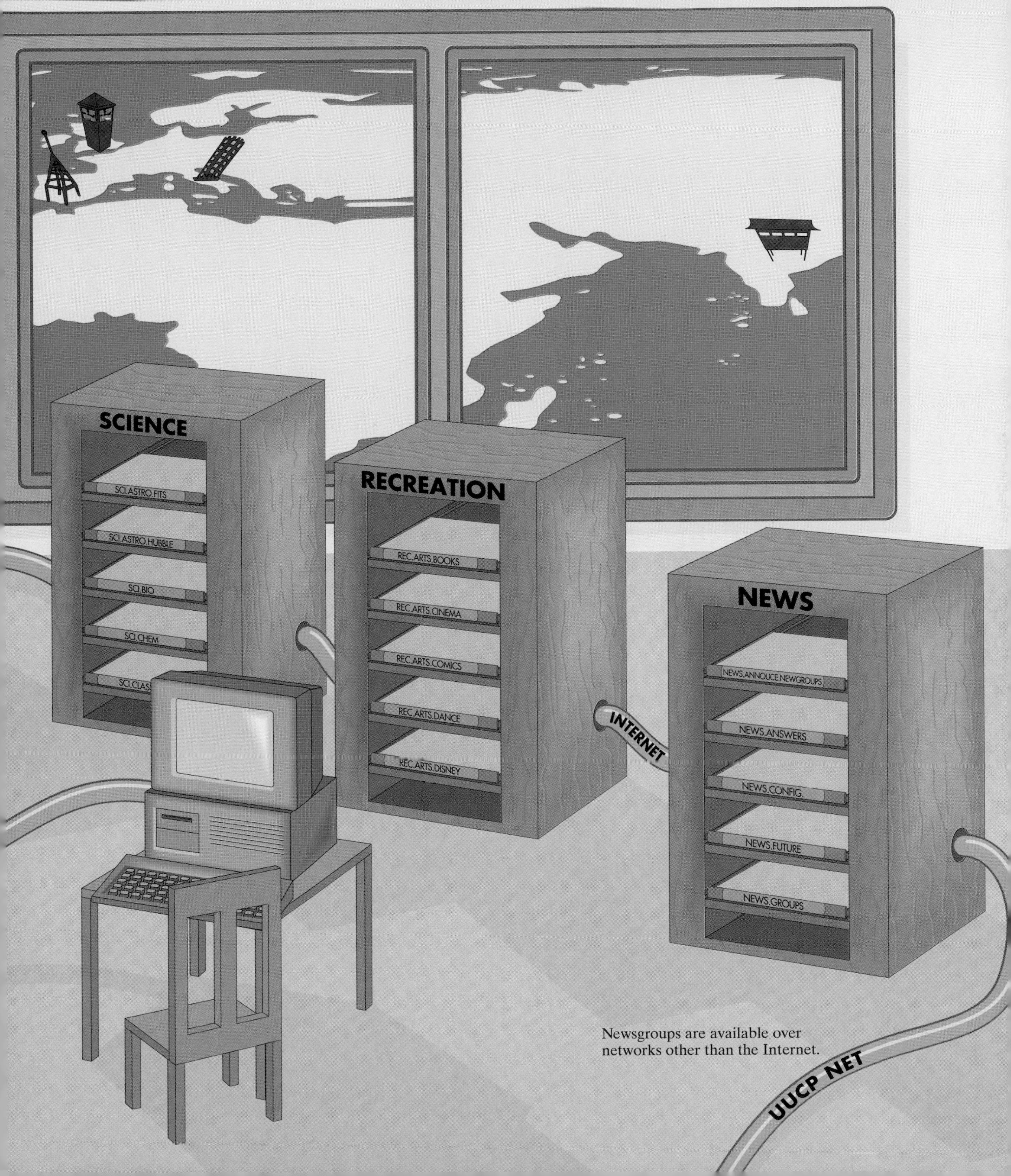

SCIENCE
SCI.ASTRO.FITS
SCI.ASTRO.HUBBLE
SCI.BIO
SCI.CHEM
RECREATION
REC.ARTS.BOOKS
REC.ARTS.CINEMA
REC.ARTS.COMICS
REC.ARTS.DANCE
REC.ARTS.DISNEY
INTERNET
NEWS
NEWS.ANNOUCE.NEWGROUPS
NEWS.ANSWERS
NEWS.CONFIG.
NEWS.FUTURE
NEWS.GROUPS
UUCP NET

Newsgroups are available over networks other than the Internet.

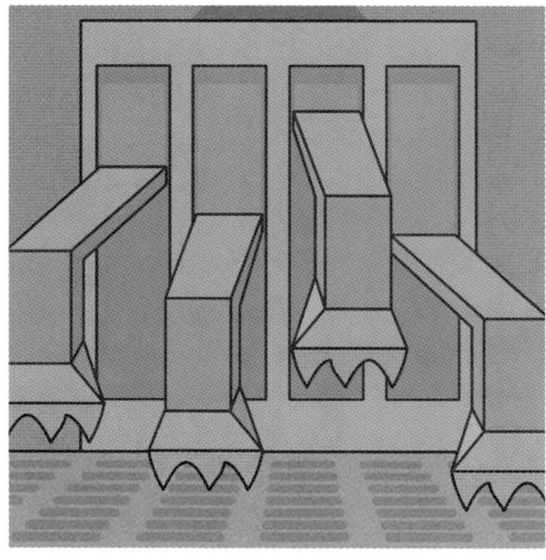

CHAPTER 20

Netiquette

NETIQUETTE REFERS TO the etiquette you should observe when using e-mail, especially e-mail sent to UseNet. Your messages may reach tens of thousands of people all over the world. Their impressions of you are based on the tone and content of your messages. Always remember that you are not communicating with computers, but with people who have feelings just as you do.

As a novice computer user or a newcomer to a particular newsgroup, you'll find that most of your questions have already been asked and answered. Experienced members of mailing lists or newsgroups have made a list of all the common questions and answers and have posted them as FAQs, or frequently asked questions. These FAQs may be available in back issues of the newsgroup, or you might have to lurk for a while until an updated list of FAQs gets sent out, usually once a month. When you are investigating a new mailing list or newsgroup, FAQs will help answer your technical questions about a newsgroup that is unfamiliar to you, or they will give you an idea of the range of topics in the newsgroup.

Be sure to "listen" to an ongoing conversation before you jump in and start posting messages to a newsgroup or mailing list. Check to see that you're not duplicating someone else's response. Also, be sure you know who you're responding to. Lastly, consider whether it's necessary to respond to the entire newsgroup.

The volume of traffic is one of the biggest problems with UseNet. *Noise*, or useless information on the net, can be a specific bottleneck. Keep in mind that it's often most efficient to send one e-mail response to the person who posted the question. You don't need to burden the whole group with your comments.

E-mail sent to newsgroups or mailing lists can convey a range of emotions. People often argue over the Internet in what are called *flame wars*. Text written in capital letters is called *shouting*. Other emotions are expressed by *emoticons*, or TLAs (three-letter acronyms), made out of ASCII punctuation symbols. Emoticons represent human faces if you turn them sideways, and they let you add emphasis to your e-mail.

E-mail lets you join in on worldwide forums and discussions. Remember that the Internet and UseNet connect a variety of cultures. Politics, religion, and other controversial topics should be discussed tactfully.

Emoticons and the Internet

The range of expression and emotion possible in the human voice is not available when you communicate by typed characters in e-mail, newsgroups or the Internet chat mode. But that is not to say the Internet is a cold, boring place! Emoticons, acronyms, and a variety of activities bring life to the Internet on-line community.

A firefighter is someone who tries to contain a flame war. A firefighter's job is to get people to talk civilly to each other again, to cool tempers, and to get the newsgroup functioning normally once more.

SCHOOL

You may unintentionally ignite a flame. Your message may seem innocent to you, but someone else might take great offense and flame back at you.

A flame war is a free-for-all, in which flaming gets out of hand. Often many people join in, tying up the network with useless messages. Flame wars can happen over such subjects as bad spelling, different types of computers, or more serious issues. Flame wars are a waste of resources, and only result in hurt feelings.

TYPING A SENTENCE IN ALL CAPS IS CALLED SHOUTING. This is considered to be very rude. Only use this when you are ANGRY or want to emphasize a VERY STRONG POINT! Shouting exchanges can lead to *flame wars*.

If you're trying to be funny or satirical, use a smiley to convey your point. Look at a smiley sideways to see a smiley face: 8-). There are many different kinds of smileys, and they can be quite involved. In fact, entire books have been written about smileys.

SHOUTING

"That's funny!" smiley

Happy smiley with glasses

"That's sad." smiley

PART 5

OTHER APPLICATIONS

CONTENTS

OVERVIEW

TELNET, FTP, AND e-mail are the three traditional applications around which the Internet was built. As the Internet has grown along with the computer industry, these applications have been used as building blocks for new generations of applications. One of the most visible new applications for the Internet is the gopher.

A gopher is a menu system that gathers for you information on the Internet. A gopher makes the full resources of an Internet computer available to you as choices on your computer screen. One of these choices offers the option of moving to other gopher sites around the world, where a new menu will show you the resources that you can access at the new site.

WAIS, or wide-area information server, is a research application, which works a little like Medline (Chapter 7). Unlike Medline, the WAIS database is not kept at one Internet site, but is spread out among many computer sites. Files at each of these sites are indexed. A WAIS search actually looks into files for the terms you are looking for, as opposed to a gopher search, which would only search menu items. A WAIS also lets you control which databases or sources you look at, and keeps track of searches you have made.

PART FIVE

The World Wide Web, or WWW, is another application that is available on the Internet. The World Wide Web is an example of how the power of the Internet can be concentrated into one program. With WWW you can choose your own path through a book or a document or through the Internet. WWW allows you to jump from resource to resource without knowing which Internet computer you're on, or how to use Telnet. All of these tasks are accomplished via hypertext links (Chapter 23).

Talk Radio is one of the most recent innovations on the Internet. Talk Radio is a digitized daily talk show that you can access with FTP over the Internet. If you have a sound card on your computer, you can download the daily Talk Radio file and play it on your computer. There are also ways of sending both video and audio over the Internet. Because of the *bandwidth*, or the amount of room video and audio signals take up, this technology is in the experimental stage. In Chapter 25 you'll see how audio and video signals can be used to make virtual reality and other *real-time*, or live, events happen over the Internet.

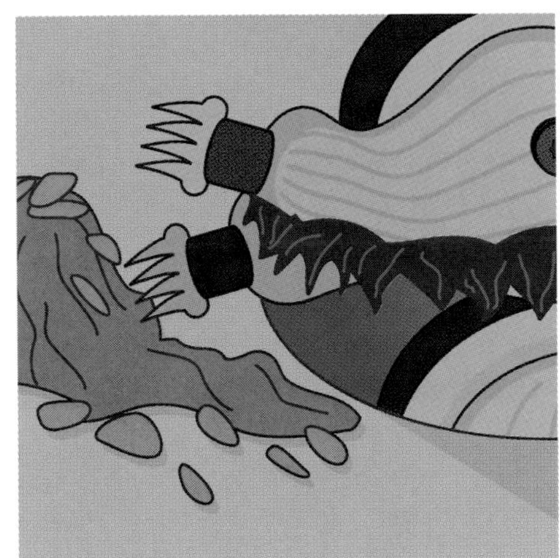

Chapter 21 Gophers

A GOPHER IS ONE type of client/server software. A gopher client runs on your computer; people usually refer to a gopher client as a gopher. A gopher server runs on the computer you want to connect with. Gopher servers exist on almost every large, publicly accessible computer system on the Internet. You can access any of these servers with a gopher, and use each system's resources, including FTP, archies, white pages, UseNet newsgroups, and much more.

Gopher clients and servers working together are properly called the *Internet gopher*. The Internet gopher consists of a fancy menu system that allows you to access resources on the Internet. If you have a character-based gopher, you'll see just simple lists of menus on your screen. Some gophers have a graphical interface that presents you with a screen containing icons and other types of images.

Gophers automatically handle Telnet and all the commands needed to connect one computer to another on the Internet. As you connect with a gopher, the log-on instructions may give you a particular account name to log on with. Entering this account name is the only work you have to do to start the gopher.

A *public gopher* is a gopher that has been set up for public access. Your computer becomes a virtual terminal of the host that is running the public gopher. You can use a modem and terminal emulation software to dial into a public gopher from your computer. You can find public gophers at many libraries and universities; many libraries set up terminals that run public gophers for your use. Contact your local college or library to obtain a phone number that will let you access their public gopher.

When you access a public gopher you do not have a full Internet connection. However, the public gopher will still take you almost anywhere on the Internet. You won't have access to the physical printers and hard disks connected to the host computer because the system administrator usually disables commands for printing and downloading. You can use the screen-capture capability of your modem's software to "capture to disk" any text that appears on your screen. You can also use e-mail to send a file from an Internet resource to an account you might have on an on-line service, such as CompuServe or America Online.

Gophers and the Internet

1 Gopher servers "serve" up information that a gopher client requests.

2 A gopher client program runs on your computer and has Telnet access to the Internet.

LIBRARY

3 If you don't have a gopher client, or don't have Telnet access to the Internet, you still can use a modem to connect your computer to a public gopher client, giving your computer almost all the same abilities as the gopher client.

4 Gophers use Telnet and other Internet applications to send streams of TCP/IP packets back and forth between the gopher server and client. This process creates on your computer a menu of the resources that exist on another computer.

Using a Gopher

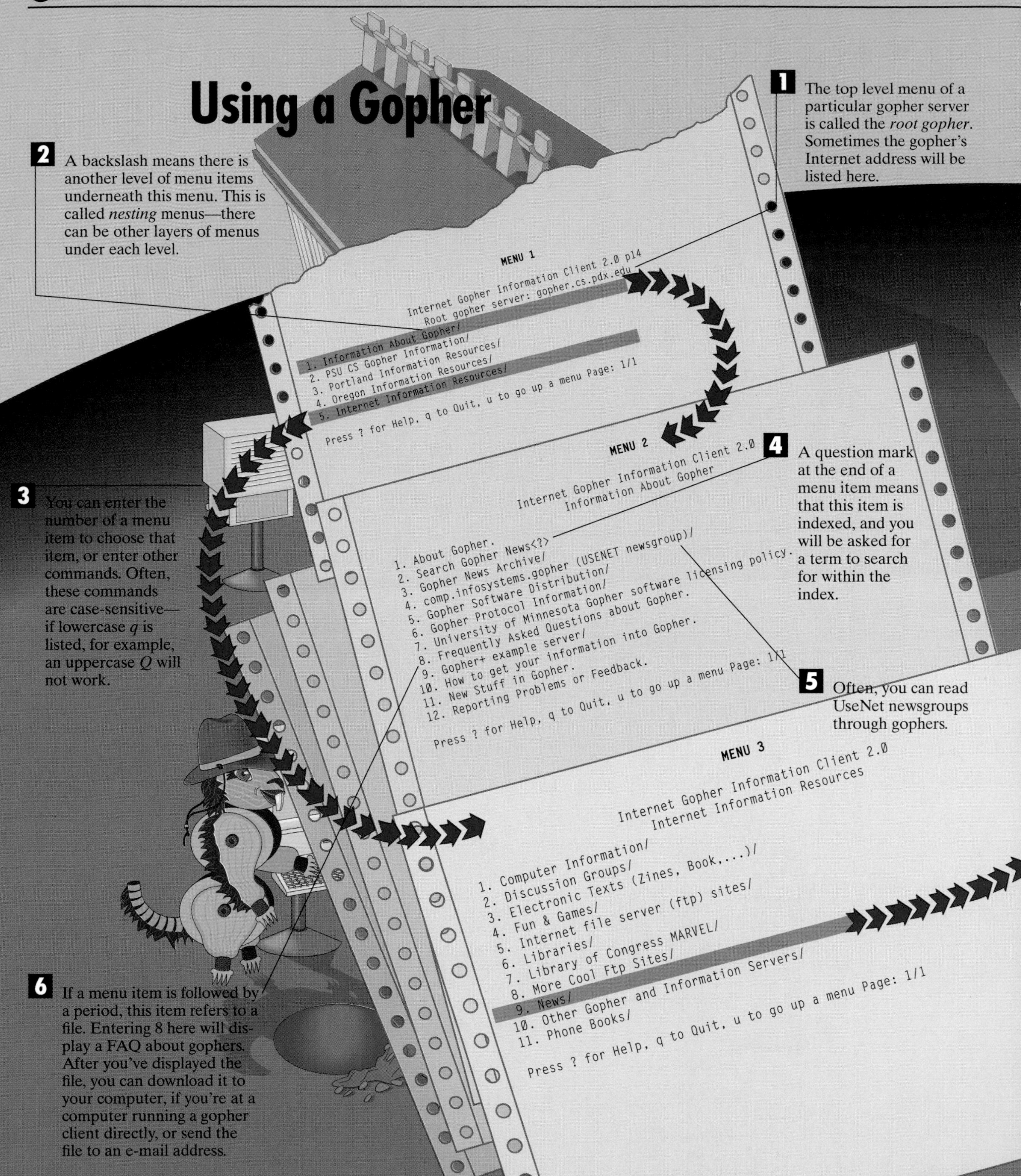
MENU 1
Internet Gopher Information Client 2.0 pl4
Root gopher server: gopher.cs.pdx.edu
1. Information About Gopher/
2. PSU CS Gopher Information/
3. Portland Information Resources/
4. Oregon Information Resources/
5. Internet Information Resources/
Press ? for Help, q to Quit, u to go up a menu Page: 1/1
MENU 2
Internet Gopher Information Client 2.0
Information About Gopher
1. About Gopher.
2. Search Gopher News<?>
3. Gopher News Archive/
4. comp.infosystems.gopher (USENET newsgroup)/
5. Gopher Software Distribution/
6. Gopher Protocol Information/
7. University of Minnesota Gopher software licensing policy.
8. Frequently Asked Questions about Gopher.
9. Gopher+ example server/
10. How to get your information into Gopher.
11. New Stuff in Gopher.
12. Reporting Problems or Feedback.
Press ? for Help, q to Quit, u to go up a menu Page: 1/1
MENU 3
Internet Gopher Information Client 2.0
Internet Information Resources
1. Computer Information/
2. Discussion Groups/
3. Electronic Texts (Zines, Book,...)/
4. Fun & Games/
5. Internet file server (ftp) sites/
6. Libraries/
7. Library of Congress MARVEL/
8. More Cool Ftp Sites/
9. News/
10. Other Gopher and Information Servers/
11. Phone Books/
Press ? for Help, q to Quit, u to go up a menu Page: 1/1

1 The top level menu of a particular gopher server is called the *root gopher*. Sometimes the gopher's Internet address will be listed here.

2 A backslash means there is another level of menu items underneath this menu. This is called *nesting* menus—there can be other layers of menus under each level.

3 You can enter the number of a menu item to choose that item, or enter other commands. Often, these commands are case-sensitive—if lowercase *q* is listed, for example, an uppercase *Q* will not work.

4 A question mark at the end of a menu item means that this item is indexed, and you will be asked for a term to search for within the index.

5 Often, you can read UseNet newsgroups through gophers.

6 If a menu item is followed by a period, this item refers to a file. Entering 8 here will display a FAQ about gophers. After you've displayed the file, you can download it to your computer, if you're at a computer running a gopher client directly, or send the file to an e-mail address.

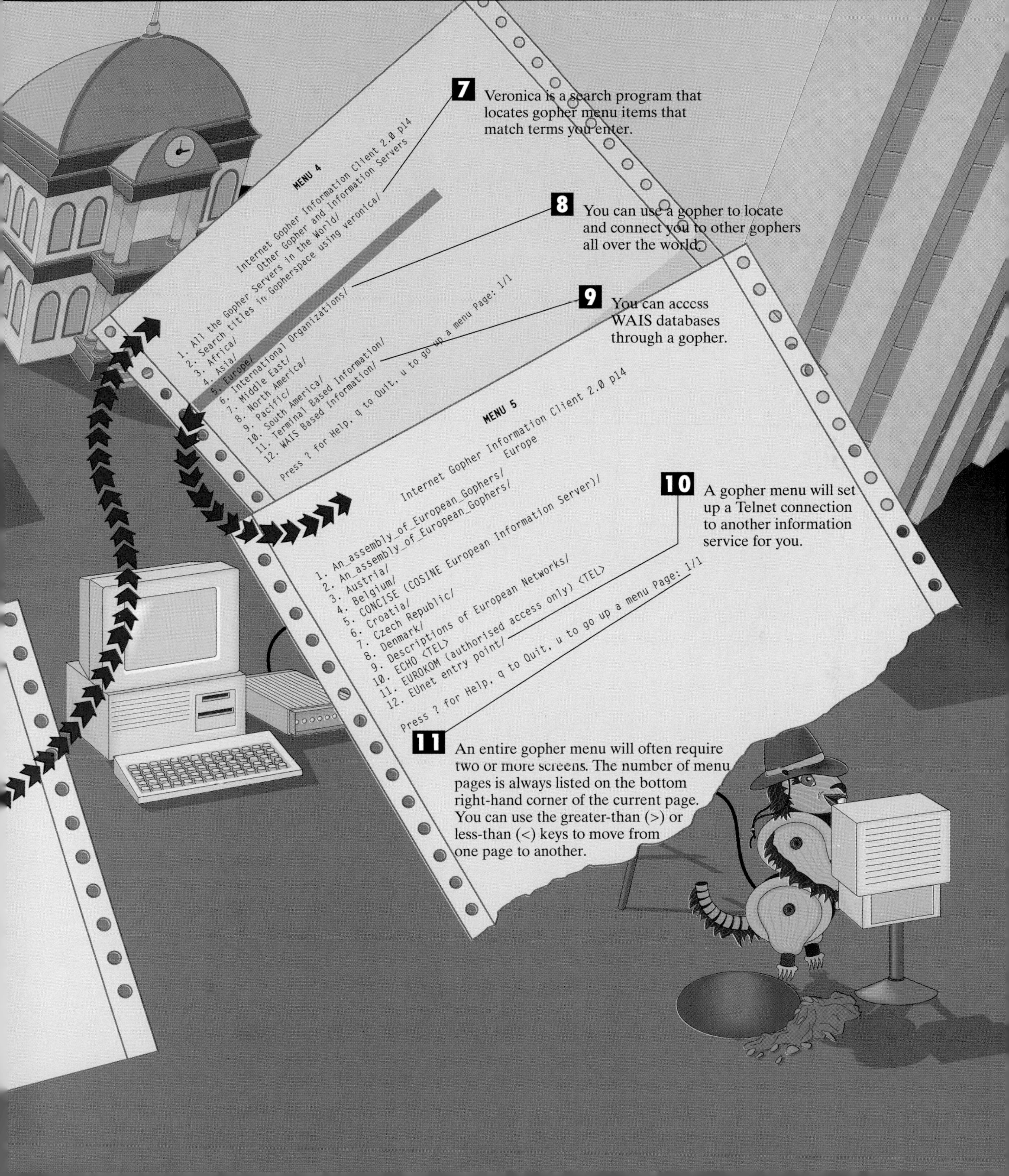

```
MENU 4

Internet Gopher Information Client 2.0 p14
Other Gopher and Information Servers

1. All the Gopher Servers in the World/
2. Search titles in Gopherspace using veronica/
3. Africa/
4. Asia/
5. Europe/
6. International Organizations/
7. Middle East/
8. North America/
9. Pacific/
10. South America/
11. Terminal Based Information/
12. WAIS Based Information/

Press ? for Help, q to Quit, u to go up a menu Page: 1/1
```

```
MENU 5

Internet Gopher Information Client 2.0 p14
Europe

1. An_assembly_of_European_Gophers/
2. An_assembly_of_European_Gophers/
3. Austria/
4. Belgium/
5. CONCISE (COSINE European Information Server)/
6. Croatia/
7. Czech Republic/
8. Denmark/
9. Descriptions of European Networks/
10. ECHO <TEL>
11. EUROKOM (authorised access only) <TEL>
12. EUnet entry point/

Press ? for Help, q to Quit, u to go up a menu Page: 1/1
```

7 Veronica is a search program that locates gopher menu items that match terms you enter.

8 You can use a gopher to locate and connect you to other gophers all over the world.

9 You can acccss WAIS databases through a gopher.

10 A gopher menu will set up a Telnet connection to another information service for you.

11 An entire gopher menu will often require two or more screens. The number of menu pages is always listed on the bottom right-hand corner of the current page. You can use the greater-than (>) or less-than (<) keys to move from one page to another.

VAIS

WAIS

WAIS, OR WIDE-area information server, is a popular method of finding information stored on computers across the Internet. WAIS is a distributed system. A *distributed system* spreads the data and information among many computers, instead of storing it at a single location. You use WAIS client software on your computer to search databases on WAIS. You select WAIS databases you want to search from a WAIS list, and you must install the addresses of these databases in your server. Many Internet computers use these databases and constantly update them. WAIS processes search requests from a WAIS client, then sends the client a "hit list" of these search requests, showing the title of each file that matches the search. You use this list to pick the files you want transferred to your computer.

Each WAIS database is a specialized library. Specialists at each WAIS site index and record each library's files in a massive computerized card catalog. If a file is not text based, a description of the file is indexed. Prepositions, articles, and words that appear very frequently in the subject matter of the database are left out of the index because they take up space and don't return any useful information in a search. Look for a FAQ or README file at a WAIS site for a list of excluded words.

You can use Telnet to access a public WAIS client, or you can use a public gopher to search WAIS database libraries one at a time. Either of these methods can be useful in a pinch, but you need to run a WAIS client program on your computer to make full use of the power of WAIS. You then can automatically spread out a single search among a group of WAIS databases, keep track of your searches over time, combine searches, or rerun a search later and catch any new data that has been added since your last search. A WAIS client program can even calculate relevancy scores that rate the "hits," or documents, that your search returns or finds based on your individual interests.

You also can use gophers to search directories of WAIS databases for individual WAIS databases that cover specific topics. You can then use the gopher to search within that WAIS database.

WAIS database searches take you inside the documents or files you're interested in. Gophers and archie searches only scratch the surface; they just look at key words in the file title and description.

WAIS

A wide-area information server, or WAIS, provides a comprehensive index for all the documents and files stored at a WAIS database. These databases are collections of materials in a single subject area. There are hundreds of WAIS databases available, covering everything from individual newsgroups to electronic books stored on an Internet computer.

WAIS
WAIS
WAIS

You can use Telnet or a gopher to access WAIS databases one at a time. This type of search can be powerful, but it can also get out of hand. If you search for a term that is two words or more, the WAIS sticks the word *or* between each word. There is no way to place the word *and* between words. For example, a search in the WAIS database that indexes the Bionet newsgroups on alpha interferon (a biochemical found in the brain) returns hits on anything that contains the word *interferon* or the word *alpha*. So you'll get articles on Alpha computers, alpha monkeys, alpha interferon, beta interferon, and just plain old interferon.

When you install WAIS client software on your computer, you can use a single search to check groups of WAIS databases. You can save your searches and run them later to see if any new data has been added.

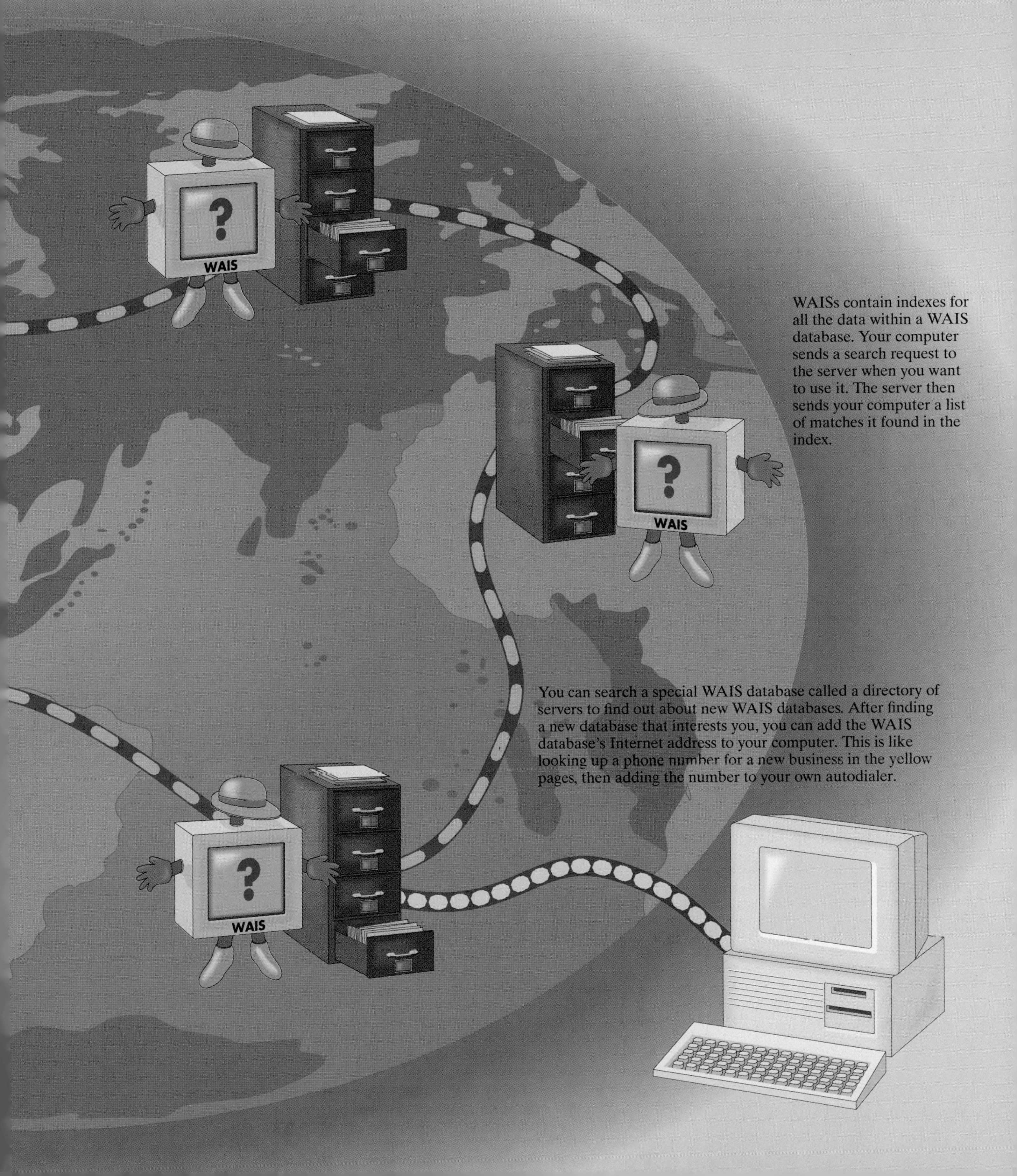

WAISs contain indexes for all the data within a WAIS database. Your computer sends a search request to the server when you want to use it. The server then sends your computer a list of matches it found in the index.

You can search a special WAIS database called a directory of servers to find out about new WAIS databases. After finding a new database that interests you, you can add the WAIS database's Internet address to your computer. This is like looking up a phone number for a new business in the yellow pages, then adding the number to your own autodialer.

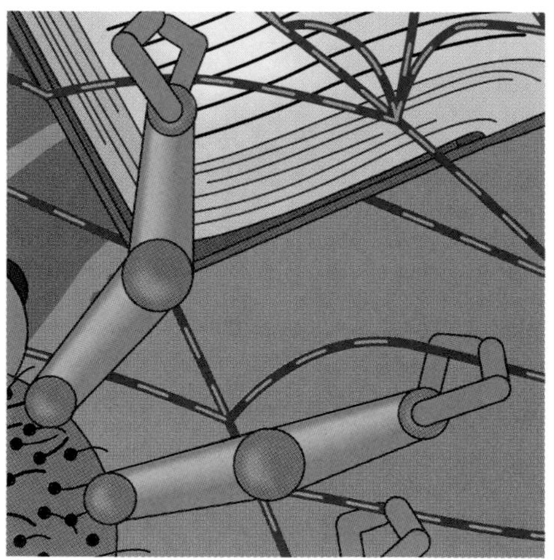

The World Wide Web

THE WORLD WIDE WEB also known as the WWW, or the W3, is a menu system. It gathers Internet resources from all over the world into a series of menu pages, or screens, that appear on your computer. The W3 is also a distributed system. A *distributed system* stores data and information on many computers. The W3 server maintains pointers or links to data that is spread out over the entire Internet, and can go out and get that data when you ask for it. Like the gopher system and WAIS, the W3 uses the client/server model. You can use Telnet to access the host computer that is running the client program.

Hypermedia is the foundation of the W3. *Media* refers to the type of data you find on the Internet. Media can be ASCII text, a PostScript file, an audio file, a graphic image, or any other sort of data that can be stored in a computer file. *Hypermedia* is a new way of connecting this media, or computer data. A hypermedia document has nonlinear links, or connections to other documents. This is in contrast to a regular document that you read linearly. You can jump around in hypermedia documents and explore related documents at your own pace, navigating in whatever direction you choose. For example, if a document mentions the space shuttle, you can choose to see a picture of the shuttle taking off, jump into a history of the shuttle program, and then jump back to the original document.

A W3 browser such as Mosaic creates a unique, hypermedia-based menu on your computer screen. A browser uses data about links to accomplish this; the data is stored on a W3 server. A W3 menu can link you to other Internet resources, not just text documents, graphics, and sound files. Gophers, white pages, and newsgroup servers can all be items on a hypermedia menu. As you choose an item or resource, or move from one document to another, you may be jumping between computers on the Internet without knowing it, while the W3 handles all the connections.

The World Wide Web

The World Wide Web is also known as the WWW or the W3. The web stretches out wherever the Internet goes, and allows you to create a menu of Internet resources that meets your needs. The W3 is similar to the gopher system, in that both are menus. But gophers are built around individual Internet computer sites. A W3 menu is based on what you, or the person who creates the menu, wants. A single menu page can refer to Internet resources scattered across the world.

You can download a free copy of a graphical browser or client for the W3 from many sites. There are graphical browsers, such as Mosaic, for Macintoshes, Windows, X Windows, NeXT, and UNIX computers. Using a mouse with such a graphical interface makes using the W3 a snap.

If you don't have a direct connection to the Internet, you still can use the W3 by e-mail. Send a message to listserv@info.cern.ch (the Internet address) with the single word *HELP* in the message. CERN's mailing robot will send a short overview of the process to your address. Using the W3 by e-mail is very slow.

You can use the web to do archie searches and find files at FTP sites. You can also find software for W3 clients or browsers from info.cern.ch. Do an archie search for WWW or Mosaic to find software at Internet computers closer to you.

A terminal-based W3 client, or browser, lets you construct your own menu pages of Internet resources. When you use a gopher or Telnet to log on to another system running a W3 client, you are browsing through menu pages set up by someone else.

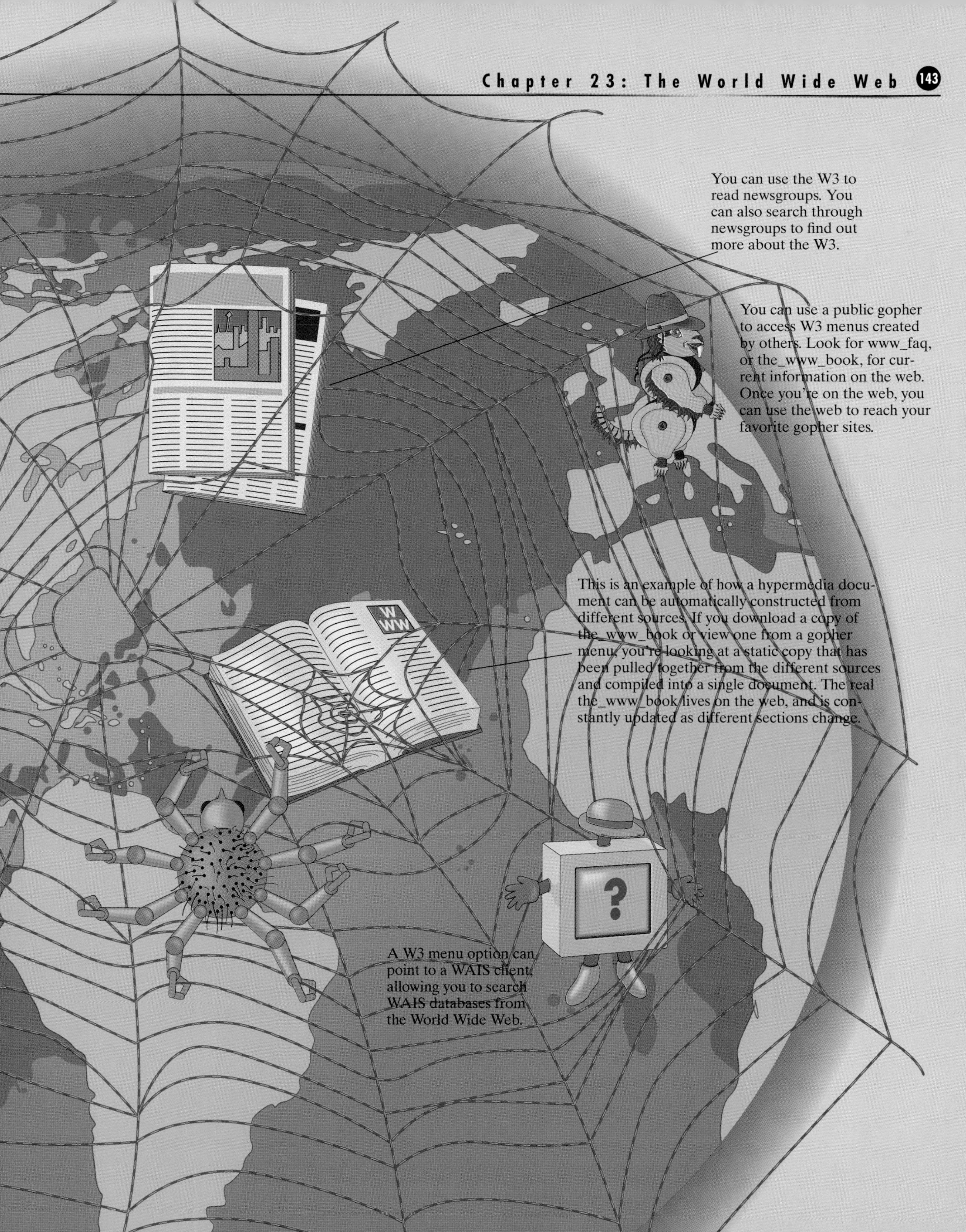
W
WW

You can use the W3 to read newsgroups. You can also search through newsgroups to find out more about the W3.

You can use a public gopher to access W3 menus created by others. Look for www_faq, or the_www_book, for current information on the web. Once you're on the web, you can use the web to reach your favorite gopher sites.

This is an example of how a hypermedia document can be automatically constructed from different sources. If you download a copy of the_www_book or view one from a gopher menu, you're looking at a static copy that has been pulled together from the different sources and compiled into a single document. The real the_www_book lives on the web, and is constantly updated as different sections change.

A W3 menu option can point to a WAIS client, allowing you to search WAIS databases from the World Wide Web.

CHAPTER
24

Audio/Video on the Internet

AN ANALOG SIGNAL usually transmits audio, or sound. The signal, or wave form, is continually varied in both frequency, or speed, and amplitude, or strength. This signal must be changed into a digital format before a computer can use it. *Digitizing* involves sampling the signal by chopping it into slices a set number of times per second. The frequency and amplitude of each sample are recorded in a file to create a digital signal. The Internet carries digitized audio information at 8,000 samples a second for Internet Talk Radio.

Internet Talk Radio (ITR), patterned after National Public Radio (NPR), is the first regularly scheduled radio station on the Internet. ITR offers programming that reaches over 100,000 people in 30 countries. The first program was "Geek of the Week," a weekly interview with an Internet expert. ITR has also broadcast public affairs programs and specials such as the eight-part "Hell's Bells: A Radio History of the Telephone." Like NPR, ITR acknowledges underwriters, or sponsors of their various programs.

Each day ITR broadcasts 15 to 45 megabytes of programming over the Internet to various FTP sites. ITR posts the audio program file to UUNET, a commercial Internet service provider that runs part of the Internet. The file is moved to other regional service providers around the world during off-peak hours. System administrators of local FTP sites can then copy the file to their servers. Ideally, you can find new ITR audio program files on your company's or school's network each morning. If not, or if you have a personal computer at home, look for a local FTP site that carries ITR programs, and download the files to your computer. If you have a SPARCstation or a NeXT computer, you can play ITR programs right on your workstation; otherwise, you must convert the program file to a format your computer's sound board can play. A *sound board* is a device that transforms digital files back into analog ones, so the signal can be sent to a speaker.

While transmitting audio over the Internet is fairly new, transmitting video is even newer, and not as common. In fact, video broadcasts are pretty much limited to experimental broadcasts or broadcasts of special Internet events, such as conferences or shows. Video requires expensive equipment and takes up lots of space on the Internet backbones, but uses the same theory as audio. A process similar to audio sampling changes an analog video signal into a digital stream of packets.

Many institutions on the Internet are cooperating to form the *mbone*, a multimedia backbone that bypasses Internet backbones and links to carry video traffic around the country and the world. Someday soon we'll probably see some sort of Internet TV, as well as other amazing innovations on the Internet.

Internet Talk Radio

You can tune in to daily radio programs from ITR by downloading audio program files from the Internet to play on your computer. Modeled after National Public Radio (NPR), ITR provides professionally produced interviews and coverage of events and people of interest to the Internet community.

RADIO CITY

Many FTP administrators will voluntarily store ITR audio program files at their sites. Distributing the files over the Internet to these sites spreads out the load of 45-megabyte files that many people want to access. Instead of crowding the lines from your home to the ITR station, you need only look up an FTP site that is close to you on the Internet. You may have to do a little detective work to find a local FTP site. Study the domain names of sites you find through a gopher or archie. You may need to poke around for FAQs or other information at several servers. Try not to download ITR files from a distant FTP server if you can help it, because this ties up the Internet.

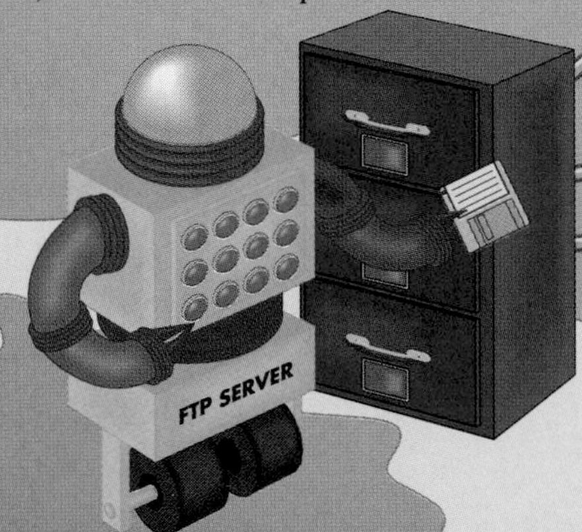
FTP SERVER

The ITR station is located at the National Press Building in Washington, D.C. Just like a regular radio station, ITR uses professional audio equipment to produce professional shows. In the field, ITR reporters use *DAT* (digital audio tape) recorders that digitize the audio signal right in the field, providing high-quality sound from the very beginning. After a program is edited, rerecorded, and mixed (all on digital equipment), the program is put into a digital file and transferred to the Internet.

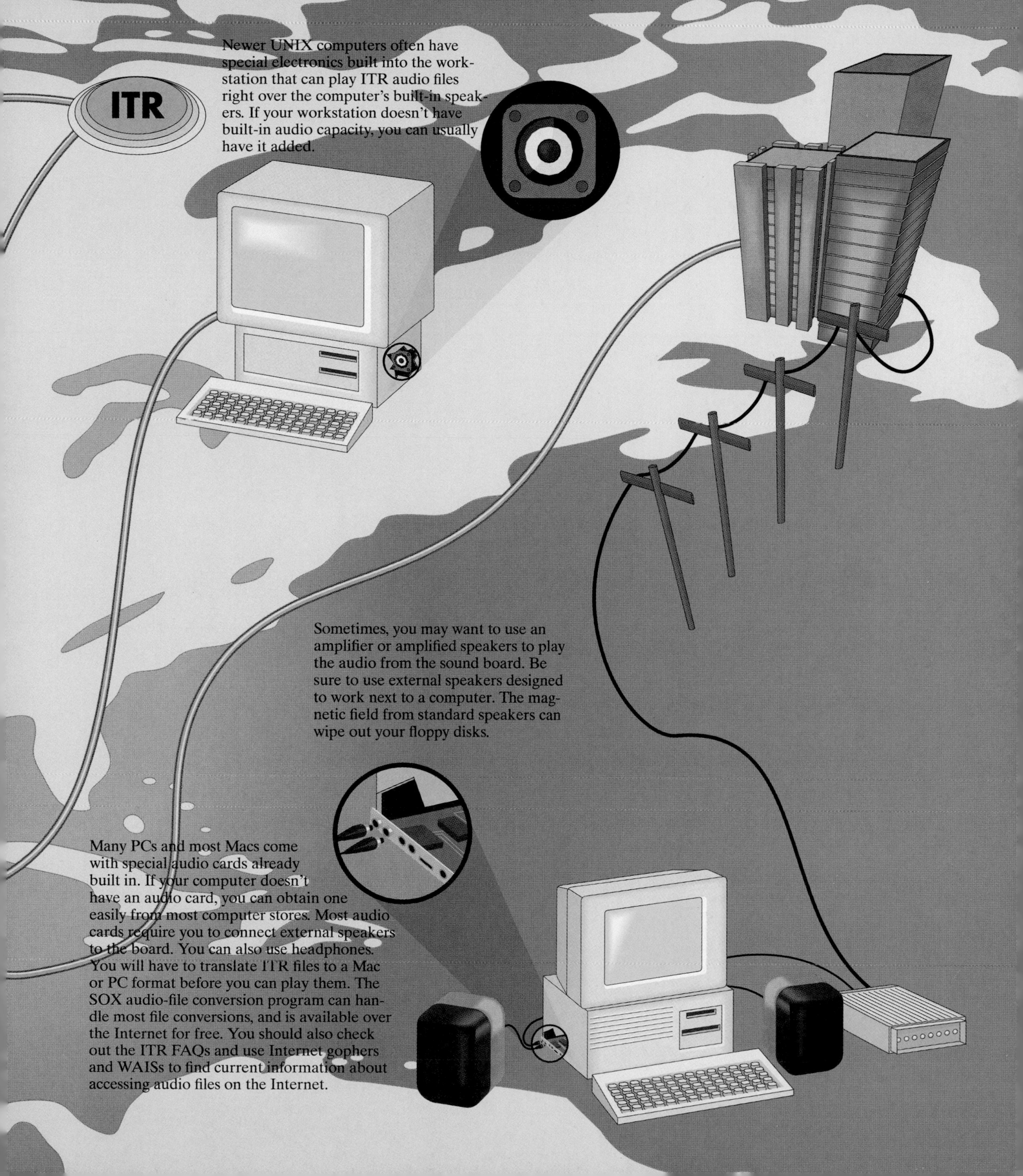

Newer UNIX computers often have special electronics built into the workstation that can play ITR audio files right over the computer's built-in speakers. If your workstation doesn't have built-in audio capacity, you can usually have it added.

Sometimes, you may want to use an amplifier or amplified speakers to play the audio from the sound board. Be sure to use external speakers designed to work next to a computer. The magnetic field from standard speakers can wipe out your floppy disks.

Many PCs and most Macs come with special audio cards already built in. If your computer doesn't have an audio card, you can obtain one easily from most computer stores. Most audio cards require you to connect external speakers to the board. You can also use headphones. You will have to translate ITR files to a Mac or PC format before you can play them. The SOX audio-file conversion program can handle most file conversions, and is available over the Internet for free. You should also check out the ITR FAQs and use Internet gophers and WAISs to find current information about accessing audio files on the Internet.

Video Conferencing

2 A computer with the appropriate digital hardware captures the stream of TCP/IP packets off the Internet, reassembles the information into a digital signal, then displays the signal on a TV monitor. The audio is also transformed into an analog signal that can drive speakers.

3 The video signal can be displayed on a large screen so a group of people can view the event. Another audio or A/V link can be established from the remote site to the speaker's site to allow two-way communications.

The Internet can transmit conferences and special events between Internet computers. This requires special hardware and coordination between the parties involved. Some groups are also experimenting with broadcasting educational classes over the Internet or other high-capacity digital networks. As the use of video hardware on personal computers becomes widespread, these kinds of transmissions will occur more commonly.

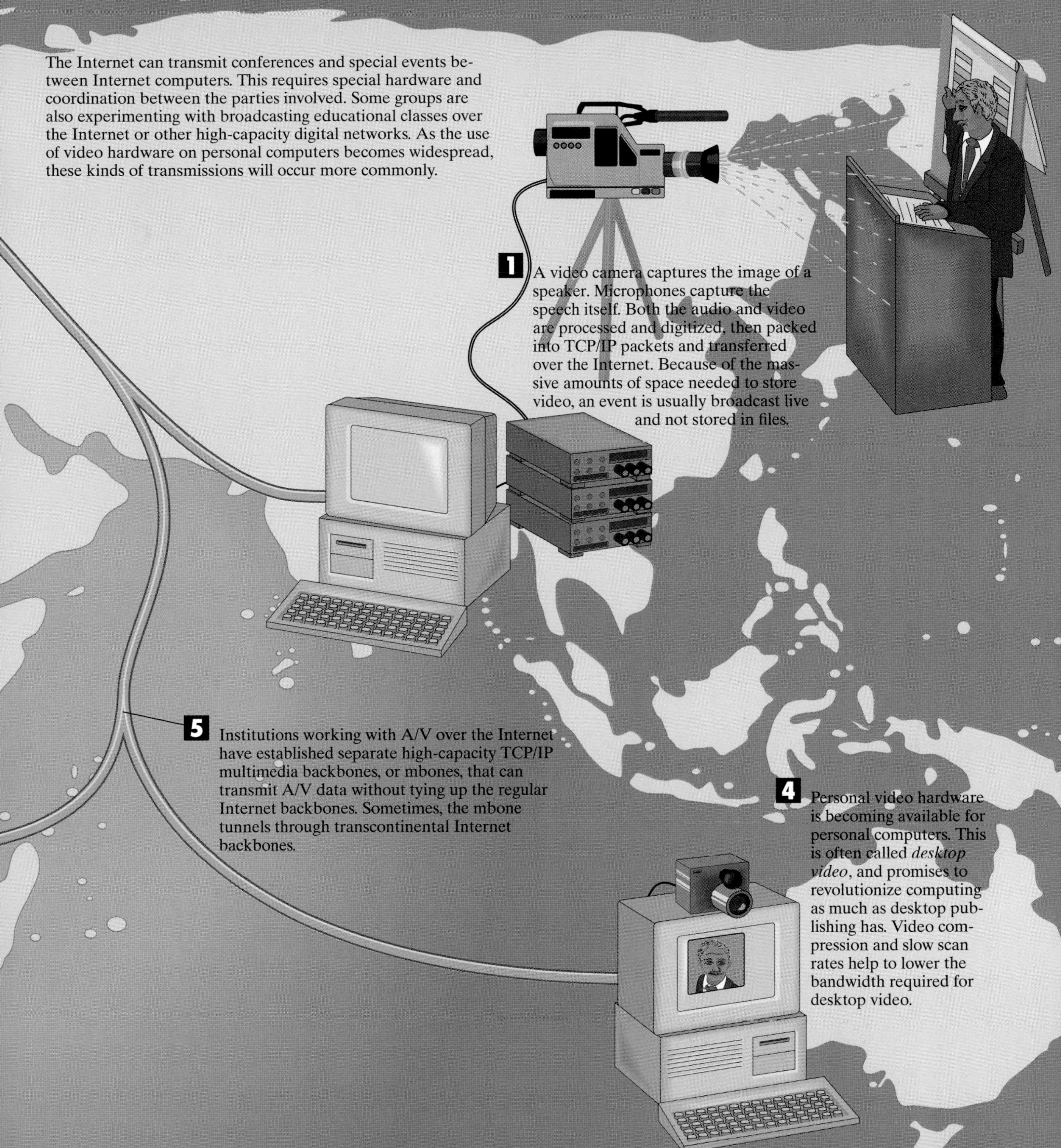

1 A video camera captures the image of a speaker. Microphones capture the speech itself. Both the audio and video are processed and digitized, then packed into TCP/IP packets and transferred over the Internet. Because of the massive amounts of space needed to store video, an event is usually broadcast live and not stored in files.

5 Institutions working with A/V over the Internet have established separate high-capacity TCP/IP multimedia backbones, or mbones, that can transmit A/V data without tying up the regular Internet backbones. Sometimes, the mbone tunnels through transcontinental Internet backbones.

4 Personal video hardware is becoming available for personal computers. This is often called *desktop video*, and promises to revolutionize computing as much as desktop publishing has. Video compression and slow scan rates help to lower the bandwidth required for desktop video.

CHAPTER
25

Virtual Reality and the Internet

VIRTUAL REALITY (VR) uses a computer to simulate an interactive environment that appears to the observer as another reality. A VR system uses special hardware and software to give your senses enough information to allow you to suspend your disbelief about other realities and imagine yourself present in another world. In a sense, VR systems pick up where watching a movie or reading a good book leave off.

Telepresence uses a video camera mounted on a robot to send pictures to an operator at another location who manipulates the robot by remote control. Telepresence and VR both require many of the same hardware devices, such as head-mounted video displays and data gloves that sense the position of the wearer's hands and transmit that information to a computer. Telepresence differs from VR in that the computer *duplicates* the interactive environment rather than *simulating* it.

Telepresence requires video data and commands for positioning and controlling the robot to be transmitted between the operator and the robot. Telepresence gives the operator a sense that he or she is present with the robot; the robot's arms are an extension of the operator's arms, even if the robot is located across the world. More and more virtual-reality applications are becoming practical, and as audio and video transmission over the Internet become commonplace, the Internet and VR will meet in many areas. Telepresence surgery, where a doctor at one hospital operates on a patient located at another on the other side of the world, will be possible in the future.

VR allows large amounts of data to be sent back and forth quickly between many sites, permitting groups of people to enter the same virtual world. This technology is already being used in education, business, and games.

You can use the massive amounts of information the Internet provides to create a virtual environment. A good example of this is the virtual library. Many libraries around the world are computerized, making many of their services, such as card catalogs, periodical indexes, and special holdings, available over the Internet. Gophers, wide-area information servers (WAISs), and the World Wide Web (W3) all offer ways of integrating this information into your own virtual library.

Many people working with VR also use the Internet to communicate with each other via e-mail and newsgroups, to discuss various VR topics. You can also find FAQs, or lists of frequently asked questions with well-thought-out answers that cover all sorts of VR topics. Use the term *VR* or *virtual reality* to search WAISs, archies, or gophers for the latest relevant FAQs, information, and software available on the Internet.

Virtual Medicine on the Internet

Telepresence surgery requires three-dimensional video; fine motor control; and tactile, or touch, feedback to be successful. This information can be digitized and sent across the Internet between two distant sites, allowing a specialized doctor at a major hospital to operate on a patient at a rural clinic.

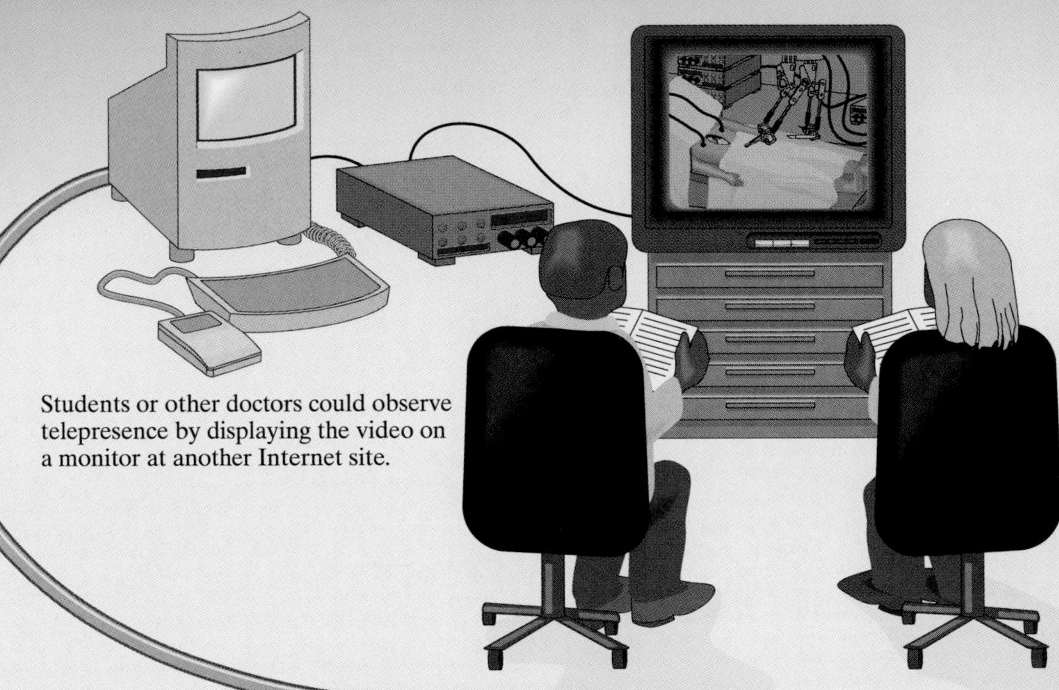

Students or other doctors could observe telepresence by displaying the video on a monitor at another Internet site.

The doctor's motions will be duplicated by the robot. The robot will be equipped with a stereoscopic camera that provides the two images the doctor's VR goggles need to create a three-dimensional image. The doctor will operate in a virtual operating room as if he or she were present at the remote operating room. The robot's arms will be fitted with tactile sensors that will send information about position to tactors in the doctor's data gloves so he or she can feel what the robot's "hands" feel.

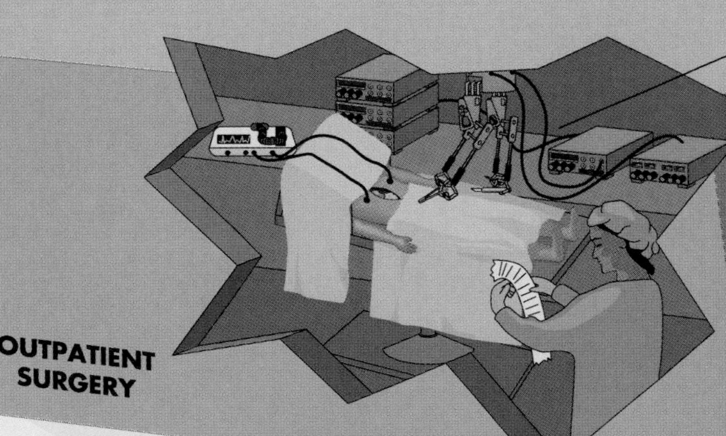
OUTPATIENT SURGERY

Sometimes it is impossible, or very difficult, to get a patient to a specialist. Telepresence surgery would allow a single specialist to treat patients all over the world, without the patient or doctor having to travel far; they wouldn't even need to be in the same room.

The clinic will need a remote manipulator or robot, along with special equipment to process all the signals that will have to be sent across the Internet for telepresence surgery. In addition, a surgical team will need to be present to handle the surgical prepping and other tasks.

The doctor will wear VR goggles containing small video screens that create a three-dimensional image of the patient. Sensors in the doctor's data gloves will detect the position of the doctor's hands and fingers. *Tactors*, or tactile feedback devices in the data gloves, create a sense of feel and resistance to touch based on what sensors on the robot report back to the doctor. The doctor's movements will be digitized and sent to the robot, while the image of what the robot sees and the pressure it feels will be sent to the doctor through special equipment that communicates via TCP/IP packets over the Internet. The Internet will provide a secure path for these packets. If a pathway fails, routers on the Internet will instantly choose another path, just as they do for regular traffic.

MEDICAL CENTER

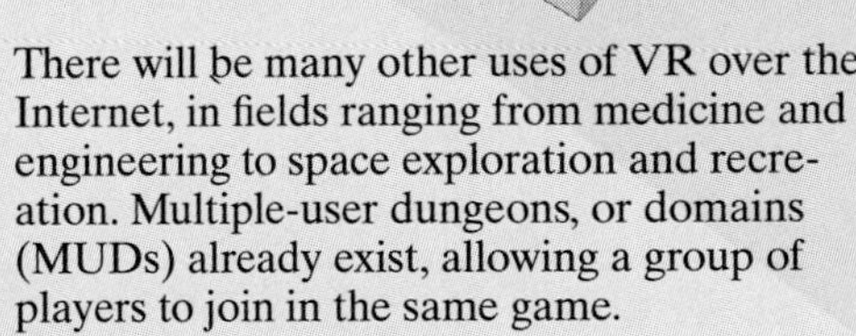

There will be many other uses of VR over the Internet, in fields ranging from medicine and engineering to space exploration and recreation. Multiple-user dungeons, or domains (MUDs) already exist, allowing a group of players to join in the same game.

The Virtual Library

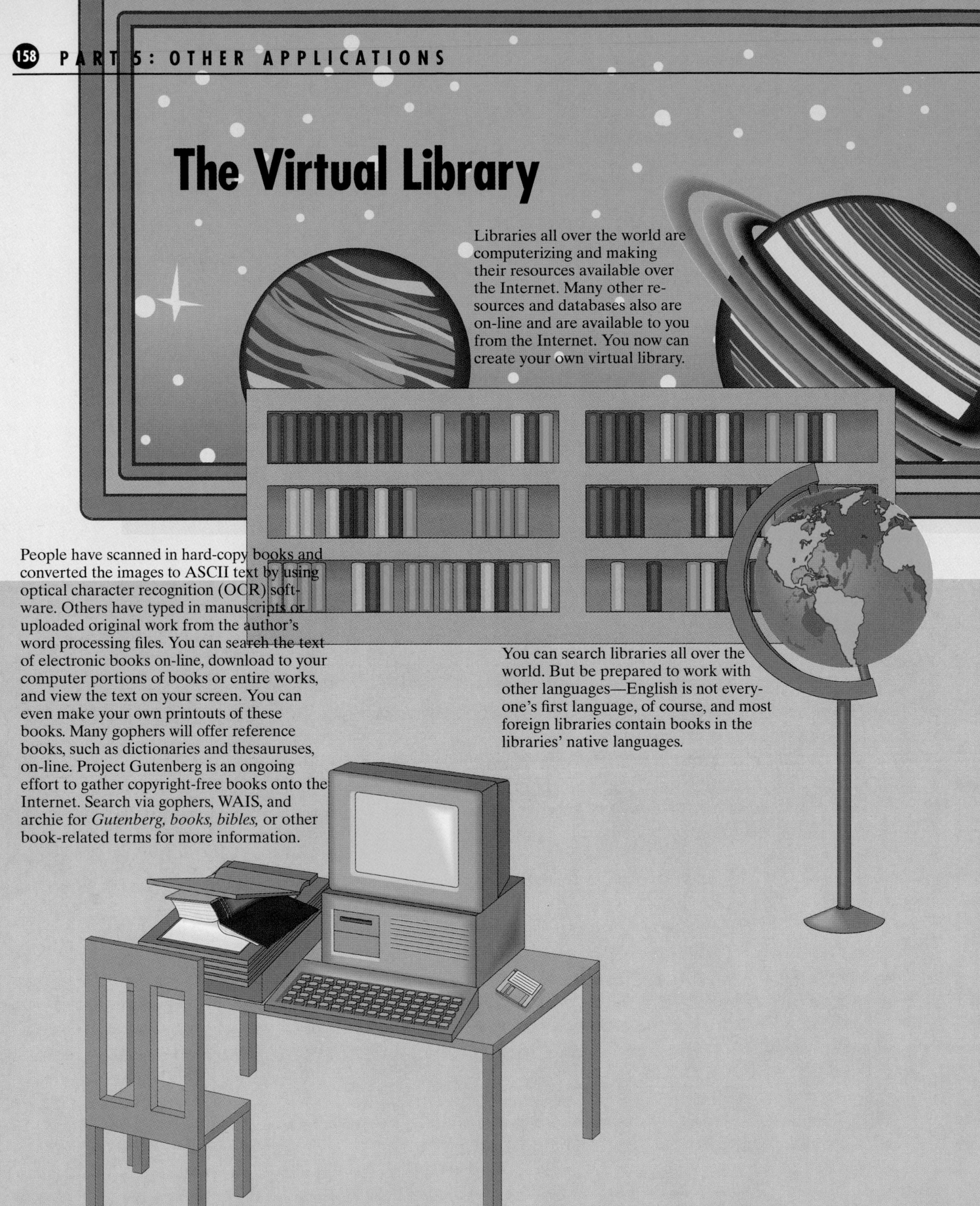

Libraries all over the world are computerizing and making their resources available over the Internet. Many other resources and databases also are on-line and are available to you from the Internet. You now can create your own virtual library.

People have scanned in hard-copy books and converted the images to ASCII text by using optical character recognition (OCR) software. Others have typed in manuscripts or uploaded original work from the author's word processing files. You can search the text of electronic books on-line, download to your computer portions of books or entire works, and view the text on your screen. You can even make your own printouts of these books. Many gophers will offer reference books, such as dictionaries and thesauruses, on-line. Project Gutenberg is an ongoing effort to gather copyright-free books onto the Internet. Search via gophers, WAIS, and archie for *Gutenberg, books, bibles,* or other book-related terms for more information.

You can search libraries all over the world. But be prepared to work with other languages—English is not everyone's first language, of course, and most foreign libraries contain books in the libraries' native languages.

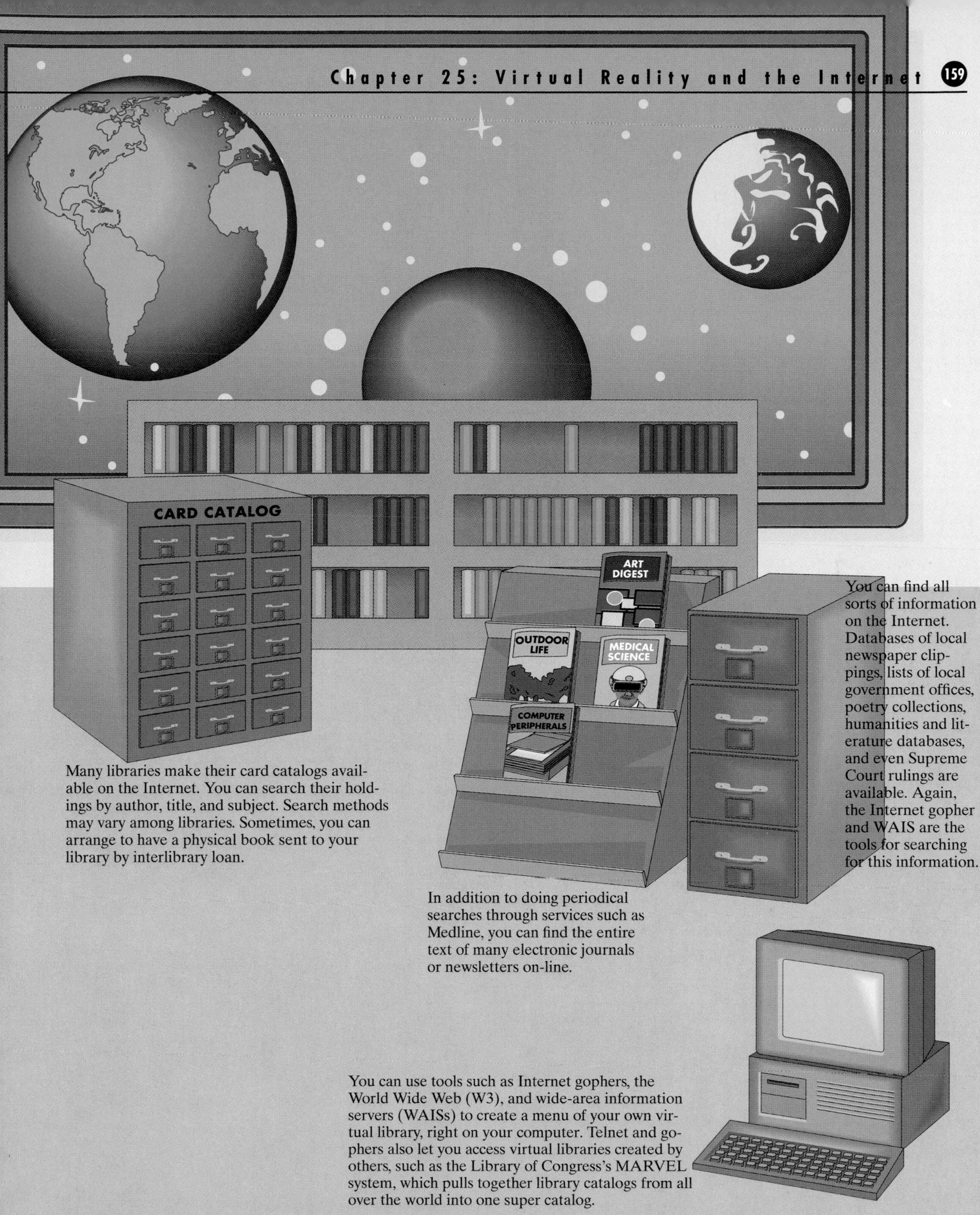
CARD CATALOG
ART DIGEST
OUTDOOR LIFE
MEDICAL SCIENCE
COMPUTER PERIPHERALS

Many libraries make their card catalogs available on the Internet. You can search their holdings by author, title, and subject. Search methods may vary among libraries. Sometimes, you can arrange to have a physical book sent to your library by interlibrary loan.

In addition to doing periodical searches through services such as Medline, you can find the entire text of many electronic journals or newsletters on-line.

You can find all sorts of information on the Internet. Databases of local newspaper clippings, lists of local government offices, poetry collections, humanities and literature databases, and even Supreme Court rulings are available. Again, the Internet gopher and WAIS are the tools for searching for this information.

You can use tools such as Internet gophers, the World Wide Web (W3), and wide-area information servers (WAISs) to create a menu of your own virtual library, right on your computer. Telnet and gophers also let you access virtual libraries created by others, such as the Library of Congress's MARVEL system, which pulls together library catalogs from all over the world into one super catalog.

SECURITY ISSUES

CONTENTS

OVERVIEW

THIS PART TAKES a look at issues of computer security in order to protect your computer and the networks and computers on the Internet. Chapter 26 discusses proper use of the Internet. "Proper use" meant not for profit when the Internet was small and consisted only of academic and research institutions. With the explosive growth of the Internet, proper use now means using the Internet purposefully to avoid tying it up unnecessarily. The distinction between for-profit and educational use of the Internet has been blurred by the large numbers of for-profit companies using the Internet today. It's no longer possible to determine which parts of the Internet are strictly for commercial or educational use, because traffic of the two is almost indistinguishable at the packet level.

Many kinds of users have come into contact with the Internet as the Internet has grown. Some don't have the best of intentions, and are not content to use the system properly. *Crackers* abuse the Internet by writing programs to "crack open" other people's computers in order to obtain access to them. Other abusers create computer viruses. A *computer virus* is a harmful computer program capable of replicating itself by infecting other programs and computers.

PART SIX

Computer scientists have come up with a variety of ways to combat these security problems. One of the first methods, and by far the most common, is the use of passwords. Without your password, no one else can access your account. But even passwords can be discovered.

Private networks, as opposed to public networks that can be accessed by anyone over the Internet, are the only secure networks. Sometimes, private networks are connected to the Internet by special gateways that prevent TCP/IP packets from passing between private and public networks.

Finally, in this part, you will see how cryptography allows you to encrypt your data to protect it.

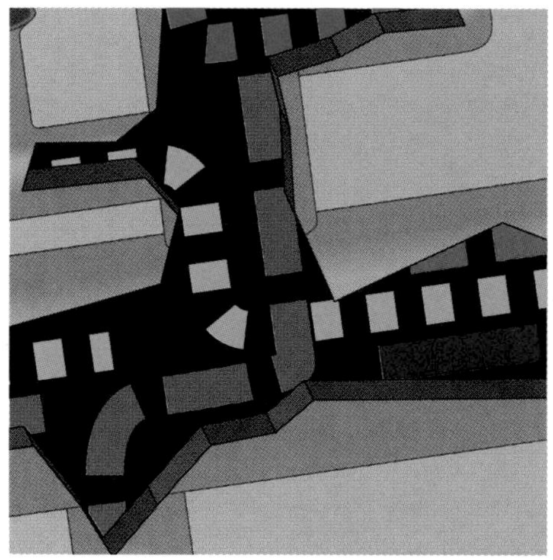

Proper Use of the Internet

IN THE PAST, educational institutions that provided substantial portions of the Internet were concerned about inappropriate commercial use of the Internet. This is one reason for the educational community's reluctance to subsidize business use of the Internet. However, the commercial community has officially embraced the Internet, often entering into partnerships with educational institutions and providing funds to help run the Internet.

The commercial and educational pathways of the Internet have intertwined as the Internet has grown. Sorting out which packets carry commercial or educational traffic is impossible due to the size and nature of the Internet. While statements or policies of appropriate use as it pertains to education or business still exist, most people are not as concerned about them as they once were. A good example is the Internet Talk Radio (ITR) practice of acknowledging underwriters, just as National Public Radio (NPR) does. In the past, this would have been considered a commercial use of the Internet. Now, no one is concerned about this particular issue. However, when ITR performs large transfers of its files over commercial portions of the Internet, ITR uses special storage sites for distribution.

Today, appropriate use versus abuse of the Internet refers more to the effective and practical use of the Internet's bandwidth, or capacity to carry traffic. The growing numbers of individual users, educational institutions, and businesses on the Internet require a higher bandwidth of transmission in order to avoid overloading the Internet. Packet-switching networks such as TCP/IP slow down when packet traffic starts to build up. Mirrored servers are often set up to distribute the load across the Internet to help keep down traffic. A *mirrored server* is an Internet computer that contains duplicate, or mirrored, data and files from a distant FTP site or other server.

Abuses of the Internet include downloading large files, particularly across the long-distance links between continents, or sending frivolous or questionable e-mail to large mailing lists or newsgroups.

If you're using the Internet for fun or your own projects, try to use it at night. You won't contribute to daytime traffic, and you'll find the response time faster. When you try to log on to different resources, you will be less likely to see the message "Too many connections open. Try again later."

Try to be aware of the consequences of what you are doing. Don't transmit a video image across the world just because you have access to the equipment. If you abuse the system, don't be surprised to get a harsh e-mail note from another Internet user. You may also find your local system administrator breathing down your neck.

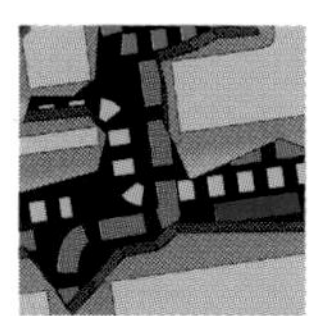

Proper Use of the Internet

A mirrored server contains the same files and information as another server. Often, you will find that a popular foreign site, perhaps in Europe, will have a mirrored server on the other side of the Atlantic. Internet users in North America can access the mirrored server, instead of tying up transcontinental links by accessing the European server.

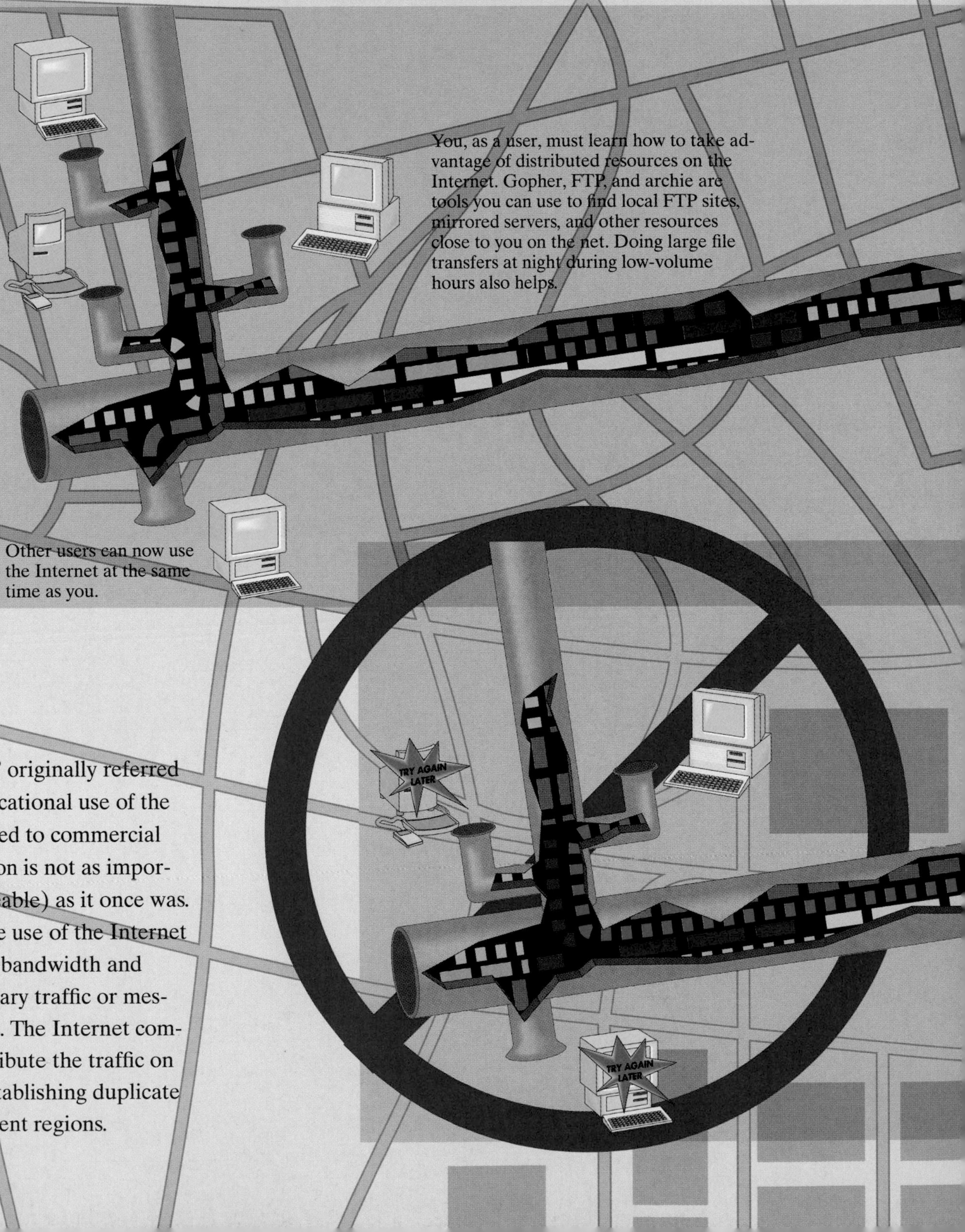

You, as a user, must learn how to take advantage of distributed resources on the Internet. Gopher, FTP, and archie are tools you can use to find local FTP sites, mirrored servers, and other resources close to you on the net. Doing large file transfers at night during low-volume hours also helps.

Other users can now use the Internet at the same time as you.

TRY AGAIN LATER
TRY AGAIN LATER

"Appropriate use" originally referred to research or educational use of the Internet, as opposed to commercial use. That distinction is not as important (or as enforceable) as it once was. Today, appropriate use of the Internet means conserving bandwidth and avoiding unnecessary traffic or messages on networks. The Internet community helps distribute the traffic on the Internet by establishing duplicate resources in different regions.

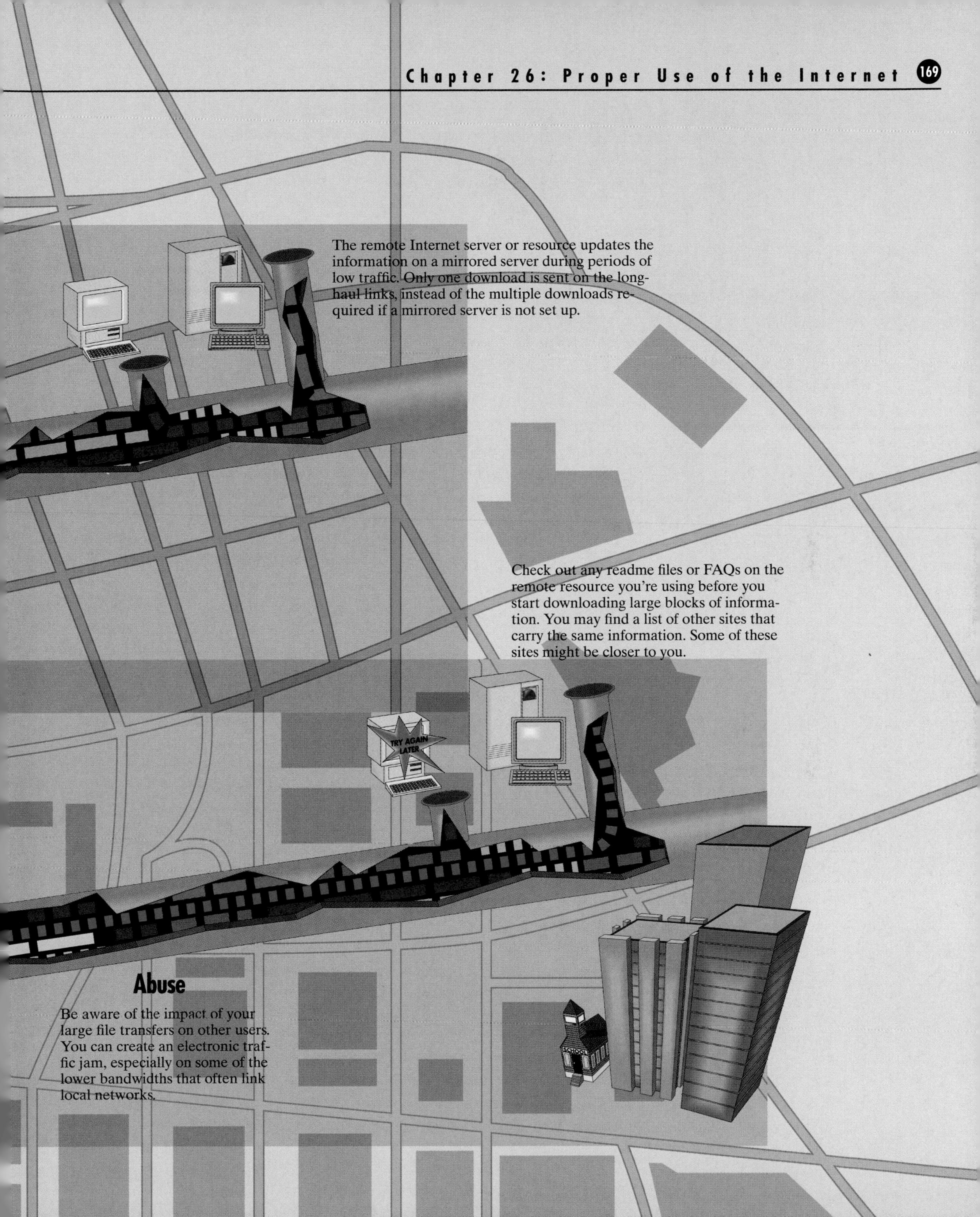
TRY AGAIN LATER
SCHOOL

The remote Internet server or resource updates the information on a mirrored server during periods of low traffic. Only one download is sent on the long-haul links, instead of the multiple downloads required if a mirrored server is not set up.

Check out any readme files or FAQs on the remote resource you're using before you start downloading large blocks of information. You may find a list of other sites that carry the same information. Some of these sites might be closer to you.

Abuse

Be aware of the impact of your large file transfers on other users. You can create an electronic traffic jam, especially on some of the lower bandwidths that often link local networks.

Protecting Computers and Networks

There are many reasons why people need to limit access to and protect the data on computers and networks connected to the Internet. A new user could unknowingly wreak havoc by trying out unfamiliar commands. Commercial on-line services may control access so they can charge customers. Companies and schools may restrict access to their employees or students because of license conditions or costs based on the number of users. Finally, computers need to be protected from people who willfully try to damage or steal information.

A cracker is someone who tries to break into computers. Crackers can range from students out for an electronic joyride on the Internet to professionals who steal computer data for a living. They can steal data for industrial or political espionage, for personal gain, or for fun. Crackers often know how to program. If they do, they may also be hackers. A *hacker* is a programmer who is addicted to computers and spends unusual amounts of time programming. Most hackers are not crackers, but they have been given a bad name by crackers' unethical activities.

A password system is the main line of defense against crackers and other abusers of networks and computers on the Internet. A *password* is a predetermined word you must enter when prompted before you can log on to a computer system. When you make arrangements to use a computer system, the system administrator may give you a password, let you pick a password, or have a computer-generated password sent to you by mail. The computer system keeps track of all users' current passwords. You should change your password occasionally, in case someone else has discovered it; you can do this while you're logged on. Don't use an obvious password, such as your name, and be careful where you write it down. Crackers often try to guess passwords, and have also been known to ransack office desks looking for them.

A private network is the only kind of network that is completely safe. A private network is self-contained and is not part of any public network. There are no connections to outside computers, not even to the Internet. Many networks install a firewall between a private network and a public one. A *firewall* is a gateway between two networks that buffers and screens all information that passes between the networks. Firewalls block attempts by crackers or others to break into the private network. However, firewalls will allow information from the private network's system administrator to pass through.

Cracking, Firewalls, and Passwords

There are ways to secure computers and networks and there are also ways to break into them. A properly used password system goes a long way toward protecting a computer system. When passwords alone are not enough to protect a system from crackers, or other abusers, a private network can be set up by disconnecting all links to the Internet or any public networks. A firewall provides a bridge between a public network and a private one, allowing some traffic to cross while keeping crackers out.

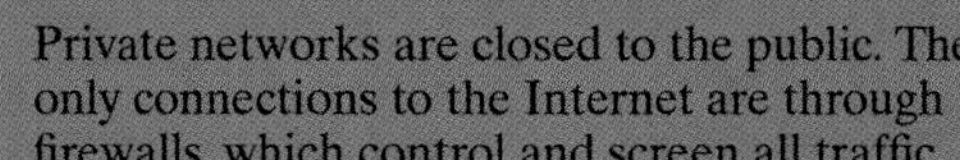

Private networks are closed to the public. The only connections to the Internet are through firewalls, which control and screen all traffic.

Public networks are accessible via the Internet and TCP/IP. You may still need a password to use some of the services of a public network.

Firewalls are gateways or special computers that let only certain types of traffic through. A firewall is designed to stop crackers from accessing a private network. Like passwords, firewalls must be used properly by the system administrator to ensure the security of the private network, while allowing as much access as possible to the users of the private network.

Clifford Stoll, in his book *The Cuckoo's Egg*, recounts tracing a 75-cent discrepancy in a computer account across the globe to a cracker in Germany. This cracker was accessing Stoll's computer and then using it to access American military computers over the Internet. This map shows the paths this cracker used to span the world. Stoll also relates how the cracker stole lists of passwords from computers and personal files and used these passwords to break into other systems.

On many computer systems, you are asked for your account name or number and password when you log on. These form your unique key for accessing that computer. Guard your password carefully and change it occasionally, so no one else can discover it. A cracker can break into a computer system with your account number and password, run up charges to your account, read your e-mail, destroy your personal files, and even cause damage to the computer system.

login:
password:

CHAPTER
28

Viruses, Trojan Horses, and Worms

MALICIOUS LOGIC CONSISTS of harmful or senseless computer programs that plague individual computers as well as the larger Internet community. There are three types of malicious logic: computer viruses, Trojan horses, and worms. A computer virus is the form of malicious logic that you are most likely to run into today. Just as their biological counterparts attack cells, *computer viruses* are programs that invade and attach themselves to legitimate programs. Some viruses interfere with the operations of their host programs. Others wreak havoc by altering the operations of the host computer. All viruses try to infect disks or executable programs. They usually infect one of three areas of your computer's software: your executable program files, the system or boot records your computer runs when you turn it on, or the file-directory system that keeps track of the location of your files.

You may unwittingly transfer an infected file to your computer in one of several ways: when you download program files by using FTP, by using a local area network, or by using a non-Internet BBS. A virus may enter your computer system from a floppy disk that was used in an infected computer. Infected disks have even been found in shrink-wrapped packages straight from a software store. You can use a special program called a *scanner* to check disks or new programs for known viruses. Often, you can then use a disinfectant program to remove the virus from the program or disk before using it on your computer. You can also use a monitoring program to safeguard your computer. *Monitoring programs* run in the background behind your regular programs, warning you of unusual changes in memory use or odd activities. An *integrity checker* detects changes in your program files and warns you when it suspects a program has been modified. Sometimes, integrity checkers can restore an infected file to its disinfected state.

It is practically impossible to get a virus by downloading *text files*. So if you're using the Internet to find information and read e-mail, you need not worry about viruses. However, if you regularly download *program files* or share disks with others who download, you might consider checking out some of the antivirus software available from software stores or over the Internet.

Trojan horses are related to viruses but are not as common, as they don't replicate themselves automatically. A *Trojan horse* is a program whose name sounds harmless or even tantalizing, tricking you into starting the program. Once started, the program occupies your attention with something cute on your screen while, unseen by you, the Trojan horse erases all your files or does something equally damaging. *Worms*, on the other hand, usually do not try to cause damage to a computer. Their primary task is to move copies of themselves between computers connected by networks. Worms are not common, and infest only computers that are connected to a network. Hackers feel challenged to design worms that can escape detection by system administrators; they get a thrill out of seeing their programs spread to other computers.

Computer Viruses

If you copy program files over the Internet either from FTP sites or from other computers, or use floppy disks to transfer data between computers, there is a strong chance that your computer will catch a virus. You don't have to worry about catching computer viruses when you're downloading text or data files over the Internet, though.

2 Once you run an infected program or boot from an infected disk, the virus attaches copies of itself to other programs and disks that your computer uses.

3 Viruses can damage your software, corrupting program or data files so they will behave erratically, not work at all, or even cause more damage. A virus can change the system files that your computer needs when it is turned on. A virus can also mess up the directory system on your disks, causing your computer to lose track of your files.

4 Software programs called scanners check for viruses and alert you to their presence. Some scanners check all incoming files for viruses. Monitoring programs watch your computer at work, looking for any signs that a virus attack might be underway.

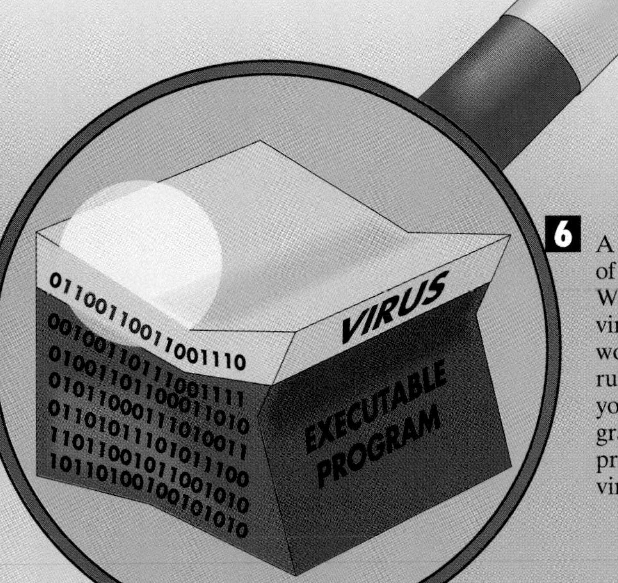
VIRUS
EXECUTABLE PROGRAM

6 A virus attaches itself to the top of an executable program. When you run that program, the virus program starts its dirty work. Once the virus program is running, it takes over the rest of your original executable program. You may not realize your program is infected until the virus starts causing problems.

DISINFECTANT

BACKUP

7 An excellent way to protect your software is to make regular backups of all your files. If you find that your computer has been infected, you can dump the infected files, reformat your disk, and reinstall your software from the backup disks. It's a lot of work, but sometimes this is the only choice.

5 Some software programs disinfect, or remove viruses from, software. Disinfectant programs do not work on all viruses, though.

1 A program file you download from the Internet or transfer from any other computer may be infected by a virus. Floppy disks used by other computers are also liable to be infected. Viruses are platform-specific because the program files they infect are designed to run on one type of computer. Computers running MS-DOS seem to be at higher risk than other types of computers, probably because of the larger number of MS-DOS computers in the world. However, other types of computers—especially Macintoshes, UNIX systems, and Amigas—are also at risk.

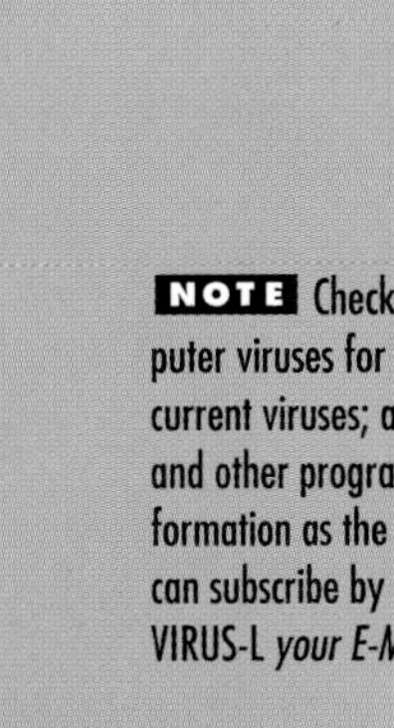

NOTE Check out the newsgroup comp.virus for a FAQ on computer viruses for detailed information on how viruses work; lists of current viruses; and where to look for virus scanners, disinfectants, and other programs. The mailing list VIRUS-L contains the same information as the newsgroup, and posts the FAQ once a month. You can subscribe by e-mail to VIRUS-L by sending the message "SUB VIRUS-L *your E-MAIL address*" to LISTSERV@LEHIGH.EDU

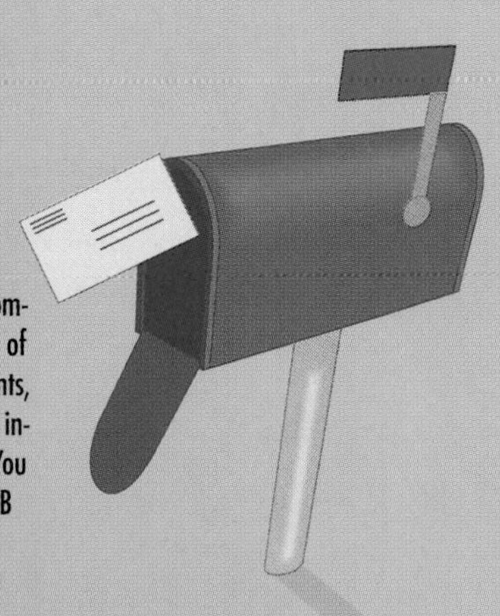

The Internet Worm

On November 2, 1988, a graduate student named Robert Morris let loose a computer worm on the Internet. This worm quickly copied itself to UNIX and DEC computers all over North America, and soon clogged the bandwidth of the Internet backbones and networks, slowing all infected machines to a crawl. Morris did not design the worm to cause harm, but he did not understand what the program would do to the Internet. This worm is now called the Internet Worm.

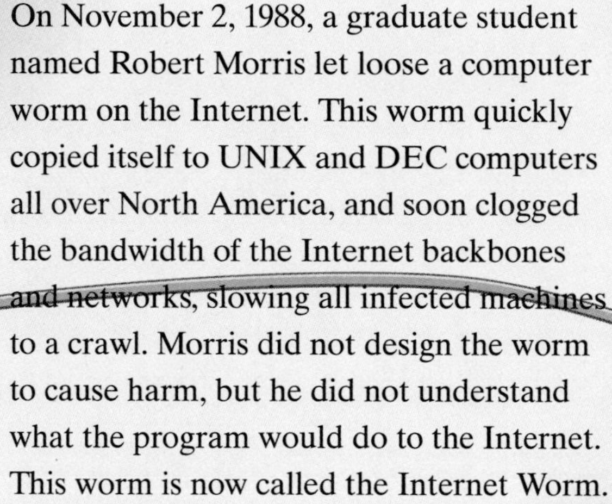

4 At first, the system administrators of the infected computers tried to use the Internet to communicate among themselves. However, their computers and the Internet pathways were jammed by the worm and many system administrators had no experience with viruses or worms. Fortunately, they were able to talk by telephone and send files to each other by modem over direct lines. Within half a day, a team of programmers at the University of California at Berkeley were able to slow the spread of the worm. Teams at Berkeley, MIT, Purdue, and other universities came up with ways to stop the worm. The Internet was back to normal in a few days, though everyone was talking about the Internet Worm for quite some time.

5 Computer scientists across the country quickly disassembled the worm, or transformed it back into a computer language programmers can read, to find out just what the worm did. The worm exploited security holes, such as "trap doors" in mail programs, that allowed the worm to send its program code to a remote computer. Once on a computer, the worm would guess passwords of any other computers connected. With the right password, the worm could use UNIX copy commands to copy and start itself on the other computer. System administrators quickly plugged up these holes so their systems would be immune to any future attacks by this method. Computer scientists now take worms and viruses much more seriously, and try to plug up any holes they discover before another worm beats them to it.

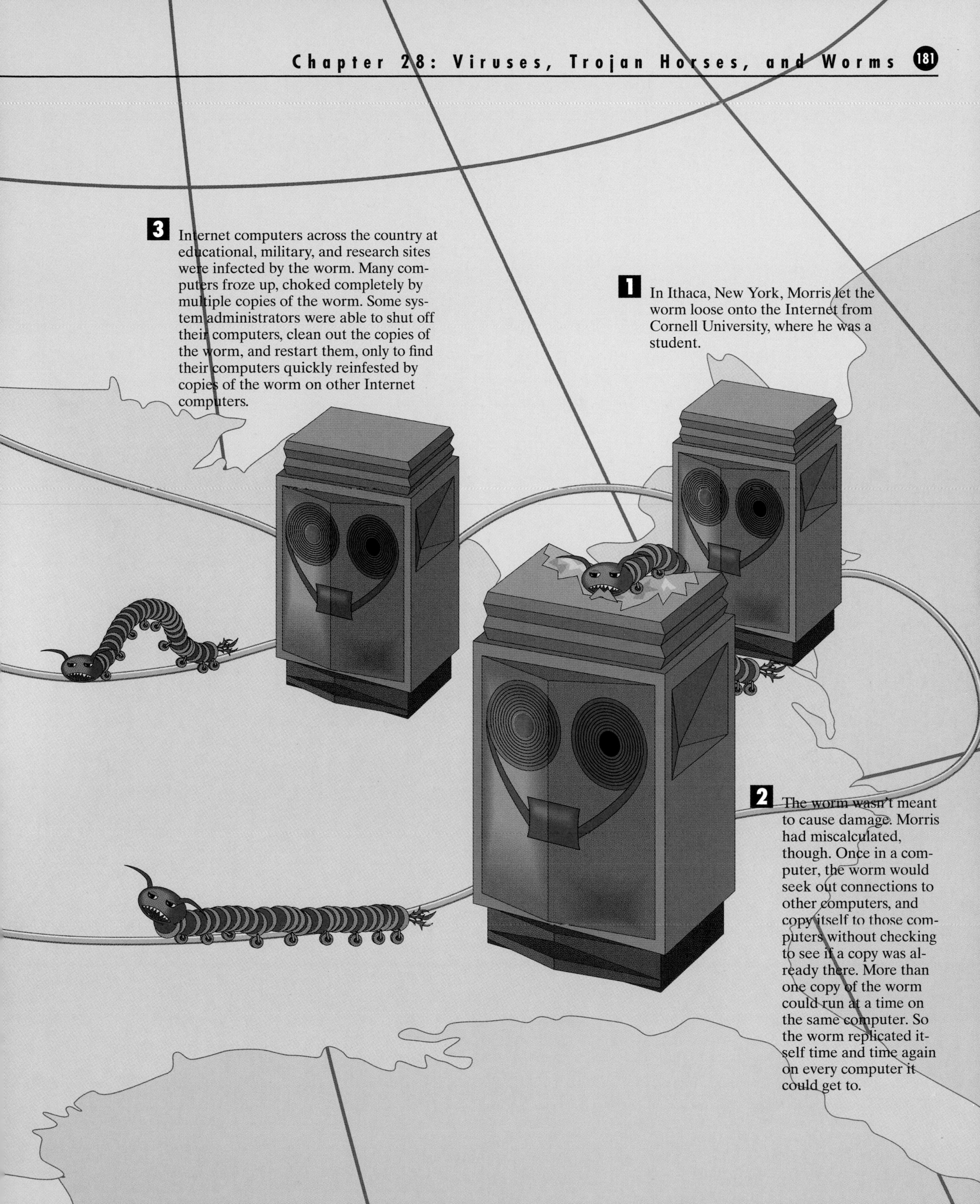
3 Internet computers across the country at educational, military, and research sites were infected by the worm. Many computers froze up, choked completely by multiple copies of the worm. Some system administrators were able to shut off their computers, clean out the copies of the worm, and restart them, only to find their computers quickly reinfested by copies of the worm on other Internet computers.
1 In Ithaca, New York, Morris let the worm loose onto the Internet from Cornell University, where he was a student.
2 The worm wasn't meant to cause damage. Morris had miscalculated, though. Once in a computer, the worm would seek out connections to other computers, and copy itself to those computers without checking to see if a copy was already there. More than one copy of the worm could run at a time on the same computer. So the worm replicated itself time and time again on every computer it could get to.

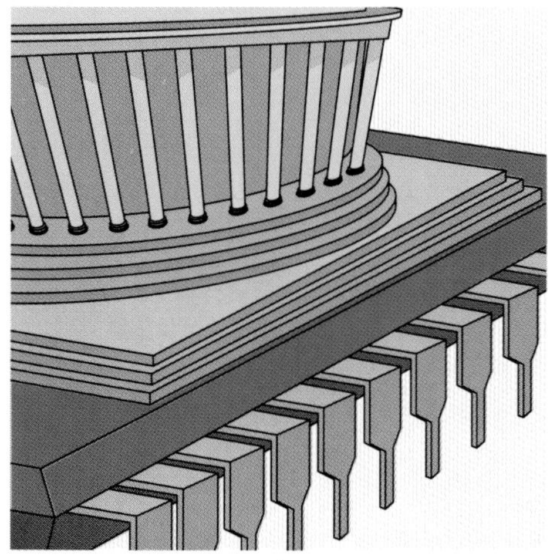

Cryptography

CRYPTOGRAPHY IS THE process of converting a message into a secret code and changing the encoded message back to regular text. The original conversion is called *encryption*. The unencoded message exists as *plaintext*. The encoded message is referred to as *ciphertext*. *Decryption* converts ciphertext back into plaintext.

You can protect messages and files sent over the Internet with cryptography. A *cryptosystem* is a software package that uses an algorithm, or mathematical formula, plus a key to encrypt and decrypt messages. A cryptosystem's algorithm must pass scrutiny by experts. A key usually consists of a large number—the larger and more mathematically complex a key is, the harder a cryptosystem is to break. The algorithm is calculated with the key and the ASCII code of every character of the plaintext to create the ciphertext. There should be a large pool of numbers, or key space, from which to choose a key; only someone with the correct key should be able to decode the ciphertext. Good ciphertext appears to be nothing but random numbers.

Public-key cryptosystems are the most secure. They use two keys: a public key that can be listed on the Internet, and a private key that is kept secret. To send you secret messages, senders need to know your public key, which they may find on the Internet, or have you send it to them. Senders must encrypt their plaintext messages with your public key, and the resulting ciphertext can be decrypted only with your private key. Your private key must never leave your computer in order to keep this system very safe.

Cryptosystems can be strong or weak, depending on how easily eavesdroppers can decrypt the system's ciphertext. Cryptosystems are strong if the private key can be kept secret. If someone discovers or steals a private key, the system is compromised. Third parties or *eavesdroppers* are people who attack ciphertext mathematically, trying to guess the key or decode the ciphertext without a key. If an eavesdropper tries every possible key, he or she might give up trying to find the right combination if the key space is large enough. Eavesdroppers use very sophisticated mathematical tools to find hidden patterns, and reveal the original plaintext that was hidden in the ciphertext. An attempt to decipher a message is called an attack; a strong system resists all known attacks, but once someone learns how to break into a system, it becomes weak.

It takes a lot of computer time to encrypt and decrypt strong systems, and you don't actually need a strong cryptosystem for everyday communications on the Internet. Weak systems do not require as much computer time. The older single-key approach is often used in weak cryptosystems built into UNIX and word processing software. A single-key cryptosystem uses the same key to encrypt and decrypt a message. If you want to send someone else a message, you must also send a copy of your key. If that key falls into anyone else's hands, they too can decrypt your ciphertext. Weak systems are great for hiding files from casual browsers, but they do not stand up to an attack by an expert eavesdropper.

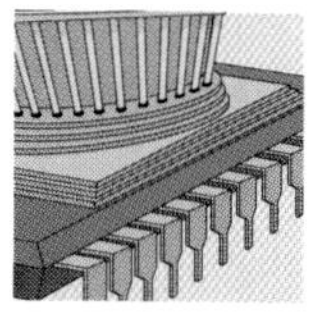

Cryptography and the Internet

Cryptography is the art of transforming messages into secret code so that no one other than the intended recipient can figure out what the message says. Today, computers help create codes that can be broken only by other computers.

The clipper chip is a cryptosystem proposed by the White House as a national standard. Its keys and algorithms would be built into a computer chip that could encrypt and decrypt data sent between telephones or computers. The clipper chip proposal has caused massive controversy in the computer community for two reasons. The clipper algorithm is secret, so people can't scrutinize the process to determine how good it is. Also, the clipper chip has a back door, allowing law enforcement agencies or others in the government to use a master key to decrypt private messages.

PLAINTEXT

Plaintext consists of messages or text that is not encrypted. Plaintext can be encrypted, or coded into ciphertext by a cryptosystem. A key provides a unique number that makes this ciphertext unique. The ciphertext can only be decrypted, or changed back into plaintext, with the proper key.

FOR MORE INFORMATION

Search your gopher for cryptography-faq. The sci.crypt newsgroup publishes this FAQ every month.

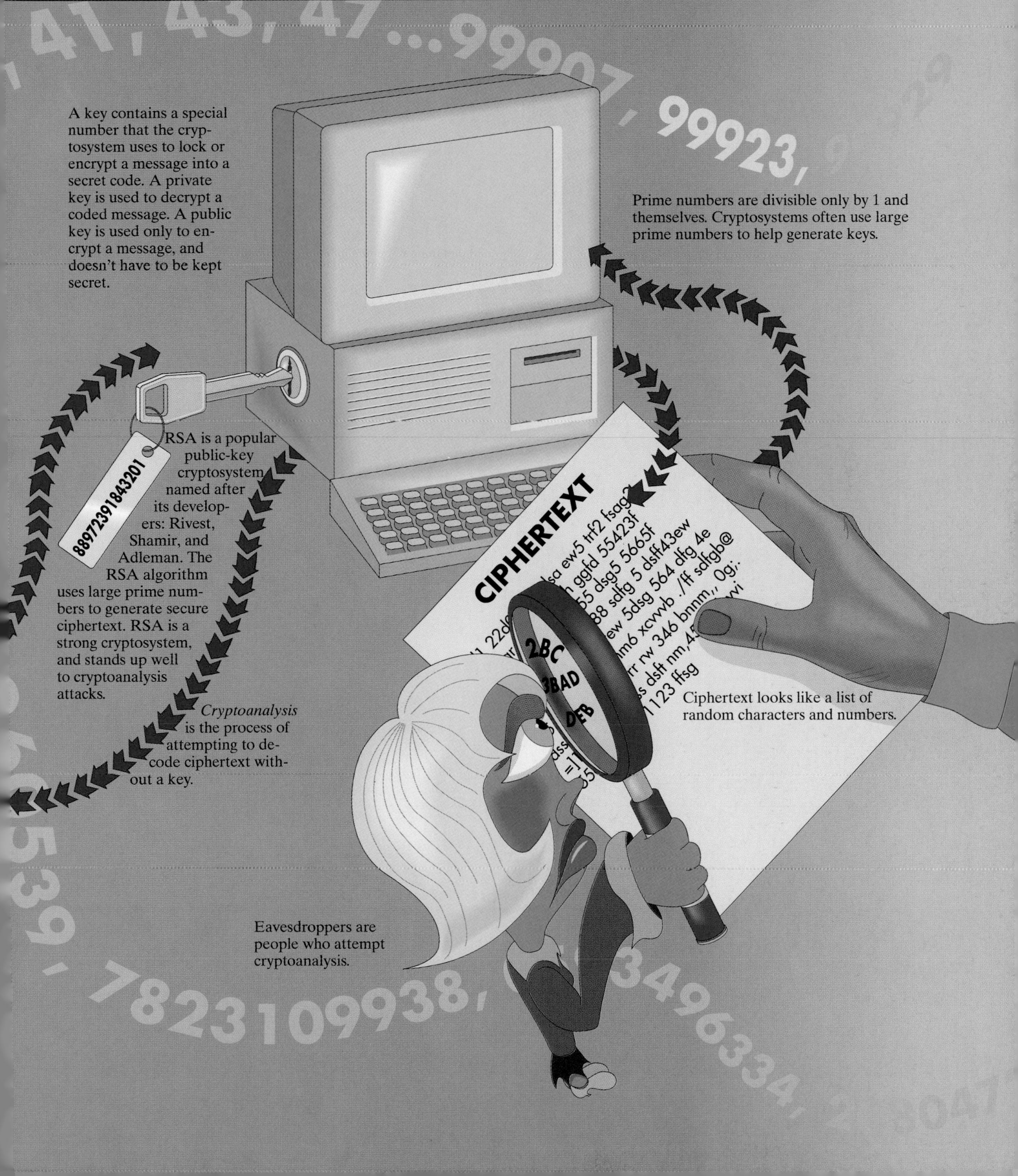

A key contains a special number that the cryptosystem uses to lock or encrypt a message into a secret code. A private key is used to decrypt a coded message. A public key is used only to encrypt a message, and doesn't have to be kept secret.

Prime numbers are divisible only by 1 and themselves. Cryptosystems often use large prime numbers to help generate keys.

RSA is a popular public-key cryptosystem named after its developers: Rivest, Shamir, and Adleman. The RSA algorithm uses large prime numbers to generate secure ciphertext. RSA is a strong cryptosystem, and stands up well to cryptoanalysis attacks.

Cryptoanalysis is the process of attempting to decode ciphertext without a key.

Ciphertext looks like a list of random characters and numbers.

Eavesdroppers are people who attempt cryptoanalysis.

CABLE TV
LIBRAR
ATM
ASYNCHRONOUS TRANSFER MODE
E-MAIL
E-MAIL
SCHOOL
NBS

PART 7: MANAGEMENT AND FUTURE TRENDS

OVERVIEW

MOST NEWCOMERS TO the Internet ask: "Who pays for the Internet?" "Who manages it?" and "Where is the Internet going?" These are good questions. However, the answers are neither simple nor straightforward.

The organizations that use the Internet manage and pay for it via a system that is not unlike an anarchy. There are no binding rules, centralized authority, or tax collectors—there is no single switch that turns the Internet on or off. Each organization has authority only over itself. Each organization pays for its own computers and networks, and cooperates with its neighbor networks to pay for the communications lines that connect them. Many smaller institutions and networks form loose confederations to provide service to their members; a regional network is an example of this type of organization. In fact, the National Science Foundation (NSF) provides and pays for the backbone that links regional networks within the United States. NSF does this to encourage educational and scientific communications and research. There are similar organizations throughout the world with the same goal.

PART SEVEN

All of the organizations and networks that the Internet connects cooperate to share resources and send e-mail and data to each other. The Internet is actually the sum of all these networks and organizations. They voluntarily follow protocols that allow TCP/IP packets to travel from one network to another, so you can connect your computer to any other computer on the Internet. There are also voluntary groups that have no authority, but serve as a forum for discussions about the Internet. For example, the Internet Society is one of many groups that makes decisions that guide the operation and growth of the Internet.

The question "Where is the Internet going?" is best answered by looking at the Information Superhighway. A lot of people are talking about this superhighway, including the U.S. Congress. The U.S. Congress will provide initial funds and some ongoing funds for the superhighway in the hope that the commercial sector will also join in. The Information Superhighway will be the infrastructure—the basis for networked computing across the United States—and will also reach out to the rest of the world. When finalized, it will be a very high-capacity system of backbones that will carry digital data, including computer data, audio, and video. The NSF backbone is one of the major components of the Internet that will soon be expanded into the Information Superhighway.

It is not yet known just how the Information Superhighway will change the look of the Internet. What is clear, though, is that the Internet will continue to grow and change. More people will have access to the Internet, and it will continue to create a global communications and research system by connecting more and more parts of the world.

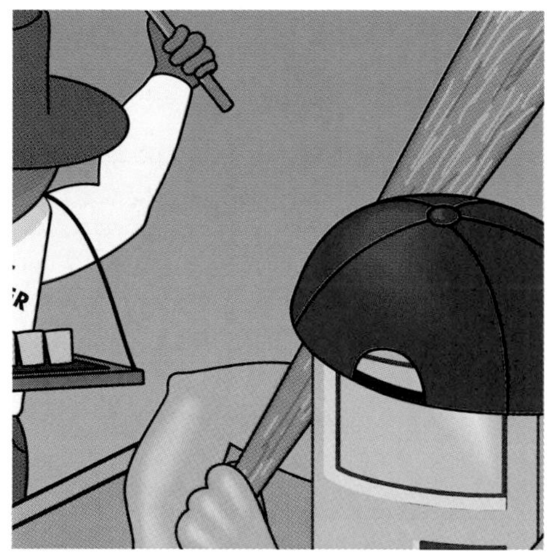

Running the Internet

THE INTERNET IS a society of thousands of organizations and networks that work together without government or centralized management. It functions like an anarchy because there is no single office or group that has authority over the whole Internet. Rather, each member organization manages and pays for its own network, and voluntarily works with its neighbors to direct Internet traffic back and forth. Networks and organizations follow protocols that Internet users have established via RFCs. For example, if your network damages your neighbors' networks because of improperly implemented Internet protocols your neighbors will quickly disconnect their networks from yours. Peer pressure can be a very powerful force in keeping the Internet running!

The Internet Society is perhaps the largest of many groups that exist to educate others about the Internet and to help guide its growth. The Internet Society is a private nonprofit organization composed of member organizations and individuals who are connected to the Internet. Membership is voluntary and it is supported by membership dues. The Internet Society does not run the Internet, but it does support the Internet Activities Board (IAB). The IAB consists of the Internet Engineering Task Force, which is concerned with the ongoing evolution of the TCP/IP protocols, and the Internet Research Task Force, which works on advancing network technology. The IAB operates the Internet Assigned Numbers Authority, which oversees the assigning of network IP addresses. The IAB also operates the Internet Registry, which keeps track of the root database of the Domain Name System, and is responsible for associating domain names with IP addresses.

The local network is the building block of the Internet. These networks connect computers in universities, private companies, or local Free-Nets, and each network is operated and paid for by the organization it serves. Dues from users, public tax money, grants, and university or corporate monies are all sources of funding for local networks.

Leased lines connect local networks to each other and to regional networks. Regional networks are consortiums of local networks and organizations that pool their purchasing power for obtaining leased lines, streamline network services in an area, and offer better support to their members than they could obtain individually. Very high-capacity lines are leased by government agencies and large corporations to create national or intercontinental backbones. Some organizations provide these backbones for their own needs, such as NASA, which uses backbones to link NASA sites all over the world. Other organizations, such as the National Science Foundation, provide backbones as part of their mandate to serve the academic or scientific community. Commercial service providers often lease lines from telecommunications companies to resell to others, or may build and maintain their own telecommunications systems and lines. A service provider may lease a single line to you, provide lines for a regional network, or offer global connections and backbones for a small company or a multinational corporation.

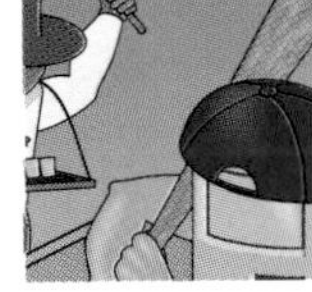

A leased line may be a single telephone line or a circuit using fiber optic cable, microwave links, or even satellite transmission to carry the equivalent of many telephone calls at a time. You are charged for a leased line on a monthly basis, not by the amount of data you actually send. The distance a line travels and the bandwidth, or amount of data a leased line can carry, determine its actual cost. Neighboring networks may share the cost of a leased line between themselves. Once you've leased a line, you are free to send as much data as the bandwidth allows, day or night, for the entire month.

Most organizations don't mind sharing some of their bandwidth with Internet traffic, because this kind of cooperation allows Internet users access to these organizations, and it helps keep the Internet running. Besides, most organizations have already paid for their leased lines.

The Internet Players

Connecting to the Internet is like participating in a baseball game. You participate in a worldwide game by contributing to the teamwork of the thousands of networks and organizations that make up the Internet. At a baseball game, you encounter referees, spectators, and peanut vendors; the Internet consists of service providers, information centers, referees, and others that keep the Internet running.

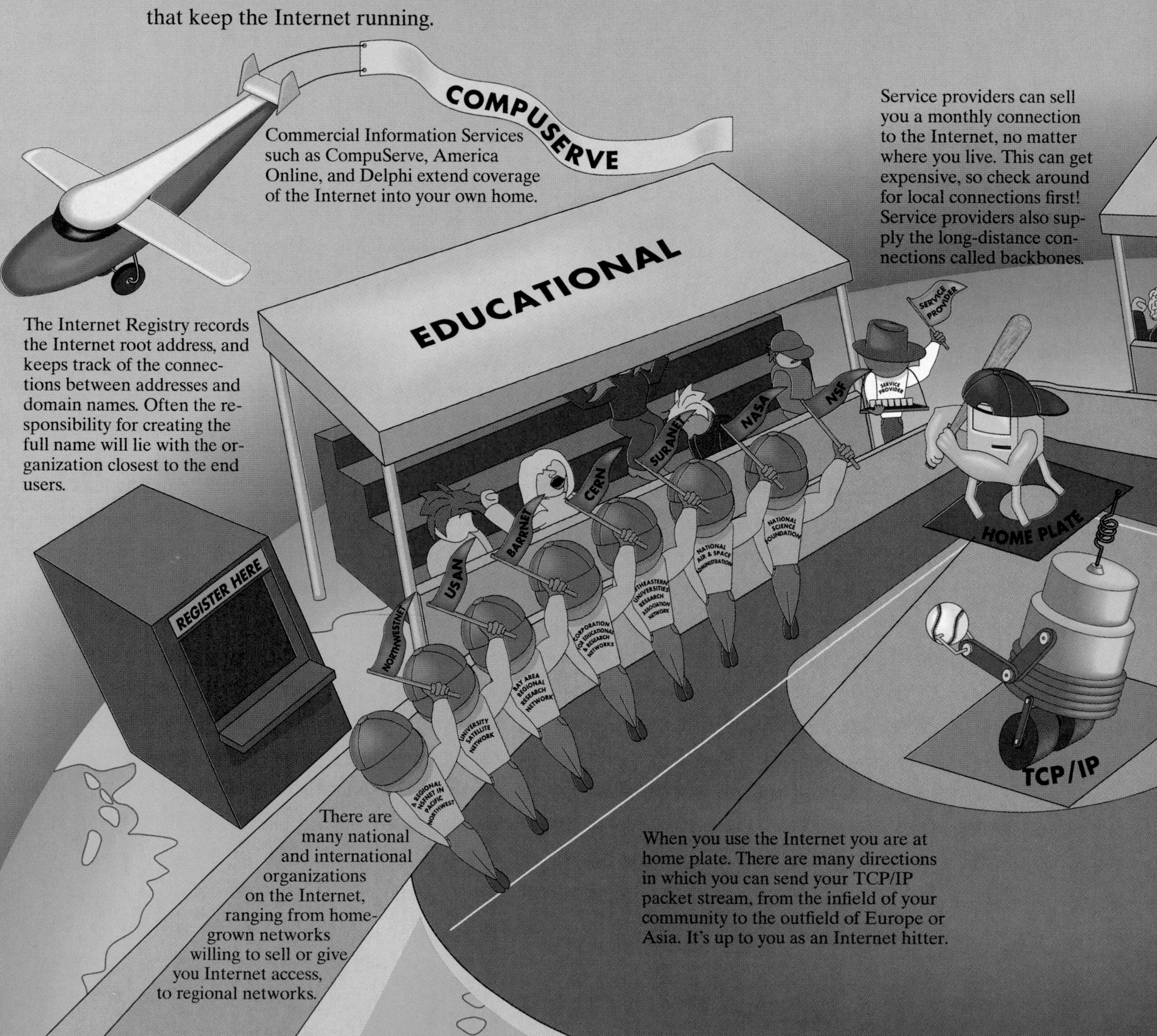
COMPUSERVE
Commercial Information Services such as CompuServe, America Online, and Delphi extend coverage of the Internet into your own home.
Service providers can sell you a monthly connection to the Internet, no matter where you live. This can get expensive, so check around for local connections first! Service providers also supply the long-distance connections called backbones.
EDUCATIONAL
SERVICE PROVIDER
The Internet Registry records the Internet root address, and keeps track of the connections between addresses and domain names. Often the responsibility for creating the full name will lie with the organization closest to the end users.
NSF
NASA
SURANET
CERN
BARRNET
USAN
NORTHWESTNET
NATIONAL SCIENCE FOUNDATION
REGISTER HERE
HOME PLATE
TCP/IP
There are many national and international organizations on the Internet, ranging from home-grown networks willing to sell or give you Internet access, to regional networks.
When you use the Internet you are at home plate. There are many directions in which you can send your TCP/IP packet stream, from the infield of your community to the outfield of Europe or Asia. It's up to you as an Internet hitter.

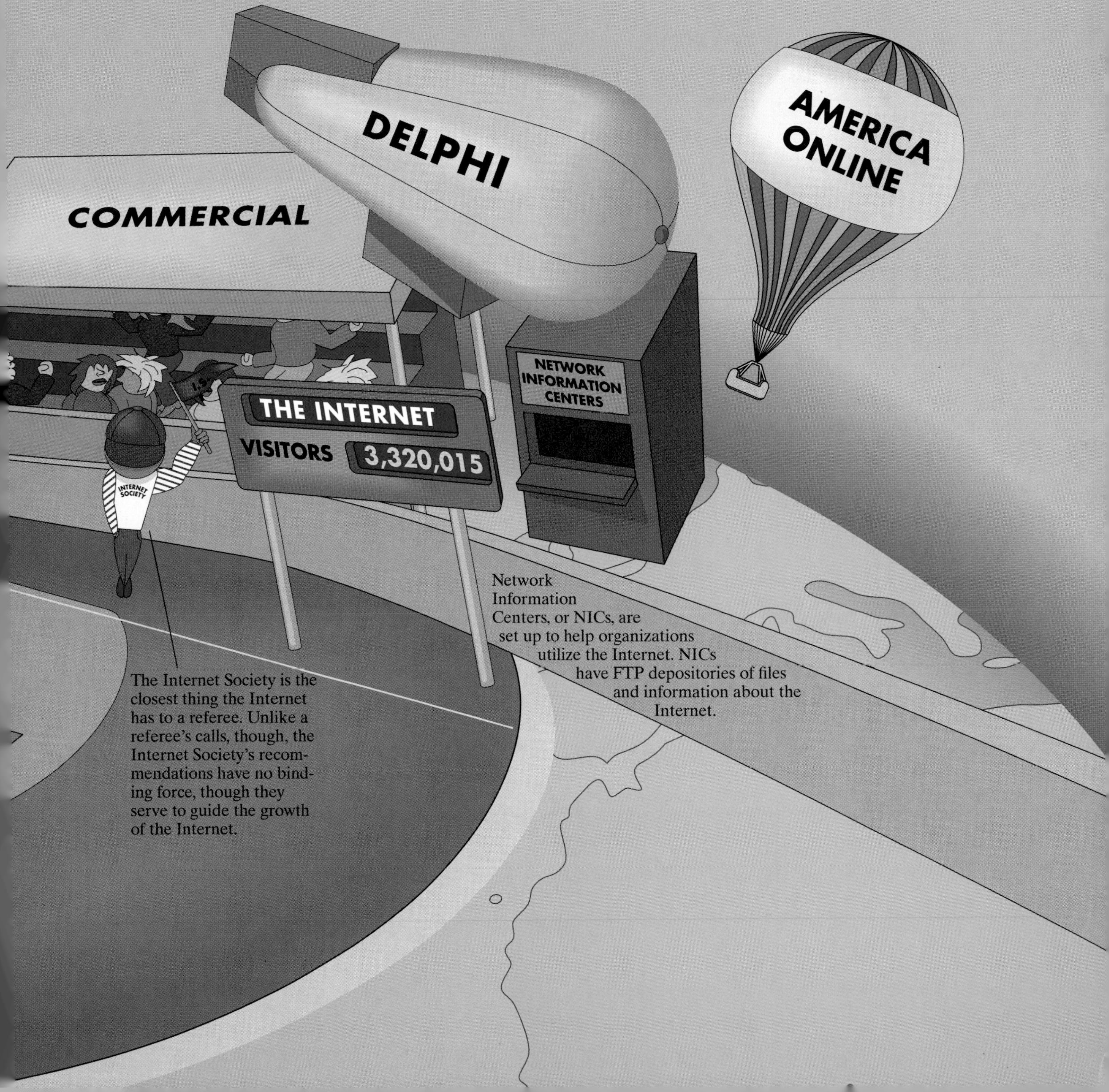

DELPHI
AMERICA ONLINE
COMMERCIAL
NETWORK INFORMATION CENTERS
THE INTERNET
VISITORS 3,320,015

Network Information Centers, or NICs, are set up to help organizations utilize the Internet. NICs have FTP depositories of files and information about the Internet.

The Internet Society is the closest thing the Internet has to a referee. Unlike a referee's calls, though, the Internet Society's recommendations have no binding force, though they serve to guide the growth of the Internet.

Who Pays for the Internet?

Organizations pay for their respective Internet sections. Some organizations are mandated by their charter to provide public access. Others share their resources with the Internet community in exchange for getting to use other resources available on the Internet.

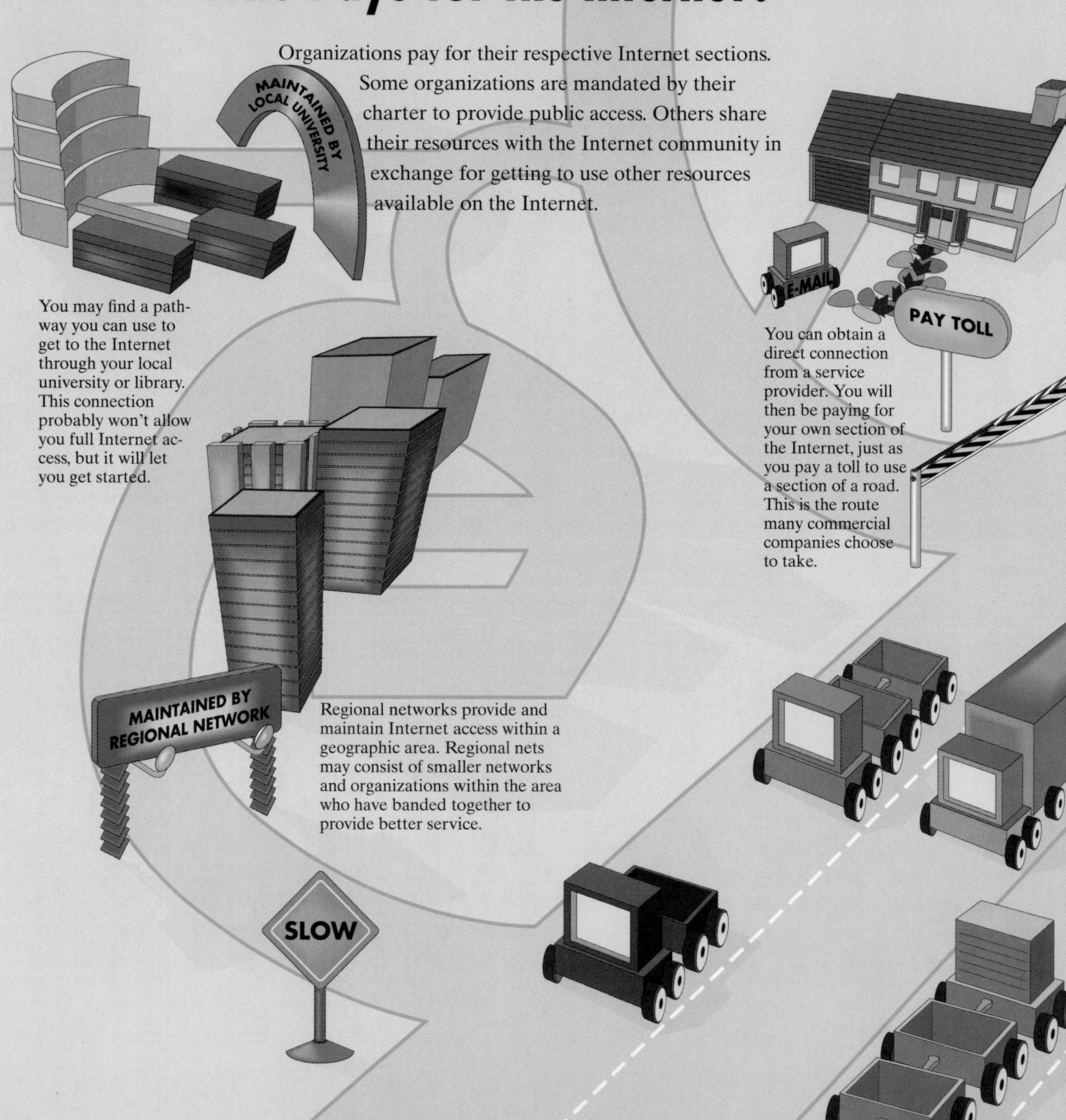
MAINTAINED BY LOCAL UNIVERSITY
E-MAIL
PAY TOLL
MAINTAINED BY REGIONAL NETWORK
SLOW

You may find a pathway you can use to get to the Internet through your local university or library. This connection probably won't allow you full Internet access, but it will let you get started.

You can obtain a direct connection from a service provider. You will then be paying for your own section of the Internet, just as you pay a toll to use a section of a road. This is the route many commercial companies choose to take.

Regional networks provide and maintain Internet access within a geographic area. Regional nets may consist of smaller networks and organizations within the area who have banded together to provide better service.

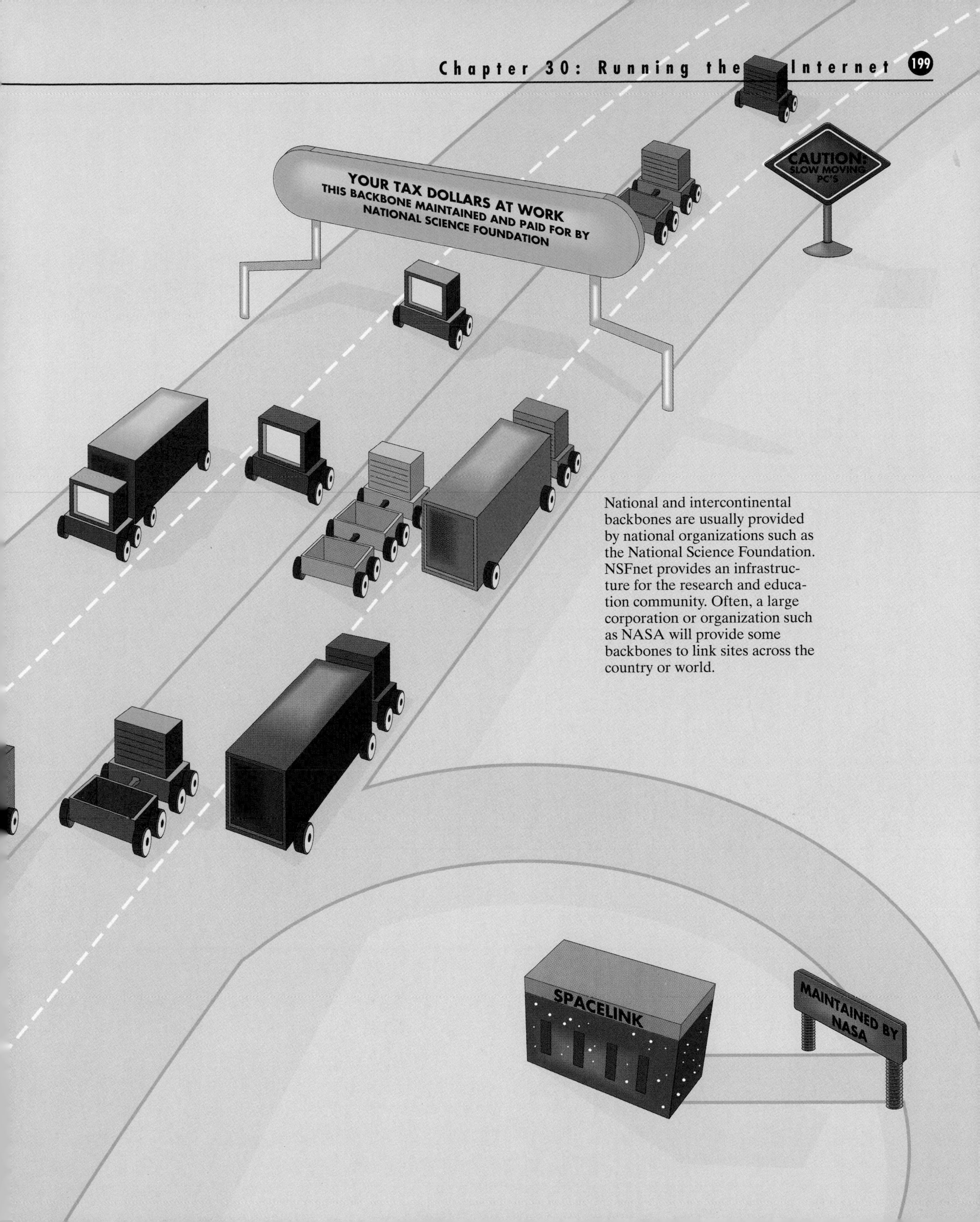
YOUR TAX DOLLARS AT WORK
THIS BACKBONE MAINTAINED AND PAID FOR BY
NATIONAL SCIENCE FOUNDATION
CAUTION:
SLOW MOVING
PC'S
SPACELINK
MAINTAINED BY
NASA

National and intercontinental backbones are usually provided by national organizations such as the National Science Foundation. NSFnet provides an infrastructure for the research and education community. Often, a large corporation or organization such as NASA will provide some backbones to link sites across the country or world.

CHAPTER
31

The Information Highway

The Internet's explosive growth into a global communications and research network has caught the world by surprise. The Internet now ties together a variety of the world's information communities, with e-mail and data flowing in English, Spanish, French, Japanese, and many other languages. Both the U.S. Congress and the business community are also showing considerable interest in the Internet's growth.

Congress wants to develop and fund the National Information Highway (NIH), or Information Superhighway as it would extend to other parts of the world, to foster economic and scientific growth within the United States. The U.S. Congress is hammering out how to run the Internet on the NIH. In 1991, Vice President Gore, then a senator, proposed the High Performance Computing Act. While that bill passed, other related legislation that will modify the original High Performance Computing Act is still being worked out. Congress hopes the NIH will achieve the same results as the legislation in the 1950s that paved the way for the interconnection of major cities across the United States by a federally funded interstate highway system. The interstate highway system helped strengthen the economy, encouraged growth of transportation industries and the companies they served, and spurred local governments to build secondary roads. Congress also hopes that establishing the NIH will promote industry investment in the NIH's infrastructure and in new applications and ways of using it. How much the highway will cost, and who will pay for which part, is one of the key points in the congressional debate.

Big businesses want to provide the infrastructure of the NIH in order to tap the potential markets, so they have watched Congress closely. Large communications companies, regional phone companies, long distance companies, cable TV companies, and others are getting into the picture. These types of companies are jockeying for position, merging, and setting up new divisions to help provide the infrastructure, even as Congress deregulates the traditional boundaries that have existed between them. Many companies will find niches providing unique information and services via the Internet and the Information Superhighway.

What does this all mean? In the future, access to the Internet will be as universal as telephone access. Not everyone had a phone 50 years ago, and calling long distance was not easy. The Internet is following the same growth curve as the telephone system, and it has faced similar problems. Anyone can get access to the Internet today, but the Internet cannot handle the load of everyone using it at the same time; the Information Superhighway will change that. The growth of the Information Superhighway will also bring new ways of using the Internet, such as connecting from your cable TV. In fact, pilot projects are already testing this approach.

The Internet and the Information Superhighway will provide a wide-open highway from your doorstep to the rest of the world.

The International Internet

Would you like to play
a game of global
thermonuclear war?
NO!
How about mah-jongg
instead?

The Internet has quickly grown into a worldwide research and communications network. English is the most common language you will encounter on the Internet, but be prepared for other languages if you journey far!

In the late 1960s the Internet began as the ARPANET, the Advanced Research Projects Agency Network, supported by the Department of Defense. In the mid-1980s the National Science Foundation became interested and helped fund the growth the Internet. By the late 1980s the Internet was starting to reach countries around the world. The original ARPANET was abandoned in 1990, as NSF backbones took its place.

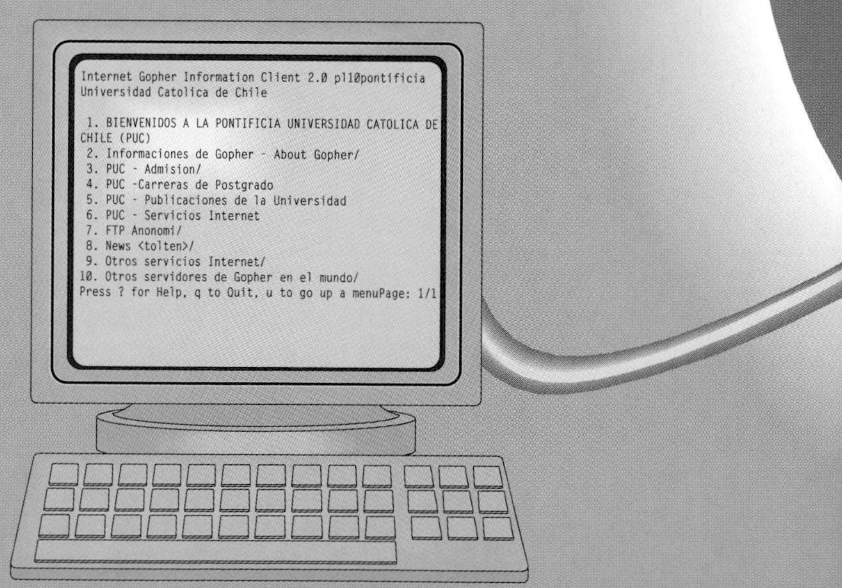
Internet Gopher Information Client 2.0 pl10pontificia
Universidad Catolica de Chile
1. BIENVENIDOS A LA PONTIFICIA UNIVERSIDAD CATOLICA DE
CHILE (PUC)
2. Informaciones de Gopher - About Gopher/
3. PUC - Admision/
4. PUC -Carreras de Postgrado
5. PUC - Publicaciones de la Universidad
6. PUC - Servicios Internet
7. FTP Anonomi/
8. News <tolten>/
9. Otros servicios Internet/
10. Otros servidores de Gopher en el mundo/
Press ? for Help, q to Quit, u to go up a menuPage: 1/1

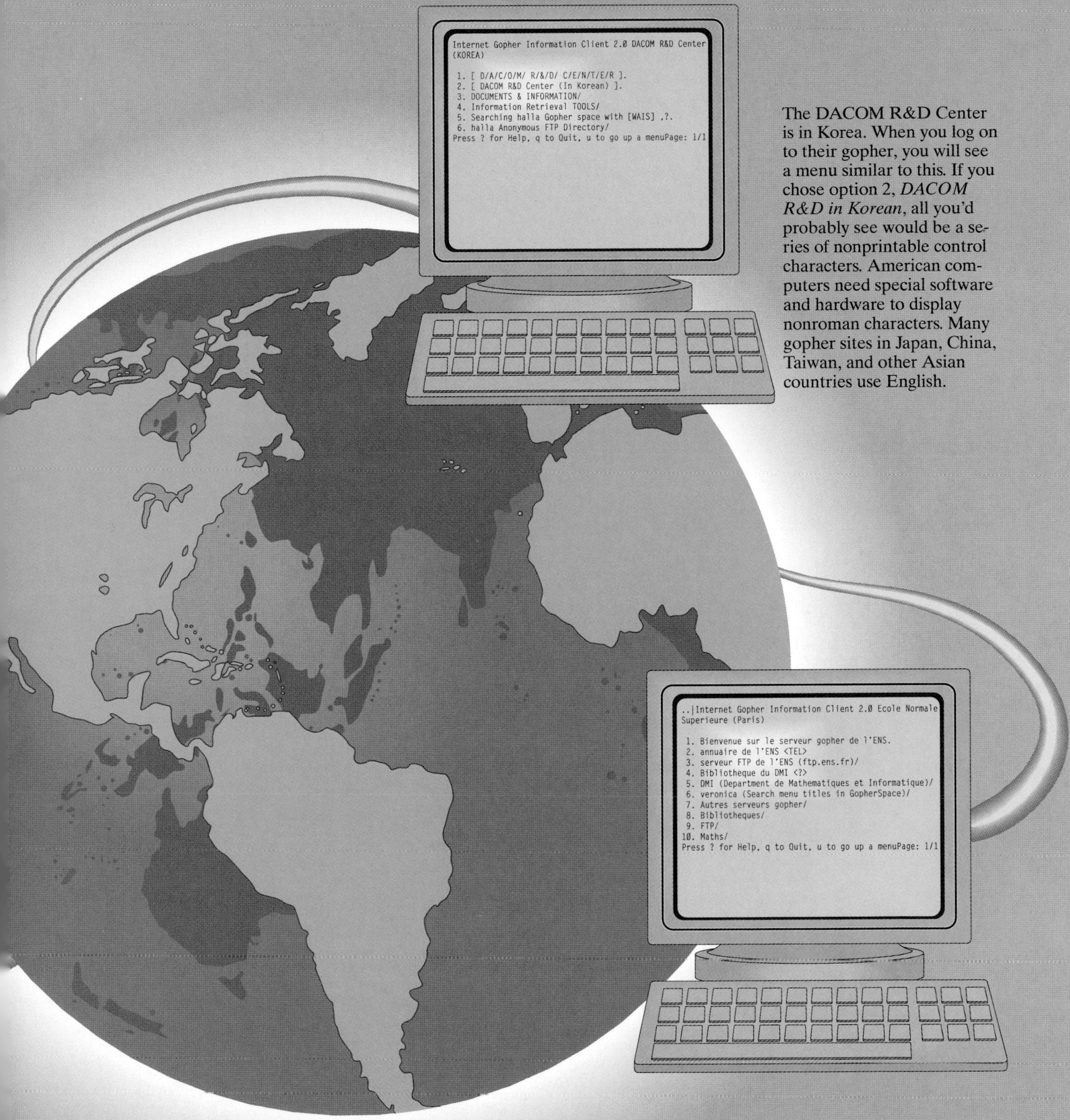

```
Internet Gopher Information Client 2.0 DACOM R&D Center
(KOREA)

 1. [ D/A/C/O/M/ R/&/D/ C/E/N/T/E/R ].
 2. [ DACOM R&D Center (In Korean) ].
 3. DOCUMENTS & INFORMATION/
 4. Information Retrieval TOOLS/
 5. Searching halla Gopher space with [WAIS] ,?.
 6. halla Anonymous FTP Directory/
Press ? for Help, q to Quit, u to go up a menuPage: 1/1
```

The DACOM R&D Center is in Korea. When you log on to their gopher, you will see a menu similar to this. If you chose option 2, *DACOM R&D in Korean*, all you'd probably see would be a series of nonprintable control characters. American computers need special software and hardware to display nonroman characters. Many gopher sites in Japan, China, Taiwan, and other Asian countries use English.

```
..|Internet Gopher Information Client 2.0 Ecole Normale
Superieure (Paris)

 1. Bienvenue sur le serveur gopher de l'ENS.
 2. annuaire de l'ENS <TEL>
 3. serveur FTP de l'ENS (ftp.ens.fr)/
 4. Bibliotheque du DMI <?>
 5. DMI (Department de Mathematiques et Informatique)/
 6. veronica (Search menu titles in GopherSpace)/
 7. Autres serveurs gopher/
 8. Bibliotheques/
 9. FTP/
10. Maths/
Press ? for Help, q to Quit, u to go up a menuPage: 1/1
```

You will run across other languages besides English if you explore the Internet in any depth. Your software's commands will still work in English, so you can always back out of something you don't understand. Often English instructions are only a menu away. Knowing even a little of other languages can be very helpful in journeying through the Internet.

A Wide-Open Highway

Congress and the White House want to see the National Information Highway fuel high-tech economic growth in the United States. The Information Superhighway will ensure a solid infrastructure for future growth of the Internet, and many companies and technologies are already contending for their piece of this pie. Because the Internet connects the world, the whole world stands to benefit from increased accessibility to the open highway.

CITY BUS
INTERNET SOCIETY
CABLE TV
PHONE COMPANY
CALL US
SCHOOL

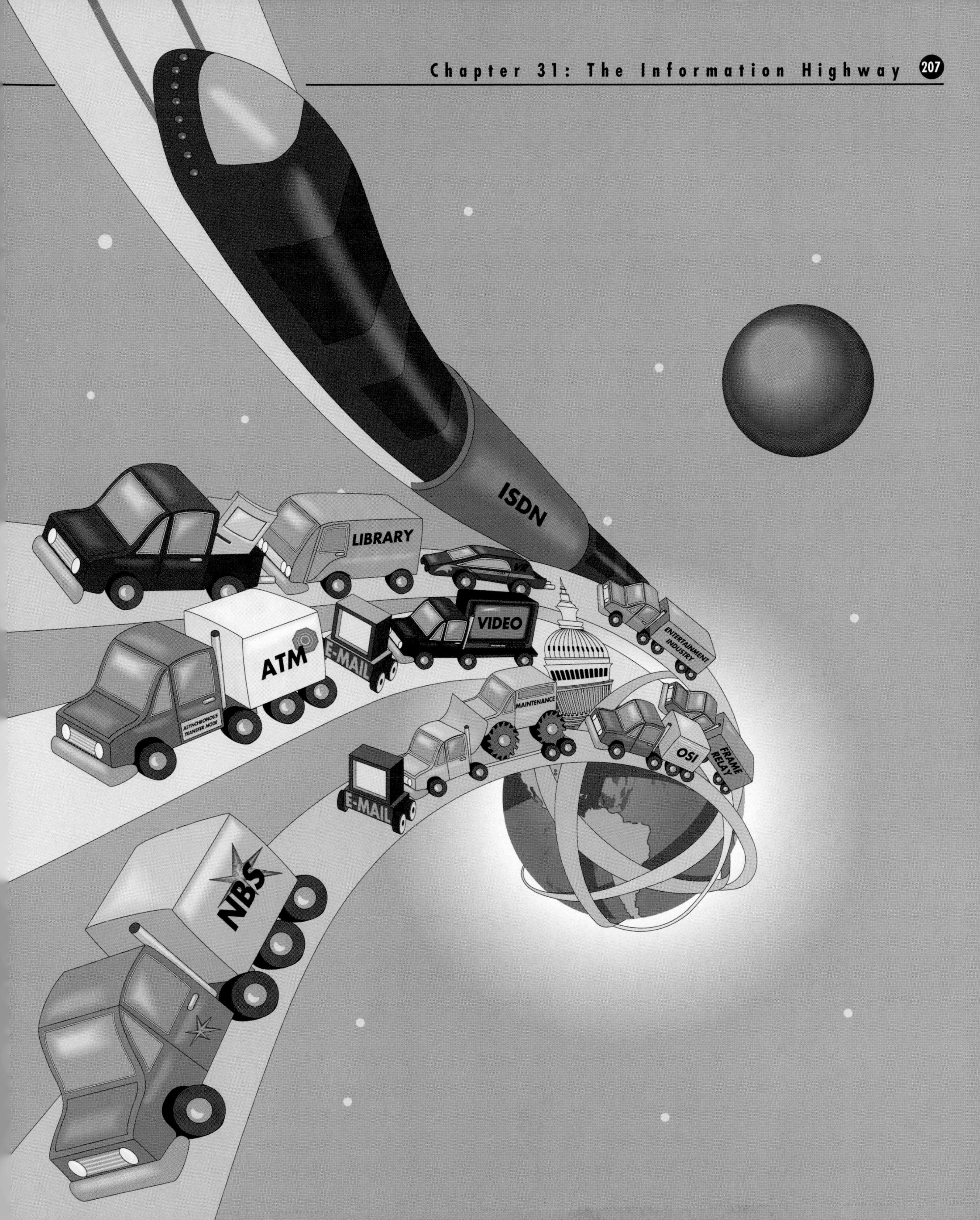
ISDN
LIBRARY
VIDEO
E-MAIL
ATM
ASYNCHRONOUS TRANSFER MODE
ENTERTAINMENT INDUSTRY
MAINTENANCE
OSI
FRAME RELAY
E-MAIL
NBS

G

H

I

K

L

X

Y

Z

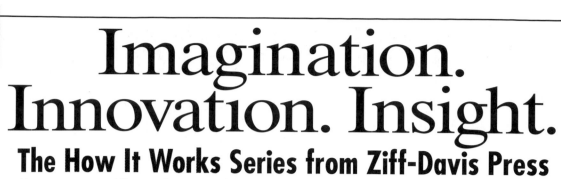

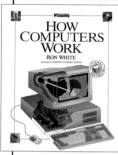

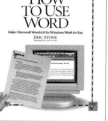

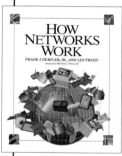

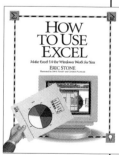

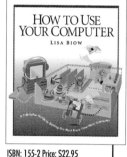

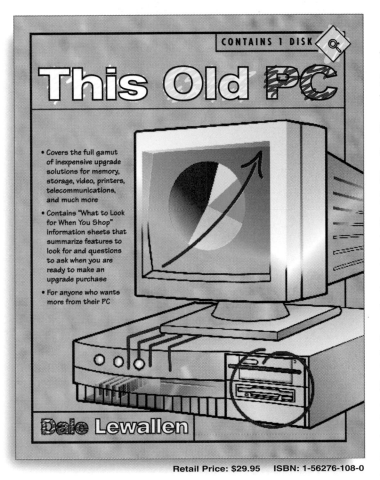

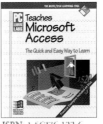

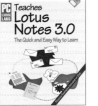

Cut Here

Cut Here

Ziff-Davis Press Survey of Readers

Please help us in our effort to produce the best books on personal computing. For your assistance, we would be pleased to send you a FREE catalog featuring the complete line of Ziff-Davis Press books.

1. How did you first learn about this book?

Recommended by a friend	☐	-1 (5)
Recommended by store personnel	☐	-2
Saw in Ziff-Davis Press catalog	☐	-3
Received advertisement in the mail	☐	-4
Saw the book on bookshelf at store	☐	-5
Read book review in: ________	☐	-6
Saw an advertisement in: ________	☐	-7
Other (Please specify): ________	☐	-8

2. Which THREE of the following factors most influenced your decision to purchase this book? (Please check up to THREE.)

Front or back cover information on book	☐	-1 (6)
Logo of magazine affiliated with book	☐	-2
Special approach to the content	☐	-3
Completeness of content	☐	-4
Author's reputation	☐	-5
Publisher's reputation	☐	-6
Book cover design or layout	☐	-7
Index or table of contents of book	☐	-8
Price of book	☐	-9
Special effects, graphics, illustrations	☐	-0
Other (Please specify): ________	☐	-x

3. How many computer books have you purchased in the last six months? ______ (7-10)

4. On a scale of 1 to 5, where 5 is excellent, 4 is above average, 3 is average, 2 is below average, and 1 is poor, please rate each of the following aspects of this book below. (Please circle your answer.)

Depth/completeness of coverage	5	4	3	2	1	(11)
Organization of material	5	4	3	2	1	(12)
Ease of finding topic	5	4	3	2	1	(13)
Special features/time saving tips	5	4	3	2	1	(14)
Appropriate level of writing	5	4	3	2	1	(15)
Usefulness of table of contents	5	4	3	2	1	(16)
Usefulness of index	5	4	3	2	1	(17)
Usefulness of accompanying disk	5	4	3	2	1	(18)
Usefulness of illustrations/graphics	5	4	3	2	1	(19)
Cover design and attractiveness	5	4	3	2	1	(20)
Overall design and layout of book	5	4	3	2	1	(21)
Overall satisfaction with book	5	4	3	2	1	(22)

5. Which of the following computer publications do you read regularly; that is, 3 out of 4 issues?

Byte	☐	-1 (23)
Computer Shopper	☐	-2
Corporate Computing	☐	-3
Dr. Dobb's Journal	☐	-4
LAN Magazine	☐	-5
MacWEEK	☐	-6
MacUser	☐	-7
PC Computing	☐	-8
PC Magazine	☐	-9
PC WEEK	☐	-0
Windows Sources	☐	-x
Other (Please specify): ________	☐	-y

Please turn page.

Cut Here

Cut Here

PLEASE TAPE HERE ONLY—DO NOT STAPLE

6. What is your level of experience with personal computers? With the subject of this book?

	With PCs		With subject of book	
Beginner	☐	-1 (24)	☐	-1 (25)
Intermediate	☐	-2	☐	-2
Advanced	☐	-3	☐	-3

7. Which of the following best describes your job title?

Officer (CEO/President/VP/owner) ☐ -1 (26)
Director/head ☐ -2
Manager/supervisor ☐ -3
Administration/staff ☐ -4
Teacher/educator/trainer ☐ -5
Lawyer/doctor/medical professional ☐ -6
Engineer/technician ☐ -7
Consultant ☐ -8
Not employed/student/retired ☐ -9
Other (Please specify): ________________ ☐ -0

8. What is your age?

Under 20 ☐ -1 (27)
21-29 ☐ -2
30-39 ☐ -3
40-49 ☐ -4
50-59 ☐ -5
60 or over ☐ -6

9. Are you:

Male ☐ -1 (28)
Female ☐ -2

Thank you for your assistance with this important information! Please write your address below to receive our free catalog.

Name: ________________________________

Address: ________________________________

City/State/Zip: ________________________________

Fold here to mail.

1927-13-08

NO POSTAGE NECESSARY IF MAILED IN THE UNITED STATES

BUSINESS REPLY MAIL

FIRST CLASS MAIL PERMIT NO. 1612 OAKLAND, CA

POSTAGE WILL BE PAID BY ADDRESSEE

ZIFF-DAVIS
ZD
PRESS

Ziff-Davis Press
5903 Christie Avenue
Emeryville, CA 94608-1925
Attn: Marketing